D0475464

ROMANS
AND BARBARIANS

Also by Derek Williams

The Reach of Rome

ROMANS
AND BARBARIANS

Four Views from the Empire's Edge
1st Century AD

Derek Williams

St. Martin's Press
New York

ROMANS AND BARBARIANS: FOUR VIEWS FROM THE EMPIRE'S EDGE 1ST CENTURY AD.
Copyright © 1998 by Derek Williams. All rights reserved. Printed in the United
States of America. No part of this book may be used or reproduced in any manner
whatsoever without written permission except in the case of brief quotations
embodied in critical articles or reviews. For information, address St. Martin's
Press, 175 Fifth Avenue, New York, N.Y. 10010.

Williams, Derek, 1929-
    Romans and Barbarians : four views from the empire's edge, 1st
century A.D. / Derek Williams.
        p.   cm.
    Incliudes bibliographical references and index.
    ISBN 0-312-19958-9
    1. Rome—History—The five Julii, 30 B.C-68 A.D.—Sources.
2. Rome—History—Flavians, 69-96—SOurces. 3. Europe—
Civilization—Roman influences—Sources. 4. Rome—Boundaries—
History—Sources.   I. Title
DG59.A2W57   1999
937'.07—dc21   98-50773
                                                               CIP

First published in Great Britain by Constable and Company Ltd

First U.S. Edition: February 1999

10 9 8 7 6 5 4 3 2 1

To Matthew, Haidi and April

CONTENTS

LIST OF MAPS

LIST OF PHOTOGRAPHS

Photos 2–4 courtesy of Hermitage Museum, St Petersburg; 9 generously provided by the Kulturgeschichtliches Museum, Osnabrück; 11 copyright the British Museum; 1, 14 and 15 by the author, with kind permission of the Muzeu de Istorie Natsionala si Arheologie, Constantsa; others from the author's collection or taken by him for the purpose of illustrating this volume.

ACKNOWLEDGEMENTS

As with many a second book, *Romans and Barbarians* owes its inception to excessive zeal in writing the first. When sketches for a work on the Roman frontier (published in 1996 as *The Reach of Rome*) promised to be unmarketably long, associates and colleagues (especially Dr Andrew Dalby and my literary agent, Caroline Davidson) pointed to the lands and peoples outside the imperial boundaries as valid subjects for a book in their own right. Though hesitating to accept so strenuous a challenge, it was undeniable that certain incidents arising from the Roman-barbarian connection were rich in interest; and that, rather than forgo the fruits of long study, the best of them could be shaped into a second book of less studious but more human character. Owing to historical chance and the even more haphazard accidents of textual transmission (by which some accounts of ancient history survived the centuries, but so many did not), several of the most memorable events fell into a group approximating to the 1st century of the Christian era. This served both to limit the canvas and offer the unity of a single period: that of the first ten caesars, when Rome's power reaches its zenith, and dominance over the outside world, begins, almost imperceptibly, to slip.

These two collaborators, then, are the first to be thanked. I acknowledge the assistance of a distinguished philologist, Anna Partington, who advised on a variety of origins and meanings. It is my loss that she was not consulted till the eleventh hour, when the book's closing date was drawing near. I am also grateful to Samantha Hopkins for typing the text, to Alexander Stilwell and Imogen Olsen for perceptively reading and correcting it; to its Editor, Claire Evans, for co-ordinating and augmenting al our efforts; and to many friends whose reception of my earlier effort emboldened me to pursue its sequel. My work is especially fortunate in its Editorial Director, Carol O'Brien of Constable Ltd, whose view is that writing need not be the monopoly of career authors, nor history the sole province of professional scholars.

The book draws on mainstream Greek and Roman sources, supplemented by archaeological findings and recent thinking. Most of its authors are to be found in the Loeb Classical Library (original texts with translation), with some published in translated form by Penguin Classics. The *Tristia* and *Ex Ponto* appear in volume VI of the Loeb *Ovid* and, in freer form, in D. R. Slavitt's *Ovid's Poetry of Exile* (Baltimore, 1990). While grateful for the many insights afforded by parallel efforts, the author's translation of these and other source material attempts to steer a middle course between the precision of the Loeb and the boldness of the less formal renderings.

Insofar as this book can claim originality it lies in the marshalling of random historical incidents (none unknown, but all deserving to be better known) into a single study. More unusual is its chosen ground, where classical and Iron Age scholarship meet. Throughout the 20th century there have of course been books on Rome in plenty, including many aspects of the empire and its provinces. More recently these have been complemented by a growing body of work on European late prehistory, notably the Celtic, Germanic and Sarmatian Iron Ages. While both zones of knowledge are indispensable, the student of antiquity's no-man's lands has largely been left to build his own bridges across the Rhine and Danube: rivers which once separated Roman from outsider and now sunder one academic discipline from another. Accordingly, the remarkably small group of works which emphasize interrelationship and examine the Mediterranean-Northern interaction has proved unusually valuable. These include H. D. Rankin's *The Celts and the Classical World* (London, 1987) and B. W. Cunliffe's *Greeks, Romans and Barbarians* (London, 1988).

In his *Concluding Thoughts* on the proceedings of a conference about the impact of the Roman invasion on Iron Age communities in Britain (BAR 73, 1979), Professor Cunliffe writes:

If one came away from the conference with only one impression it would be that Roman Britain is too important to be left to the Romanists! The divide between Romanist and prehistorian (or for that matter between Romanist and Dark Age specialist) is far too abrupt for the health of our discipline [. . .] It is, I think, above all the result of laziness, breeding a defensive arrogance [. . .] The disciplines have diverged to such an extent during the last half century that the mental effort required to master both is more than many scholars are prepared to make [. . .] There are however signs that this unfortunate divide is breaking down.

Nearly twenty years on, the divide remains. No thoroughgoing merger has occurred in research and the secondary literatures largely reflect these separate courses. Could it be that the origins of this divergence lie far deeper than our own century? Is it perhaps the legacy of Rome's 400-year frontier, whose presence accentuated and perpetuated the distinction between the two worlds: one recoverable from the page, the other from the soil? The activities, motives and achievements of these two sets of peoples (those inside, and those outside the Roman empire) have survived in different proportions and degrees, with each unlockable in its own way. It behoves the ancient historian and the archaeologist of the future to carry both sets of keys.

Finally, I would like to thank those who helped me during the assembly of illustrations: in Germany our friends Otto and Annegret Kollecker for kind hospitality and much practical assistance; also Professor Wolfgang Schlüter for valuable advice and for arranging to make pictorial material available. My visit to Romania was greatly facilitated by the co-operation of the Museum of National History, Constantsa and the Adamclisi Museum, to whose officers I am indebted. Detail of photo-credits is given with the Photographic List.

LIST OF ROMAN EMPERORS
1st AND 2nd CENTURIES

Augustus	27 BC–AD 14
Tiberius	14–37
'Caligula'	37–41
Claudius	41–54
Nero	54–68
Galba	68
Otho	69
Vitellius	69
Vespasian	69–79
Titus	79–81
Domitian	81–96
Nerva	96–98
Trajan	98–117
Hadrian	117–38
Antoninus	139–61
Marcus	161–80
Commodus	180–92
Pertinax	193
Didius Julianus	193
Septimius	193–211

Romans and Barbarians

THROUGH WAR, TRADE, EXILE OR accident, Romans parted
the curtain between their world and that of the outside peoples and
occasionally left accounts of what they saw and did. Best known
are Caesar's. This book moves forward to the century following,
presenting four episodes from the early imperial period, which
straddle Europe from the Black Sea to the Scottish Highlands, offering portraits of Rome's Sarmatian, German and Celtic neighbours.
Its setting is the empire's northern margins and beyond, where Mediterranean certainties falter and history hesitates. Though supplemented by recent findings and modern thinking, these glimpses
from the rim of the classical world retain the almost accidental quality of snapshots, afforded us not only by Rome's wide expansion
but also through the chance presence of individuals, who ventured
or were sent beyond the imperial pale. The first two episodes are
dated to the ninth year of our era, but their context harks back to
27 BC: the accession of Augustus and the empire's commencement.
The final episode ends at the beginning of Hadrian's reign in AD
117 when, with his emphasis on neutrality, large-scale intervention
in barbarian affairs diminishes.

Mindful of the distinction between prehistory and history, based
on the absence or presence of a written record, one is double-tongued
from the outset. On the Roman side one speaks historically, of men
and women with names, of known events and established dates; on
the barbarian side prehistorically, of uncertainty and anonymity, of
peoples called after their burial practices and cultures known from
their type-sites. This reflects a deep division in the study of antiquity.

On the one hand classics students are heirs to a long and noble textual tradition. Those who live in Europe are surrounded by reminders of Rome. If they are Westerners their languages and customs are studded with reference points. Quite different are students of the barbarians, whose discipline is recent, whose text is the soil and, though some of their languages live on in ours, whose pursuit is often of faint traces. Yet, allowing for these discrepancies, it is odd that those who study the Rhine's left or Roman bank should seemingly require a different terminology from those studying its right or barbarian bank. At university they would be members of different faculties, attending different lectures and sitting different exams. Such is the compartmentalism of classical and Iron Age learning which has blurred our understanding of the north-south interaction and fogged our view of the Roman empire's edges.

There are of course bridges across the scholastic river. Most prominent are the writings of Roman historians and geographers, crucial contributors to knowledge of the barbarian side: crucial because archaeology's findings seldom match the power of language to penetrate minds and motives. This does, however, present a snag. While the Roman empire bequeathed words by the hundred thousand, those outside its European borders left none. Nor have barbarian oral traditions survived from this time. So classical authors became the spokesmen for the barbarian by default; and it could rightly be said that they hijacked our way of seeing his world. In comparing Roman and barbarian one must therefore allow for the partiality of the written sources; and it may help to remember that the Romans themselves were by no means superhuman, that they were not invariably ahead of their time and that where a gap between them and the barbarians existed it was sometimes smaller than Romanists might have one believe. What, then, was the nature of the Roman imperial state?

The 20th century is a time of unprecedented growth in the complexity of officialdom, dominated by organizations of all kinds, mesmerized by experts and obsessed with theory. Modern conditioning ill prepares us for the crudity of imperial Rome: successful beyond all rivals yet backed by rudimentary bureaucracy, unsupported by political or economic thought, without parties to give voice to new aspirations or the flexibility to produce new institutions. In a constitutional sense this amounted to underpowered machinery carrying majestic coachwork; a mighty empire propelled by a governmental engine more fitted to driving a petty province, chauffeured by one man. It was without ministers or ministries; without home, foreign or colonial offices; without chiefs of staff, admiralty or war office; with an army lacking a professional officer corps, its command based on the principle of impermanence and its officials hamstrung by the limits placed on personal power. It is not surprising that, according to Dio,[1] Rome's vital statistics could be contained in a notebook, carried perhaps on the emperor's person.

The modern economist's tendency to equate wealth with industry, and poverty with failure to industrialize, has no ancient counterpart. The Roman empire resembled the barbarian lands in being dominantly agricultural. Produce, rents and property accounted for at least 90 per cent of GNP. Farming was the basis of the state. Yet even here, though Rome did not lack the skills of husbandry, she was backward in applying invention to its processes. The Gauls had already devised a mechanical reaper: in effect a wooden comb mounted on wheels and drawn by animals. The corn stalks slid between the teeth and, reaching the end, the ears snapped off and fell into a tray. By contrast the Romans did not know the wheelbarrow. Farmers did not have the horse collar and oxen were used for heavy work. During the entire imperial period there were no major improvements in agronomy or farming technology. In the sense of yield in relation to work, Rome marked time. The problem was fiscal rather than nutritional. Because taxes on land payed for the empire's defence, agriculture's success or failure determined the size of the armed forces. These would continue to be modest in relation to Roman responsibilities. Without growth through productivity, wealth could only be augmented spatially; and avenues for easy conquest were now few.

Given the absence of inventiveness, Rome's problems would not be solved – nor the barbarian decisively outclassed – by technical or commercial revolution. Industry was undercapitalized, its processes bucolic and its standing low. Here, as in agriculture, the existence of slavery removed the incentive to seek labour-saving processes. Considering that the empire was history's biggest single market, with a unified currency, trading performance was poor. Manufacture, business and commerce would continue to account for no more than 10 per cent of wealth-creation. It would of course be wrong to exaggerate Rome's limitations or to suggest that the barbarians were better off. The point is that neither in economic nor military terms was Rome likely to transform herself, to leave her neighbours standing, or so to dwarf the outside world that the barbarian danger would recede.

Neglect of industry, conservatism and lack of innovative thinking cast their shadow over learning; and it is little surprise that the twelve centuries of Rome produced no scientist to whom posterity is in serious debt.[2] Education was literary and hidebound. There were no universities. In mathematics the numerical system and absence of the zero impeded advance. There was no notion of theoretical chemistry. Physics was strong in the study of stable forms but weak in dynamics, equipping its students to understand structure but not mechanism. Despite prodigious feats in aqueduct, bridge and sewerage construction, many techniques were crude. Most lamentable was metallurgy. Rome's soldiers used untempered weapons, and in annealing, alloying, forging and welding, German products would eventually outclass Roman.[3] The quality of machinery was woeful. Gearing was wooden. Vitruvius described the machine as 'a combination of timbers, lashed together'.[4] Progress had been made in crane and mill design, but there were no other applications of water power, and steam remained theoretical. With Romans strong on practice and Greeks on theory, the empire which bound them together was curiously weak at giving Roman substance to Greek speculation.

At sea there was no compass, sextant or chronometer. Captains clung to coasts. Better ships were being built in Scandinavia. There was no mechanical clock and concepts of time were hazy. Daylight was divided into twelve, with the hour varying in length between winter and summer. Though Rome dominated the Mediterranean (and in due course the Black and Red Seas also), beyond Gibraltar the 'outer ocean' was a source of dread which she was slow to overcome, even in the instance of the English Channel. Other than the solitary advance by the Greek navigator Hippalus (1st century AD) in understanding the monsoonal winds and regularizing the India trade, disinterest in deep water meant there would be no such thing as Roman overseas discovery.[5] Consequently she could never call a New World into existence to redress the balance of the Old.

In war Rome had no secret weapon. She prevailed not through technical advantage but by discipline, pertinacity, organization and reputation. She was in some respects inferior to her eastern rival Parthia (Iran); even to the steppe nomads, for the West was first to produce neither saddle, stirrup, girth, horseshoe, nor the reinforced shortbow (for use on horseback). One may guess at a Chinese or central Asian origin for the saddle because riders of the Bactrian camel, mounted between humps, are especially stable. The idea of a saddle, with its front and rear pommels, could then be applied to the horse; and footrests, attached to or hanging from it, became a natural appendage. Saddles and stirrups, absent from Trajan's Column, may be seen on Chinese pottery horses at least as early as 600 BC. Without a saddle to steady the rider, mounted archery is ineffectual. Without stirrups, the lancer is projected backwards at the shock of contact. Without shoes, the horse is lamed by hard surfaces, forcing the rider to use the soft verges and reducing the advantage of Rome's famous road network. Cavalry was valued for scouting and pursuit but was slow to be applied as a weapon of attack and manoeuvre.

By contrast Roman excellence lay in infantry training and skills. To these could be added developments in torsion artillery, though throwing-weapons were only to prove decisive in sieges. The third Episode will show *scorpio* and *ballista* in action. Complementing military prowess was a talent for political cohesion (unknown to the barbarians and denied the bickering Greeks) plus an impressive record in the manipulation and co-option of other nations. Indeed this is how the juggernaut was made, for more manpower than was ever born in Central Italy would be required to create and serve imperial Rome. Nor must urban development and civil engineering achievement be forgotten, most memorably road building, as well as spectacular accomplishments in architecture and literature.

Accepting this, but recalling her institutional and technological backwardness, Rome's deficits almost outweigh credits. None the less, in terms of reputation, these were the credits that counted. Her military and diplomatic talents produced the territorial, and her skills in words and stone the cultural results which deeply impressed later ages, perpetuating the image of a marble Rome in a muddy world and leading to emphasis on short periods of peak achievement at the expense of two millennia of Roman and Byzantine history as a whole. It is difficult to think of another civilization where so much attention has been given to so small a part of its span.

What are the conclusions of this profit-and-loss account? Is it feasible to see Rome merely as the culminating Iron Age power; or is there some factor which appears to distinguish her from the barbarians in kind, even to give her an exceptional place in the ascent of man? This is not a question which troubled the Romans. The answer was implied on every page of their history. The gods had a reason when they put Rome at Italy's centre, Italy at the Mediterranean's centre and the Mediterranean at the centre of the world. We, too, have seldom questioned Roman superiority over the outside nations, seeing it as a basic ingredient of the Western heritage. In what, then, might the Roman contribution be said to lie? Doubtless in the sphere of multinational dominion and superstate governance; in the accumulated experience arising from the breadth and variety of this management; plus the lessons learned from its responsibilities, such as co-ordination of parts and grasp of long-term goals. Added to this are contributions to civil order, internal stability and (surprisingly for a structure welded by war) to international peace. Finally there is Rome's role as the conduit by which Greek thought and Judaeo-Christian belief reached the future West. In all the above respects it is the Roman empire's extent and longevity, as much as the talents and efforts of its individuals, which permitted enrichments to civilization unmatched by tribes lacking literacy, unity, or continuity.

By the accession of Augustus, Rome owned most of the Mediterranean seabord, Gaul to the Rhine and Syria to the Euphrates. Acquisition had not been systematic or based on a sustained vision. A torrent of territory had fallen to the Republic during its later years, the result of spectacular victories by generals like Pompey and Caesar. In fact they had been moves in a power game, ambitions on a collision course both with the Senate and each other. These were the forces over which the consuls lost control, compelling Rome toward the thirty-five-year *débâcle* of dictatorship, assassination and civil war which encompassed the Republic's dissolution; leading to the emergence of Octavian, Julius Caesar's great nephew and heir, as Rome's first emperor (later to be named Augustus).

Including the additions made by Augustus and his successors, the empire would be among history's more extensive, covering three-and-a-half million square miles of land and sea, with a land area about the size of the United States and Alaska. This Augustus managed with a peculiar mixture of strength and tact, wishing to be known by no more imposing a title than *princeps* (first citizen), though posterity, dismissing subterfuge, bluntly called him emperor: first of some seventy holders of that office between his taking power in 27 BC and the fall of Rome some five centuries later. From *princeps* there comes the term 'principate', meaning either the reign of an individual emperor or the early imperial period generally. This regime, described by Tacitus as 'neither of total slavery nor total liberty',[6] would vary in its ratio of freedom to tyranny with each occupant of the throne.

Augustus, probably Rome's most successful emperor, charmed the Senate with generous amnesty and gentle persuasion, allowing it to retain the inner empire and its members to lead legions and govern provinces as before, while he controlled the high command and the outer territories, including the frontiers. The forces were overhauled and the Western world's first standing army created, consisting of 150,000 legionary and a similar number of auxiliary soldiers. The concentration of power in one man, who controlled the military machine, as well as the permanence of that machine, would deter both internal and external challengers. Augustus' reforms thus offered a genuine prospect of peace, though long habits of strife and the pursuit of glory would render Rome incapable of grasping it fully.

The expression *pax Romana*, adopted from the elder Pliny, was used by that writer incidentally, in describing plants 'now available to the botanist from all corners of the world, thanks to the boundless majesty of the Roman peace'.[7] During the 1st century AD the principle of a universal peace will at times be honoured more in breach than observance, in the sense that most of Rome's rulers reverted at least once to external ventures. But the *pax Romana* is not to be sneezed at. Despite notable exceptions, the empire and its battlefronts would soon fall quiet for almost two centuries. This was something new to the human condition. The temple of the double-faced Janus, traditionally open in time of war, had been closed only twice in the seven centuries between the city's foundation and Augustus' accession. Within the *Barbaricum*, where feuding and raiding were facts of life, a prolonged or widespread peace was similarly unknown. Given such unpromising precedents, the imposition and maintenance of the *pax Romana* was an extraordinary feat and perhaps mankind's greatest achievement until that time.

Augustus' professional army of twenty-eight legions, assisted by some 300 auxiliary units, was now posted to the outer provinces where it would remain for three centuries and more. There the exterior nations, counting only those within reach of imperial territory, may have outnumbered Rome's soldiers by ten to one: a guess which envisages a compact corps of full-timers facing the vast potential of a prehistoric world in which all were part-time warriors.

Rome's erratic expansion had left anomalies which Augustus resolved to correct. Spain's north-west corner, the Alpine lands and much of the Balkans still lay outside the empire and would be dealt with in turn. A serious underrating of difficulties beyond the Rhine would then entice Augustus eastwards. Our second Episode recounts the disastrous outcome in Germany: the first, clear, large-scale failure of Roman imperial expansion. The shock of this rebuke led to the famous advice, contained in Augustus' will, that the empire should not be expanded further. In deference to his stepfather's wish, Tiberius turned to a foreign policy based on diplomacy, and with the exception of the British venture (described in Episode Three), the carrot would prevail till the end of the 1st century, when Trajan brought back the stick. Nevertheless, despite inconsistencies between one ruler and the next, Rome was gradually turning her back on adventurism: not only because of the absence of easy victims or dangerous enemies, but also because defence costs, coupled with economic stagnation, were reducing the means to attain more distant and difficult territorial goals.

A corollary to the cessation of expansion would be an armed frontier, soon to evolve along the Rhine and Danube. It would continue to be strengthened throughout the period and be joined by others in the Near East and North Africa. This represented an exchange of the informal boundaries of the Republican period, held by treaty and supported by bribery or menace, for a precise line of exclusion guarded by Roman soldiers. The barbarians would be allowed through its checkpoints in time of peace and in numbers acceptable to the Roman authorities, providing entry was in daylight, unarmed and after payment of dues.[8] Though the army would continue to patrol the near *Barbaricum*, gathering intelligence, mediating in disputes and paying stipends to friendly chieftains, the frontier could now be sealed at a moment's notice. However, that the mistress of the world should even consider hiding behind barriers suggests deep changes in attitude, whose origins are also described in Episode Two: a recognition of the size of the outside nations, an acceptance that the gulf between those inside and outside the empire was unlikely to be bridged and barbarian envy unlikely to be assuaged. Time confirms this pessimism. The centuries offer no example of a frontier's dismantling because improved relations made it unnecessary;

or of voluntary fusion between the empire and its neighbours brought about by the onset of goodwill.

The First Episode sees the poet Ovid looking from the wall of a Black Sea outpost onto savage but skilful horsemen. This exemplifies the security problem of antiquity. On the one hand, a cultural gap and disparity of wealth between the classical and barbarian worlds too big to promise indefinite peace; on the other, advantages in military technique too small to guarantee a permanent Roman lead. Furthermore the *pax Romana*, with it laws against the bearing of arms, created a state whose civilian majority would forget how to fight.

The situation described by Ovid will not be revived till the 16th–19th centuries, when the age of exploration takes Europeans across oceans and the Old and New Worlds collide. Most obviously, his vision of mounted archers circling the walls reminds one of Indians round a paleface stockade. But the comparison is unfavourable to Rome in two respects: the American settlers had firearms; and their support, in terms of numbers migrating from the motherlands, was almost limitless. Rome's lacklustre technology would never put a decisive weapon into her soldiers' hands; and population pressures would work not outwards against the barbarians but inwards against the empire.

At present, however, Rome still disposed of muscle enough and her astuteness in co-opting other nations and diverting their energies to advantage has been mentioned. During the century covered by these episodes the last quarter of imperial territory will be acquired. It is only as the period ends that Hadrian dares flout Rome's glorious traditions by making pacifism a plank of policy. With his successor, Antoninus, the empire reaches its floodtide of prosperity. Yet, by the end of the 2nd century, the best will be over. Military dictatorship, assassination, *coup d'état*, overtaxation and inflation mark the down-path. Rome's sickness will be sensed by the outside peoples and as she neglects the art of unity they begin to cultivate it.

However, the rebound of the barbarians and their eventual part in the formation of Europe are still centuries away. At the time of this study the peoples ranged in relative docility round the empire were, to the north, Celts, Germans and Sarmatians; to the east, various Iranian groups, most notably Parthians, plus the Arab tribes; and, in Africa, Hamitic natives of Ethiopian and Berber strains. First, however, it should be asked what Romans understood by 'barbarian'.

The actual term seems to have arisen from Greek mimicry of unfamiliar language, i.e. 'bar-bar', rather as we say 'jabber-jabber'. The Latin *barbatus* (bearded) appears to describe a barbarian characteristic rather than to supply the expression. Though the name was applied to nations outside the classical orbit, not all the empire's neighbours were considered barbarians. Apart from bedouin, the Near and Middle Eastern races were seldom so described. Literary usage suggests that 'barbarian' meant what it does today: the opposite to civilized; and that barbarians were seen as backward, wayward and dangerous. In practice, the barbarians with whom Rome had contact were largely European, though these extended indefinitely eastwards into northern Asia. In North Africa the surviving word 'Berber' implies that the interior tribes were also called by this name. However, these were fewer and further from mainstream events, as demonstrated by the guarding of North Africa (other than Egypt) by a single legion, in contrast to Europe's fourteen.[9] To concentrate on the three ethnic groups confronting the empire in Europe is to focus on the barbarians about whom most is known, whose importance for history is greatest and who offer the widest spectrum of development: from the creative Celts, on the verge of literacy, to the still nomadic Sarmatians, gruesome in their savagery.

In Egypt the barbarian problem would easily be solved by barring the Nile at its first cataract, while the Eastern and Western Deserts largely looked after themselves. In the remainder of North Africa the barrier of the Sahara shielded the Roman provinces from invasion, though nomadism on its fringes was a source of nuisance, as it was along the Syrian and Arabian frontiers. In the East, however, stability hinged on a single factor: the longstanding rivalry between Rome and Parthia, each coveting the other's nearer provinces but neither finding strength to hold them. Major conflict was in practice rare. Europe presented more complex problems, arising from fragmentation and the unsettled times. Here Rome faced a crazy paving of tribe beyond tribe, in which annexation of one simply brought her into contact with others. Continuing to advance offered conquest without conclusion; ceasing meant bribing unconquered tribes to keep the peace. It was the dilemma of power: to expand, overgrow and become unmanageable; or to halt and consolidate, but become the paymaster of covetous clans.

In recent years historians have built another bridge between classical and Iron Age studies by reinterpreting Roman influence upon the *Barbaricum* in economic terms. Whether a creature buffeted by such fickle winds as prehistoric man – or indeed man in any period – is a reliable basis for 'model' construction, is doubtful. Nevertheless this theory deserves attention because it is compatible with archaeological facts. Some 100 or 150 miles east of the Rhine there begins a zone of chieftainly graves, containing prestigious goods of Roman origin. This continues for a further 200 miles into Central Germany. A similar zone is encountered on the barbarian side of the Danube. In pre-conquest Gaul archaeology traces a corresponding band of interments across Central France at a comparable distance from Roman Provence. In each instance there is the same gap of 100 or more miles between Roman territory and the start of the splendiferous burial belt.

To explain these grave-goods, which often include objects associated with sumptuous wining and dining, there is another theory, known as 'prestige goods dependency'. According to this, a tribal society can be made dependent upon a more advanced neighbour simply by supplying novel and luxurious goods to its chieftain. For his part the chieftain will corner the supply by ensuring that no such products enter his territory other than through him. In this way he makes himself the sole source of bounty and giver of spectacular gifts, feasts and carousals, and his influence will be greatly enhanced. The situation is echoed in modern monarchy's monopoly in the bestowal of titles and decorations, except that in the barbarian case the rewards took the form of imports, which could be withheld by the outside supplier. Cessation of the flow could have dire consequences for a dependent chieftain.

Returning to the cross-frontier model: this proposes three zones and accounts for the entire near *Barbaricum*, to a depth of about 500 miles. To take the example of the Rhine: the zone nearest the river (Western Germany) was that in which the Roman army could intervene directly to influence tribal politics. It was therefore unnecessary to create an addiction to prestige goods. In any case, it would hardly be feasible for a chief to monopolize trade in a region so close to the frontier and its markets. Here coin prevailed, if not between Germans then as a medium of trade with the Romans. Chieftains would be paid in it; both to keep the peace and permit traffic through their territories to and from the belt beyond. This was the second zone (Central Germany), classic location for the exercise of 'prestige goods dependency', being too far from the frontier for general access to its markets or for coinage to be useful. Supplies for this zone are likely to have moved in guarded consignment to chieftainly recipients. It is unclear what proportion was regular commercial traffic, for example wine, and what were diplomatic gifts, such as silver goblets and dinner services of finest craftmanship. No doubt there were both. What did Rome ask in return? The answer is, of course, the implementation of pro-Roman policies; but also, almost certainly, slaves. A third zone (Eastern Germany) is therefore postulated for procurement, where slaves were seized in raids or taken as prisoners of war.

The model is buttressed by the frequency of coins in the western zone, lavish interments in the central zone and so-called warrior burials in the eastern zone, where grave-goods emphasize weaponry, suggesting a region of tension and strife. It is also consistent with the imperial economy. Because industrial development was limited and tradition forbade senators to engage in commerce, agriculture was the principal outlet for investment available to the Roman rich. This led to the formation of large estates, worked mainly by slaves. As peace became the 1st-century norm, the flow of prisoners of war to the slave market dwindled and the search for sources within the barbarian lands must inevitably have intensified.

Based on a sustained flow of luxuries toward its centre and constant slave raiding along its edge, it need hardly be added that the model seems unstable. The movement of prestige goods could be interrupted owing to troubles within the empire. The procurement zone might seek a larger share of the middle zone's benefits; or, depopulated by the constant activities of slavers, more distant tribes might be tempted to invade, leading to an implosion toward the frontier whose security the system was supposed to support.

Little is gained by testing the model against written sources, which yield few details regarding cross-frontier transactions and tell us almost nothing of the deeper *Barbaricum*. The best information is from the 1st-century BC and earlier. The huge size of wine shipments is known from the case of a merchant arraigned for non-payment of export duty;[10] while many a lost cargo tells underwater archaeology the same story. Diodorus of Sicily goes a step further in relating wine trade to slave trade:

Great guzzlers are the Gauls. They drink wine at full strength; and when sozzled either pass out or act crazy. Small wonder the

Italian merchants rate them as their most valued customers, plying the plonk upriver by the boatload and overland by the cartload. And great is their reward, for the price of one amphora is one slave.[11]

Athenaeus (quoting from a lost work by Posidonius) offers a colourful instance of chieftainly craving for popularity in his vignette of a Gaulish prince, scattering gold and silver pieces from his chariot to tens of thousands of followers; then throwing a feast, lasting many days, in a field of one-and-a-half square miles extent!

In summary there is, however, no certainty during the Roman imperial period that major frontier troubles arose from the breakdown or over-exercise of the slave trade. It seems more likely that the 3rd to 5th century barbarian invasions were a result of migrational pressures from underfed regions: a Baltic unfavoured by sunlight and a Eurasian steppe unfavoured by rainfall. As for the economic model: whether or not it will stand the test of time, there is no denying the general impact of southern upon northern Europe. The needs of the empire for metals and manpower, the scope of the slave trade, the scale of the wine trade, the native aristocracy's deepening addiction to Roman products: all had profound effects on prehistoric Europe. In the thousand years between the emergence of the Greek trading colonies and the fall of Rome, much barbarian development was in reaction to Mediterranean influences and events. The picture is of two worlds in uneasy partnership, unable to do without one another but seldom at ease with each other.

It is time to look more closely at the three ethnic groups adjacent to the empire's European provinces. First, the Celts. The terms Celtic and Gallic are virtually interchangeable, *Keltoi* being either a Greek rendering of *Galatae* or, as Caesar suggests in the opening lines of the *Gallic Wars*, it was one of the names used by the Gauls themselves. The Celtic tribes were probably a merger of incomer and native, crystallizing as a recognizable people in Central Europe around 700 BC. There was perhaps a racial relationship with the Germans, though shortly before our period the two were in conflict. A German exodus from the Baltic was squeezing the Celts out of what is now western Germany, leaving a transitional zone of mixed cultures on both sides of the Rhine. In response the Celtic centre had shifted westwards and all north-western Europe was either occupied or influenced by them. They were also in northern Italy, Austria, parts of the Balkans and even western Anatolia, as we are reminded by St Paul's *Epistle to the Galatians*.

The Celts exceeded all barbarian groups in duration and intensity of contact with the Mediterranean. The southern coasts of Gaul and Spain were Celtic, and for five centuries Greek and Carthaginian traders had been busy along them. By the 2nd century BC these coastal Gauls had towns walled in square-cut stone, crowned with towers, containing rectangular houses arranged in paved streets. Further inland were earthen forts of Celtic tradition, enclosing settlements of thatched roundhouses; some crowning hills, spurs or other defensible positions. To meet the threat of Roman expansion, many had been refurbished with massively wide, dry-stone ramparts, braced with long beams. These impressive works of earth or stone were most numerous in a long arc, from western and central Gaul, round the north of the Alps, to the middle Danube; with clusters on the Seine and Somme, as well as in Britanny and Britain. The Belgic Gauls, whose way of life was largely pastoral, proved to be among Rome's toughest resisters. They favoured oval enclosures in low-lying situations, fitted into river bends or protected by marsh.

Prompted by Caesar, who called all larger, northern European defended settlements *oppida* (towns), archaeologists sometimes describe the 2nd and 1st centuries BC as the period of the '*oppidum* culture', signifying acceptance of the widespread urbanization then emerging in barbarian Europe. This phenomenon is an important measure of advance; and there can be little doubt that the major centres, particularly the tribal capitals, contained those skills and services deserving the name of town; such as trade and manufacture, organization and administration. Some would become Roman (and in due course modern) cities. The army's practice of *deductio in plana*, the 'leading down' of hostile tribes to resettlement areas 'on the plane', meant that Roman cities would tend to be founded on flat land, sometimes in proximity to former forts.

On the Continent, the definitive phase of Celtic prehistory known as La Tène (after a site on Lake Neuchâtel) was now in flower. Society was dominated by military families. 'The common people', wrote Caesar, 'are regarded as little more than slaves.'[12] Control of trade with the Roman world enhanced princely power and gave spur to the arts. Bards were employed to celebrate the feats of the mighty. Artistry, decorative metalwork and jewellery were superb. Carpentry

Rome in Europe
Early 1st Century A.D.
Locations of Episodes, numbered
Exterior Peoples:

Britons
Germans
Sarmatians

BRITONS

GERMANS

SARMATIANS

Rhine

Danube

Tomis

0   100   200   300 MILES
0 100   500 KMS

jm'97

was advanced. Carts, agricultural vehicles and (in Britain) splendid war chariots were constructed; and a network of unpaved roads and inland waterways developed to assist trade. There were substantial corn surpluses. Tribal coinages were minted. By the eve of conquest, descent from the forts and establishment of towns in road, waterway or seaport locations suggests the triumph of trade over fear. Those strongholds would, however, be reoccupied as trouble approached. Mimicking Rome, the Gauls had begun to elect annual magistrates, and in the face of Roman invasion the tribes proved capable of forming alliances with unified leadership and concerted action. There is no knowing how far this swiftly advancing civilization might have gone had not Rome's shadow fallen across its formative years. Certainly modernity would not classify the Celts as 'barbarian' at all, but rather as an emergent group of nation states, some of which had already left the equivalent of what might today be described as a Third World condition.

Attribution of the term 'civilized' to the Iron Age must be qualified by the fact of human sacrifice, forbidden under Roman law but familiar to all who lived outside the empire's European frontiers. In the Celtic instance we have a description by the poet Lucan of a shrine near Marseilles, demolished by Caesar in 49 BC. Though poetic licence and sensational reporting must be allowed for, it indicates the luckless though perhaps occasional fate of captives:

A grove there was, untouched since ancient time,
Whose overarching boughs made roof of gloom
And chill shadow. The gods with gory rites
Were worshipped, altars heaped with grisly
Relics and every tree trunk blotched with human
Blood. Here were gods' grim likenesses, rough-hewn
From crudest timber. They said the ground
Groaned, yews yawed backwards then reared up again;
And from boughs not burning, light glowed weirdly.
Snakes twined and slithered round bare branches.
Here worshippers, fearing to worship, left
The place to the gods . . .[13]

Both Celts and Germans had earlier marched on Italy (c. 390 and 100 BC); events so bitterly remembered that one may speak of a chronic fear of the transalpine tribes, ensuring that Romans would not feel safe until northern Italy – and ultimately most of western Europe – were under control. The struggle to ingest the Celtic world had already taken two centuries and by the reign of Augustus only the British Isles lay outside the empire. Its most dramatic step, Caesar's eight-year war against Gaul, had brought Rome close to her other northern adversary, the Germans. At the time this narrative begins Augustus had reached a crossroads. Should the eagles venture the Channel against the still free Britons; or the Rhine against Germany? His choice of the latter alternative is the starting point of the second Episode.

Proud, powerful and turbulent, the Celts had equalled – even exceeded – Mediterranean norms in several aspects of technology and artistic expression. But in the more telling areas of cohesion, discipline and organization they were a step behind; sufficient to make them losers in almost every clash with the Roman army. Owing in part to geographical position, they were the chief victims of expansion; and of their wide areas or settlement of influence, only the Scottish Highlands and Ireland would in the end escape Rome's grasp.

How did the Celts fare under Roman rule? Though it was not imperial policy to extirpate the languages or customs of conquered peoples, a four or five-century occupation inevitably diluted native ways. La Tène art withered on contact as its patrons, former Gaulish princes, became Roman provincial nobodies. It would be replaced by empire-wide, melting-pot standards of artistic expression, with neither barbarian vigour nor Mediterranean maturity. On the other hand, peace, improved roads, new markets, urban growth and service in the imperial armed forces all contributed to a stability and prosperity unknown before the conquest.

In the face of Roman aggression the relatively advanced state of the Celtic and related peoples had told against them. Their lands, more developed than the German, boasted better drainage, greater woodland clearance, higher standards of grain production and transportation; all of which provided a sounder basis for conquest than the forest and swamp of central Europe. Furthermore, the Celts were victims of their own braggadocio. An impassioned sense of honour obliged them to seek battle. This was a fatal flaw, for the Roman army was at its best in set-piece encounters. By contrast the Germans surrendered readily and regrouped stealthily. They were masters of hit and run. Despite the stupendous hillforts and an array of armament which dwarfed the German arsenal, German resistance would be the more successful.

By contrast, the Germanic legacy in art, artifacts and fortifications is smaller. In stone building it is especially slight. There were no towns. Villages were of semi-sunken huts: wooden, thatched, windowless and chimneyless; plus occasional timber longhouses, with family at one end and animals at the other. Farming included tillage and animal husbandry, but its scope was subsistence and its method often slash and burn. Barley was the leading staple.

Fighting was largely on foot. Weaponry was light, with spears and shields more common than swords, and helmets or body armour rare. Germany's vast iron deposits had barely been scratched. Pottery was hand-made, while the Celtic was wheel-made. Standards in woodwork, leatherwork and textiles were relatively high. Population was considerable but concentrated in valleys between large areas of thicket. Roads, or rather prehistoric tracks, were bad and circuitous. The heartland presented major difficulties of development: a water-logged plain and, to its south, hills dense with forest. Biggest was the Hercynian Forest. Caesar was told it took nine days to cross from north to south. Eastwards no one knew its extent.[14] Though the Germans were generally sedentary, the habit of solving problems by migration remained common. The area of Germanic settlement was double that of present-day Germany. It included southern Scandinavia and what are now the Netherlands, plus Poland to the Vistula and what was till recently known as Czechoslovakia, as well as Germany proper. The Germans, barbarians of the forest, met the Sarmatians, barbarians of the grassland, near today's Slovakian-Hungarian border. (One must, of course, allow for the absence of the Slavic peoples from central Europe during Roman times, as well as those later Balkan arrivals, the Magyars, Bulgars and Turks.)

Cornelius Tacitus (whose approximate dates were AD 55–120) is rightly regarded as a supreme literary stylist as well as Rome's greatest historian. A master of minimalism, he pared description and squeezed comment, gaining in expressive power but losing something of the juice from which history is brewed. His fascination with the Germans perhaps began in youth, when his father may have governed *Gallia Belgica*, a province adjacent to the Rhine. In the *Germania*, an ethnographic work, Tacitus makes important observations on Germanic society: notably that it was in some respects egalitarian, with shared decisions and a sense of personal liberty, unknown to the Celts. He also wrote of the German campaigns of Augustus and Tiberius in his last and greatest work, the *Annals*, recognizing how the combination of intransigent tribes and intractable terrain, plus a non-existent infrastructure, made Germany a poor prospect for absorption.

A century earlier it had been less easy to judge the German War as a mistake. History seemed to lead Rome toward it. A record of success on every front, in all climates and terrains, against a wide range of enemies, lent it support. This was, nevertheless, deceptive. Rome's Mediterranean and Near Eastern subjects had largely belonged to the Punic or Hellenistic empires. They were accustomed to obedience and taxation. For them, as for the Celtic underclass, conquest merely meant a change of master. By contrast Germany had never known a foreign yoke and it made her an obdurate resister. The conflict would remind the caesars that the easy way to get an empire had been to acquire someone else's; the hard way to chase irreconcilable barbarians through bog and bush.

In summary, we need not disparage Germanic attainment either in artisanship or cultural levels. The final centuries of the Iron Age were a time of substantial advance, in which the Germans participated; though less than the Celts who were, after all, the Mediterranean's nearest neighbour. In the early decades of our era, however, with Rome in Gaul and on the upper Danube, free Celtica dwindles and it is Germany's turn to be the nearest neighbour. Development accelerates accordingly. As time passes the Germans will prove better learners than the Romans. In this sense they will be the Japanese of antiquity: absorbing from the Roman west the ability to combine; from the Sarmatian south the skills of horsemanship; from their own, Scandinavian north, the capabilities of weapon-forging and shipbuilding; as well as being both stimulated and shaken into motion by the migratory upheavals which surrounded and involved them during the later Roman period. All this, combined with their widening world picture, points toward two momentous achievements: the 5th-century transformation of the western Roman empire into the Germanic kingdoms and – some three centuries later – the Viking Age.

It is a curious outcome of history that, while Rome herself ceased to be, her neighbours and subject-nations in many cases still exist. The Sarmatians are an exception. Settling in Europe's least stable corner, they have long been overwhelmed by later travellers along the same Eurasian corridor from which they had themselves emerged during the 2nd century BC. Nomads leave few traces; indeed nomadism itself is today a half-forgotten way of life. Nevertheless the Sarmatians are of special interest, being visitors from deeper inside barbarian space and further into prehistory than Europe's other barbarians. Their arrival anticipates even more dangerous enemies, like Huns and Turks, ultimate extinguishers of classical antiquity.

The first Episode describes the steppe, its western end now lost beneath the wheatfields of southern Russia and the Ukraine. In former times it offered the shepherd an alley of grass, linking China to Europe via their respective back doors. In the classical age of Greece it had been the Scyths who travelled this road; in the early Roman period the Sarmatians. Wanderers could of course join or leave the pastoral pipeline almost anywhere on its 5,000-mile flow. The Sarmatians, an Indo-European people, perhaps originated in Afghanistan or north-eastern Iran. By the period of this study their leading tribes had penetrated the Balkans, settling in Thrace (Bulgaria) and Dacia (Romania). These had by now become farmers. The rearguard remained nomadic: mounted shepherds, their families in wagons, knowing no world but grass and sky. They ate, parleyed and slept on horseback. They were ferocious fighters. Women might not marry till they had slain an enemy. On their death Sarmatian kings, like their Scythian forerunners, were interred under mounds surrounded by murdered slaves and slaughtered horses.

The steppe had seen no plough and would not till the 18th century, when Russian soldiery was followed by a mattock-wielding peasantry. Only then would thickest sod be punctured to reveal the world's richest soil – the celebrated black earth, or chernozem – ending the nomadic way of life for ever. On the other hand, though without arable skills, the steppe was far from craftless. Trees in the streambeds provided timber for wagon building, while animal products (wood, hide, sinew, bone and horn) were turned to multiple uses, which included equipping the mounted archer with whip, lasso, saddle, shortbow and scale armour; the last of horn shingles, stitched to leather.

Furthermore, being the world's longest natural road, the Eurasian steppe drew influences from its entire course; from China to Greece, with echoes north from Siberia and south from Iran, the Caucasus and Asia Minor. The result was a steppe art, derivative but distinctive, familiar yet outlandish. Here the Sarmatians were heirs to the

Scyths and Cimmerians. Like them, their princes loved gold. Grave goods include adornments, plaques and vessels, typically decorated with sinuous or contorted animals. Many pieces are in the Hermitage Museum, St Petersburg, some with electrotype facsimiles in the Victoria and Albert Museum, London. Unfortunately it is sometimes difficult to distinguish steppe-made objects from those by Greek craftsmen, manufactured for the Sarmatian market.

Despite the steppe's apartness and the essential separateness of its way of life, this strange and frightening world was surprisingly penetrable. It was a short sail from the Aegean to the Black Sea; and by this period Greek commercial outposts had long been established round the entire coast at approximate 100-mile intervals, tolerated by the barbarians as their principal source of outside products.

The first and last Episodes deal with two peoples, the Getans and the Dacians, at opposite ends of the Sarmatian spectrum. The Getans, one of the tribes still spread along the Black Sea's northern coast, were among the most backward. They were also restive, for others were jostling behind and the way ahead was barred by Rome's Danubian provinces. Prudent measures would in due course reduce the tension: recruitment into the Roman army, controlled admission into the empire and diversion into the east Hungarian plain. However, these improvements would come too late for the poet Ovid, whose exile to the Black Sea in AD 9 (subject of the opening Episode) coincided with a time of exceptional disquiet.

On the other hand, the Dacians of Transylvania were in some respects the most advanced people faced by Rome across her European frontiers. In just six centuries after penetrating the Carpathian passes, this Sarmatian tribe had adopted agriculture, built stone-walled citadels, learned the rudiments of writing and created a war machine which would shatter Roman complacency on the Danube. Nothing says more about the speed of change during the late Iron Age, when the nearer barbarians were being swept into the stream of history, than the divergence between these two cousin nations after a relatively short time in different surroundings.

In the light of Rome's varying success against advanced and backward peoples, it is no surprise that her showing would be better against the settled than the nomadic tribes. The Dacians had set aside their horses and put their trust in mountains, which did little to deter an army born beneath the Appennines. Trajan would end the Dacian Wars in time-honoured fashion by striking at the enemy's capital.

By contrast the Sarmatians who still wandered the steppe had no capital, no commitment to territory, no villages to defend and no crops to be commandeered. Furthermore, Rome's cavalry, her weakest arm, could neither catch nor match these horsemen on their native prairie and did not try. By choosing to stand on the Danube, Rome was able to exclude the grasslands of south-eastern Europe which, like forest, desert and salt water, were elements in which her success rate was modest. Though it pleased her authors to assert that the gods had granted Rome the right to world dominion, in practice she would settle for what her army could handle, her tax collectors organize and her economy exploit. The consuls had been wary of saddling themselves with intractable regions and the caesars followed suit, save in rare cases where precious metals beckoned or strategic arguments prevailed.

How did Roman and barbarian see one another? Archaeology tells us little of opinions and we are obliged to look elsewhere: to written sources and monumental art. This will of course be a one-sided view, in which the barbarian survives by proxy. Most accounts were sensationalized. Few reflected the normal in barbarian life. No society was studied systematically or in detail. First-hand observation was rare. We have no direct knowledge of a barbarian language until the late 4th-century translation of the New Testament into Gothic. The very term 'barbarian' covered such divergent ways of life and levels of development that it is almost without scientific value.

The nature and sparseness of written comment on the outside peoples suggests public knowledge of them was limited and vague. This is understandable. The barbarian lands were four to six weeks' journey from the empire's centre, beyond frontier barriers and across zones which were pre-eminently military. Information was scarce and sometimes censored. The frontier's fences were supplemented by an invisible fence between the exterior provinces, governed on behalf of the emperor, and the interior provinces, administered by the senate. The effect was to sedate the inner provincials, especially the Italians, and cocoon them from the asperities of the outside world. When, in the *coup d'état* of AD 193, Septimius Severus marched on the capital, it is clear from Dio's description that the Romans had never met frontier soldiers and were astonished by what they saw: 'He flooded the city with men of many regiments: wild to look at, terrifyingly noisy, coarse and boorish of speech.'[15] These were trained troops from the Danube's Roman bank. How the citizens would have reacted to barbarians, from the further bank, is less easy to imagine.

It was of course from the inner provinces that Roman readership largely came. As with other forms of literature, it may be assumed that factual works were read aloud in private or public recital. Audiences were predominantly metropolitan and subject-matter was tailored to suit their tastes. Literary tradition was not only Rome-centred. It was also inward-looking: drawing upon past authors, classical mythology and history to produce a sometimes elaborate skein of allusion and near-quotation. Ovid is a prime example. Even in exile his verse is stitched with erudite, internal threads. The impression is of a self-contained, self-centred literature, more concerned with its own cultural legacy than with extending experience in a geographical sense.

It is hardly, therefore, surprising that comment on the external peoples is less abundant than might be expected from an active century of Latin letters or that, where it occurs, it deals less with the European outsider than with Rome's eastern relationships. Hallowed by the exploits of Alexander and Pompey, the East was the prestigious theatre, where Roman statesmanship had achieved memorable results. By contrast the tribal tangle of the northern lands made less rewarding reading and merited less careful attention. Clichés appear to have dominated the Roman view and authors to have reinforced them. Germans and Gauls were mistaken for each other. The 'noble savage' was a literary commonplace and his nobility exaggerated to scold Roman decadence. Contradicting this were beliefs that the barbarian lived on a low moral plane, with the satisfaction of bestial instincts as his stereotyped goal;[16] and that he throve upon thievery and deceit.[17] Choice between these noble or ignoble conventions appears to have varied with the effect sought by the individual writer.

The scowling barbarian, with long locks and matted beard, is a stock figure on triumphal monuments and soldiers' gravestones. It was usual to make him brave and brawny so that skill in defeating him would seem greater. His wildness was considered a result of remoteness.[18] He was thought to be more dangerous where the climate was harsher.[19] A common view was that those from regions colder than Italy were plucky but rash and those from warmer climates clever but cowardly. Only Romans, on whom divine providence had bestowed earth's fairest portion, combined courage, intelligence and farsightedness in ample measure.

So much for perceptions of the barbarian. What of relations with him? The last century and a half had seen Rome in mortal combat with her northern neighbours. The sieges and slaughters in Spain and Gaul under the late republic, and the revenge expeditions across the Rhine with which Augustus' reign culminated, were as brackets, enclosing some of the bitterest campaigns in ancient history. A Greek quip, relayed by Cicero, might best describe the Roman view: *oderint dum metuant*[20] (no matter that they hate us, as long as they fear us). The Republican and Augustan periods had been characterized by fluid warfare and *ad hoc* borders, whose very nature implied a warning to outside troublemakers that they could be engulfed by the next Roman advance. Then times began to change: the army digging in on the long rivers and fixity replacing mobility. Tiberius' rejection of foreign adventures, followed, a generation later, by Vespasian's upgrading of the earth-and-timber frontier fortifications to stone, were broad hints to the barbarians of an intention to advance no further. Calm descended over most of the borderlands, the shadow of conquest began to lift and chieftainly fear of dethronement to recede. What might replace these deterrents as a curb to barbarian insolence?

It is not feasible that Rome could switch from expansionism to the custodial role without corresponding adjustments in diplomacy. In fact, following the end of the German War in AD 16, foreign policy turns from its Republican and Augustan norms, with their overtones of world dominion and manifest destiny, toward a peaceable pragmatism. More precisely, the diplomacy of the Principate now enters its characteristic phase, in which grand assumptions are allowed quietly to lapse in favour of normalized, cross-frontier relations (though the option of tactical advance on the odd front is kept open). Thus, while retribution is retained as a warning to outsiders and the occasional pursuit of glory remains as a sop to the Romans, in practice the main play is toward *détente*. Doubtless diplomatic missions were henceforward to be seen rowing across the Rhine or Danube and the bruised barbarian was sweetened by Romans bearing gifts.

For their part the provincials must buy protection, not merely footing the bill for the frontier's upkeep but also carrying the cost of wooing the wild nations. So begins the principle of taxing Romans to pay barbarians which, though it starts modestly, will reach ruinous dimensions during the late empire. Naturally Rome's subsidies had strings attached and she still had ample power to pull them. Further-more, much of the money would be won back by Roman businessmen. The point, however, is that by admitting commercial traffic, supplying recruits, keeping the peace, accepting arbitration and a degree of supervision (as well as through the direct payment of bribes and stipends) Rome's nearer neighbours were allowing something of the empire's wealth and order to be spread beyond its borders, creating a penumbra between the classical and Iron Age worlds. This was progress of a sort. Though backed by scant sym-pathy or trust, though insufficient to alter history's eventual outcome, the Roman change from chastisement to inducement paved the way for a tolerable relationship between the empire and its northern neighbours for a century and a half to come. It was, unfortunately, no more than an official *détente*. It did not mean that the *Barbaricum* would be a safe place for Roman civilians, or that the stage was set for wider understanding. Diplomatic improvement helped make the borderlands more stable; but as the frontier hardened and gaps were plugged, its presence would ensure the estrangement of ordinary people on either side.

In opposition to the Ciceronian quotation is the elder Pliny's description of Italy as 'a land chosen by divine consent [. . .] to unify widespread empires [. . . and] to educate mankind'.[21] Written in the AD 60s or 70s, its relaxed, even altruistic tone suggests a more confident view of external affairs. Even so it cannot be interpreted as a comment on foreign policy. Unification of 'widespread empires' clearly refers to Rome's Hellenistic and Punic takeovers, on which her Asian and African power rested. Pliny is speaking not of bar-barians but of the conquered nations, for which the imposition of Roman taxation and law necessitated a swift induction into the imperial scheme. Rather than altruism, this was realistic dealing: the offer, to each new province, of protection and a variety of civilized benefits in return for disarmament, good behaviour and payment of taxes. By contrast there is no evidence of a comparable effort to uplift the outside peoples or to spread enlightenment beyond the imperial limits, at any rate until Christian missionaries began to overstep the frontiers in the late 4th century. Indeed Romans applauded barbarian ignorance, seeing it as an impediment to inter-tribal unity and an obstacle to military improvement. Mediterranean vices were another matter. Caesar had been emphatic that these softened Rome's enemies and assisted her cause. So, on the one hand, luxuries would continue to be peddled by Roman merchants. On the other, the south's more thoughtful lessons served only to hasten unwelcome advances in the north, like stone-rampart construction and confederational politics. It was in the Roman interest to 'educate mankind' as far as the last tax-paying subject, but no further.

At an everyday level, one may guess that, for those who had dealings with the outside lands, the dominant sentiment was contempt. Officials in the frontier provinces can hardly have seen the barbarian other than as a petitioner for economic aid. Trans-border contacts must largely have meant paydays. The sense of being surrounded by the paid-to-be-peaceful was a permanent obstacle to Rome's acceptance of the barbarians as equals, ensuring that cross-frontier relationships would seldom be based on mutual respect. Inevitably Roman assumptions of superiority would be reinforced, perpetuating the view that the only world which counted was the empire, its citizenship the greatest privilege to which ordinary men and women could aspire. By contrast the *Barbaricum* represented a civilizational void. Such at any rate seems to have been the official, the ruling-class, the 'Roman' view, projected in patriotic literature and government-sponsored sculpture. It was not necessarily held by ordinary provincials; for we must remember that many of Rome's subjects were themselves erstwhile barbarians. None the less, the only time most Romans saw a barbarian was as a captive or a slave. His humbled image provided the perfect foil for imperial propaganda and there was no better tonic for the army's self-esteem than the cowed and bewildered savage, whose misfortune was to be born outside the imperial boundaries.

Roman law governed conduct on the empire's soil, though only citizens enjoyed its full protection. Romans were not required to harbour scruple regarding things done beyond their borders, especially during punitive actions. Promises between Romans and barbarians were not necessarily binding. There were instances of perfidy and massacre on both sides. The army, instrument of retribution, even invoked an appropriate deity, *Mars Ultor* (Mars the Avenger). Terror was an instrument of policy and treachery a tool of diplomacy. Quintilius Varus' view of the Germans as so wild and backward 'that they have nothing in common with us but voice and limbs',[22] carries the inference that they were, in their untutored state, unworthy of humane treatment. Though extreme, it is a credible Roman opinion.

It should, however, be added that genocide was virtually unknown. Disasters resembling the European impact on Polynesia, Africa and America, the extinction or decimation of Tasmanian, Carib and other nations, seldom scarred the ancient world. Except for the Jews, whose monotheism ill-fitted them to a pagan order, religions were seen as compatible and policy as oecumenical. Annexation did not mean the substitution of one form of land use for another or the displacement of one race by another. In short, this was not comparable to the all-out collision of steam age with stone age, but a more moderate encounter between different aspects of the same age. One may also recall Rome's cosmopolitanism and cultural flexibility. Conquest had drawn together a mixed bag of customs, languages and beliefs; and by and large she let them flourish. There was no compulsory Romanization. The early empire had no missionaries and was free from proselytism or fanaticism. Power lacked the sanctimonious dimension of its 19th-century exercise. Expansion brought booty and taxes, but it was not fuelled by moral or ideological objectives.

Without a barbarian literature, outside opinions of Rome can only be guessed. Of all witnesses perhaps the Jewish historian Josephus is nearest to neutrality. Though a *protégé* of the emperor Vespasian and reporting a supposed speech by the pro-Roman Herod Agrippa II, Josephus does not hesitate to equate Rome's outward march with megalomania: 'The world itself is not big enough for them; the Euphrates not far enough east, the Danube north, the Sahara south, nor Cadiz far enough west to satisfy them; but still they must soldier on, across ocean, even as far as mysterious Britain.'[23]

It was inevitable that barbarians should stress Roman greed. All were familiar with rapacity at local level; tribe robbing tribe, as was their way. But here was a plot to take over the world. '*Raptores orbis!*' ('globe grabbers') shouts a British leader. The phrase may be an invention of Tacitus, but the sentiment is plausible. 'They pilfer and slaughter and call it empire,' he continues. 'They make a void and call it peace.'[24]

Another British leader survived capture to ask a question of imperialism, famous for its irony: 'Caratacus, a barbarian ruler, was seized and brought to Rome, but later pardoned by Claudius. Finding himself free to wander the streets of the city and taking in its size and splendour, he asked: "You who have so much; why do you covet *our* poor huts?"'[25]

The battle speech of Queen Boudicca offers an answer of a sort when she says of the legions: 'They cannot do without bread, wine and oil; and if just one of these should fail, so will they.'[26] It is doubtful whether Boudicca really said this; even whether it was true. Nevertheless, the comment reminds us that Roman imperialism was concerned not with huts but with fields. In the last resort it was agricultural. That the land and its produce were the root of taxation must have loomed large in strategic thinking. The core provinces were those which produced all three of these staples and in practice the high command showed no interest in acquisitions which could not grow at least one of them; except for a few mountain chains whose control was unavoidable.

Of the four Episodes, two will take us up to and over the Danube, one beyond the Rhine and one across the Channel. In each case, as the narrative crosses water it enters the Iron Age and its dramas are played out in the final decades of prehistory. It is an era whose violence is heightened by the approach of Rome and the splintering of tribes into pro and anti-Roman factions. That these events are known is through odd circumstance and freakish coincidence. A poet blotted his copybook, an emperor's niece married a lawyer, a writer married a general's daughter, an artist took his sketchbook across the Carpathians; and one is left with four snapshots into barbarian south-eastern, central and northern Europe, before Rome's faltering expansion drew the blinds for ever.

The Poet

THOUGH OVID'S GREATEST WORK, THE *Metamorphoses*, concerns miraculous changes to its central characters, few of those transformations match the singularity of the real one, which befell the poet himself: from fame and acclaim in Rome to obscurity and despair on the edge of the classical world.

A statue of P. Ovidius Naso, known to posterity as Ovid, stands in the Piatsa Ovidiu in the town of Constantsa, principal seaport of Romania, on the north coast of the Black Sea, 200 miles east of the Bosphorus. This medium-sized, industrial city is capital of Dobruja, the province of Romania which is held in the crook of the Danube as the great river makes its final turn toward the delta. The delta begins only ninety miles further along the coast and beyond its marshy triangle is the former Soviet frontier. The name Constantsa comes from Constantiana, sister of Constantine the Great, after whom the city was renamed. Originally it was Tomis,[1] a Greek colony founded in the 7th century BC. This was the place of Ovid's exile to which, in AD 8, he was abruptly ordered, with no reason given, without trial or opportunity for self-defence. Here he passed the December of his days, composed his last poems; and here, after a banishment of nine years, he died. These final works, known as the *Poems of Exile*, are the most direct vision we have of the classical margins during the early years of the Roman empire. To appreciate this fully we must know something of Ovid's character and career. But first one must understand the place.

The Turks call it *Kara Deniz* (Black Sea) in contrast to the Mediterranean, *Ak Deniz* (Blue Sea) and for good reason. Emerging from a

Bosphorus bright with lawns and palaces, the very act of entering seems to induce a mood change, appropriate to the sea's name in all languages except Greek and Latin. The Greeks called it *Pontos Euxinos*, the Hospitable Sea and the Romans followed their lead. But this was a publicity stunt, rather as Eric the Red was to change Whiteshirt Land to Greenland, 'so that people will go there'. Indeed, with the bluntness of men whose business was to sail rather than sell, Greek mariners had called it *Axenos*, the Inhospitable. What influenced the change?

In the absence of later arrivals (Turks, Slavs and Bulgars), the Greek lands were adjacent to the Black Sea's western end and Greek ships could penetrate its eastern. This is at longitude forty-two degrees, somewhat further east than present-day Moscow. So the Black Sea brought Greece to Inner Asia's doorstep. Not surprisingly the twin seas, Black and Aegean, though wedded by water, were culturally divorced. The Greek view of this alien world is evoked by the Golden Fleece legend, in which fear and fascination mingle. Here was a sombre sea surrounded by savages, lacking the comfort of harbours and islands, yet tempting boldness with a rich reward. The picture is darkened by Euripides' *Iphigenia in Tauris*, with death on a barbaric altar as the price of shipwreck. Eastward loomed grim mountains: Virgil's 'rugged, rock-bristling Caucasus'[2] where Prometheus endured eternal torment. Doubtless the origins of the Fleece legend may be sought in Caucasian gold, swept down in the freezing torrents, to be panned by prospectors and filtered through wool. But there were other prizes, which in the end proved richer. Where Jason led businessmen followed, pursuing, if not gold, then a golden rule: that whenever unlike peoples meet, money is to be made. Such convergences are eternal settings for commerce, since each side has something the other lacks.

To exploit this opportunity, the Greeks required anchorages, warehouses, interpreters, homes, defences; in short, the infrastructure of safe and stable business, repeated every hundred miles round this profitable shore. And to promote the exchange of goods, an exchange of adjectives, from inhospitable to hospitable, from hostile to welcoming, would encourage the colonists bound for these Pontic cities. At least five centuries before Rome's arrival, two dozen trading stations had been established. Some were at the mouths of the rivers which drain down from the immensity of what we now call Russia: the Dniestr, Bug, Dniepr and Don. Others were on the Crimean peninsula and the Sea of Asov. Yet more lay in Georgia and along the northern coast of Asia Minor. Especially active as founder of these outposts was Miletus, on the Aegean coast of today's Turkey, 'mother of more than ninety cities',[3] though herself a daughter of Athens. Tomis was a Milesian foundation. It is a process still familiar to maritime nations, whose emporia, such as the depots along the Gold and Ivory Coasts, Singapore, Shanghai, Calcutta and many more, were so placed that they could be established, defended and, if necessary, evacuated by sea. However, in these modern instances, technology and strength favoured the incomer. By contrast, the Greeks were without particular advantage and faced impossible odds, surviving because the local peoples wanted them to.

There is ample evidence of the store set by barbarian societies upon trade and the goods it brought. Strabo speaks of 'the Caucasian people taking produce to market by sliding down the snowy slopes on sledges made of animal skins'.[4] The eastern Black Sea was reputedly the terminus of a caravan route from somewhere so distant that no one knew its origin. Pliny tells us that Dioscurias (Sukhumi) was 'the common emporium of seventy tribes . . . all speaking different languages';[5] and that 'dealings were done by our businessmen, aided by a staff of 130 interpreters'.[6] Similarly Strabo on Tanais, at the Don mouth: 'It is a market for both Asiatic and European nomads . . . who bring slaves, hides and such things as they produce; the Greeks giving in exchange clothing, wine and other commodities associated with civilized life'.[7] Nevertheless, though normally tenable, and though there were also Greek colonies in unfriendly parts of the Mediterranean, the Pontic were the most precarious.

Cities like Tomis, on the Black Sea's northern shore, faced a particular problem in that the world on whose edge they were precariously poised was itself precarious; for they were liable, after a long investment in bribes and trust building, to be confronted by new and even fiercer arrivals. This can be understood by seeing geography more widely, particularly that of the former Soviet Union whose zones of natural vegetation run crosswise in broad and even bands: tundra, pine, deciduous woodland, woodland mixed with grass, and finally grassland. The last, too dry for tree growth, was known as the grassy steppe: a strip barely 150 miles deep and running the entire length of the Black Sea's northern shore. Today it is largely the southern Ukraine where, with the aid of irrigation from those mighty rivers, the landscape is one of waving wheat and heavy-

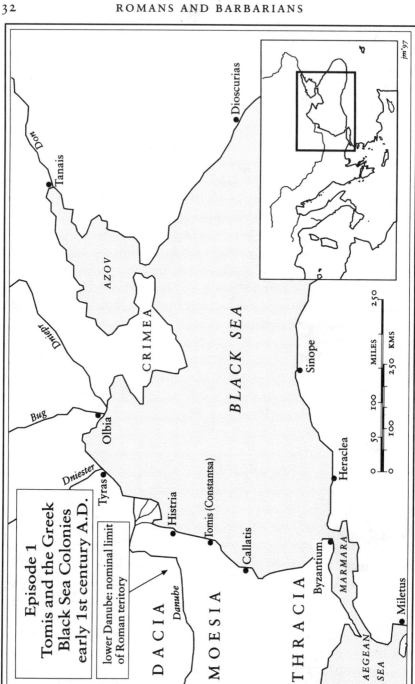

Episode 1
Tomis and the Greek
Black Sea Colonies
early 1st century A.D.

lower Danube: nominal limit
of Roman teritory

headed sunflowers; ideal for mechanized farming, though the dense and matted sod remained unbroken till the late 18th century, when Russia's southward expansion transformed the steppe way of life.

Steppe is Russian for *prairie* or *pampa*. This grassy or Pontic steppe is so flat that the Greeks called part of it the Racecourse of Achilles. Though generally more undulating, the short-grass prairie of the American high-plains states, which can still be seen in the National Grasslands of Nebraska and the Dakotas, is essentially the same. Virgin steppe, now rare in the Ukraine, survives at nature reserves like Askanya Nova; in spring melodic with lark song and vivid with wild tulip. Huge flocks of birds rest in mid journey between Northern Russia and the Middle East. Here too the Przewalski horses, pinkish-beige and white-maned, drum the dry plain. Introduced from Mongolia, these are possible descendants of the sturdy ponies of steppe prehistory.

Early summer is more spectacular still: the plain sprouting fescue, needlegrass and feathergrass; whirring with grasshoppers and bobbing with marmots. Hyacinth, lavender, sage, mint, vetch, milkweed and, most typical of all, the pungent wormwood,[8] with its grey-green leaf and yellow flower, colonizing ground made bald by lightning-kindled grass fires. Hawks hang in the bare blue and everywhere is an endless horizontality, broken only by the bumps of *kurgans* (burial mounds or round barrows) scattered widely over the vivid, green grassland.

Late summer and autumn are less rewarding, the bronze and silver steppe a sea in which the walker wades, waist-high, through tinkling grass and crackling weed, legs pricked by stalks, socks stiff with burrs and bootfuls of sharp seeds. Here unmounted man makes little headway. Winter is more savage still. Big blizzards scour the plain, reminding us that, though we may be at the latitude of northern Italy, this, after all, is close to Russia.

Such was the hinterland of Tomis and her sister colonies along the Black Sea's northern shore. The ultimate factor, however, is not the steppe's natural history, but its extent. Although narrow in a north-south sense, from west to east it is one of the longest features on earth, extending some 5,000 miles from eastern Europe to Manchuria, where the grassy strip widens to 600 miles. All told, the area is immense, perhaps 5 per cent of former Soviet territory. While the American plains run north-south, from Manitoba to Texas, the steppe, almost three times as long, lies crosswise, traversing 100 degrees of longitude, well over half the width of the Eurasian land-mass. Though its central portion is interrupted by mountains, these are crossable. As this grassy path marches eastwards it becomes higher, drier and more thinly peopled. However, the normal direction of march is westwards; for with each day's journey the winter grows minutely milder, the climate infinitesimally moister and the pasture fractionally richer. If sheep led shepherd – as doubtless they often did – greener grass would draw them gently toward Europe.

It is easy to see how these accidents of climate and geography made the steppe a feature of long-term danger for the West. Not only did it offer the Asian herd folk a corridor toward the Balkans, it brought that most irksome enemy, the mounted nomad; for such vast distances, and the tangle of summer herbage, decreed that horse-men would dominate the steppe, as cowboys would one day rule the American prairie and *gauchos* the Argentinian pampa. This is why steppe migration awaited the taming of the horse and did not begin until about 2000 B C. At least a futher twelve centuries then elapsed before a distinctive, mounted warrior emerged, using armour and weapons largely copied from Iran.

Nomads have been described as those whose animals eat grass faster than it grows. Though we are used to thinking of the pastoralist as peaceful, this may simply be conditioning. Our cultural heritage is shepherd-friendly. The bucolic[9] vein runs deep in Western art: through Virgil's *Eclogues*, Dresden shepherdesses and Beethoven's Sixth. Its theme is the unattainable: either an innocent past in one's own place, or an innocent present in some legendary place. It elevates the shepherd to an ornamental role in societies whose real business is now the drudgery of agriculture. Christianity strengthens the tra-dition by emphasis on the good shepherd.[10] And yet, as the Old Testament reminds us, there is also the bad shepherd: 'And so it was, when Israel had sown, that the Midianites came, and the Amalekites, and the children of the east [. . .] they came as grasshoppers for multitude [. . .] and they entered into the land to destroy it.'[11] These 'children of the east' were of course bedouin from the dry lands beyond Jordan, recalling the Arabian adage, 'raids are the bedouins' agriculture'. The nomad has always sought to rob the granaries of settled lands. Alas, the shepherds soon to be encountered by Ovid would bear little resemblance to those decorous products of Graeco-Roman pastoralism with which he and his colleagues had so blithely supplied their readers.

Whether squabbling over grazing and watering rights or harrying the farmers along its edges, aggression was a fact of steppe life. Though nomad populations were thinly spread, raiding parties could be mustered quickly. Doubtless they would as quickly dissolve, for lacking logistical capacity, there was little likelihood of prolonged campaigns. However, limitation was compensated by performance. These were the world's best horsemen. All adults were warriors. The steppe drew little distinction between military and civilian, man and woman. Accordingly the Pontic region supplied the ancient world with two of its abiding images: the amazon, a woman who could outfight a man; and the centaur, in which rider and horse merge into a powerful killing machine.

Seen more widely then, the Pontic steppe was part of an invasion path of long standing. This is not to say that mounted hordes were continually pouring out of Mongolia, intent on the West's destruction. Their view was local and their progress slow. Nor did they necessarily stay the course. Sometimes their wanderings ceased for centuries. Some tribes left the path midway, while others entered it. In particular the wide gaps between Caspian and Aral, Aral and Lake Balkhash, invited the northward movement of refugees from the droughts of northern Iran and Afghanistan, who joined the steppe in its central or Kirghiz portion. This was the probable origin of the Scythian and Sarmatian peoples, whose appearance in the Pontic region coincides with Greek commercial expansion. Nor did this pastoral corridor end at the Black Sea. Its natural *termini* were more ominous still: the Wallachian Plain, that part of the lower Danube where Bucharest now stands; or, branching north round the Carpathians, the Hungarian Plain and the middle Danube.

Foundation of the Pontic cities had coincided with a long lull in steppe migration caused by the settling of the Scyths, a people of sufficient power to command agricultural produce from the moister zone to the north and trade goods from the Greeks to the south. In the mid-1970s an exhibition from the Soviet Union called *Scythian Gold* caused surprise and excitement. Here were objects recovered by Soviet archaeologists from the *kurgans*. Of finest Greek workmanship and commissioned by Scythian notables, some depicted scenes from steppe life. The excavation reports are more sensational still. They describe burials of opulent barbarity, sickeningly brutal in their accompaniment of human and equine sacrificial massacre. Such findings provided a striking confirmation of Herodotus. In about 450

BC the 'father of history' visited Olbia, a Pontic city at the mouth of the Bug, three towns along from Tomis, leaving this description:

> The death and burial of Scythian kings [. . .] A great, square pit is dug. The body is enclosed in wax, the stomach cavity stuffed with fragrant herbs and incense. The bearers mutilate themselves, slashing arms, scratching faces, cutting off ear lobes and piercing the left palm with an arrow. The body is placed on a couch, with spears planted all round it and roofed with hides. A concubine, the closest servants and their horses are then garrotted and buried with the body, plus various personal treasures. Then all build an earthen barrow, vying to make it as great as possible. A year later they strangle fifty more servants and horses. The horses' bodies are propped up on posts and the men, mounted on top of them, secured with more stakes, as if riding round the king. Finally the whole grisly cavalcade is buried.[12]

The Scyths built palisaded settlements, usually within the protection of a river bend. The largest known has a perimeter of twenty miles, including grazing space for substantial flocks, wooden dwellings, smithies and leather workshops, plus a royal palace. Greek-style coins were minted, bearing the likeness of Scythian kings. Here was a developmental level not far behind that of Celtic Europe.

Two centuries after Herodotus' visit, steppe traffic began to move again. The next arrivals were the Sarmatians. Numerous, ferocious and less advanced (except in war), they defeated the Scyths and confined them to the Crimea, where remnants survived for a time. The name 'Scythia' continued to be used by classical authors both for the north Pontic coast and, more loosely,[13] for almost the entirety of the former Soviet Union. In fact the lands to the Black Sea's north would remain inscrutable. Reportedly they were the abode of races subhuman and deformed: a conventional evasion by the ancient geographer when the limits of his knowledge were reached. Antiquity probably knew more about coastal India than the hinterlands of Dniepr and Don; as in the Age of Discovery, when continents would be circumnavigated long before they were investigated. Certainly the Greek colonists did not contemplate Livingstone-like marches into the interior. They preferred to placate the nearest tribes, addicting their leaders to outside products, especially wine, so inveigling them into a dependence through which the interior could be exploited indirectly. In this way a slave trade would be set in motion and grain drawn down from the forest-steppe zone around today's Kiev, without the instigators leaving the safety of their coastal depots. The discovery of Greek objects far to the north tells of a web of trading relationships in partnership with the Scyths. Now the Sarmatians had blown the web away and a replacement must be sedulously spun.

The newcomers, however, were a trickier proposition. Though also of Iranian origin and speaking an Indo-European tongue, the Sarmatians were less likely to be influenced toward sedentary courses. The burial mounds of their chieftains are of a construction comparable to the Scythian, but less lavishly equipped. Many were opened by Soviet archaeologists in the pre-war and post-war years, mainly along the rivers and in the Kuban, yielding gold or bronze jewellery, weapons and iron chainmail; the latter confirming a formidable cavalry of knightly type. No sign of a steppe agriculture has been found. On the other hand, grave fields of two or three hundred burials imply prolonged stays. Here is something of a contradiction: a mobile people caught up in an indefinite pause. It is difficult to say whether trading and raiding among the Pontic cities provided incentives to stay. But stay they did: some eight or ten unruly sub-groups, scattered along the Black Sea's northern shore. Their vanguard, the Thracians, had reached as far as today's Bulgaria. Closest, therefore, to Greece, the Thracians tended to side with the Greeks against their own Sarmatian cousins. Another group, the Dacians, had crossed the Carpathian passes, abandoned the ways of the nomad and settled in Transylvania. Yet another, the Getans, now occupied the steppe around Tomis. Nearby were the restless Rhoxolans and Iazyges; then the Sarmatian parent tribe itself, living east of Tomis; and the Alans, probably the rearguard: together a queue of troubles awaiting Rome's eventual attention.

Such was the Pontic steppe when Jesus was a boy in Nazareth, the elderly Augustus ruled a renascent Rome and the imperial army and navy were taking the lower Danube in hand. However, their approach was slow. The coastal region between the Bosphorus and the delta would not be formally annexed for at least forty years. The date of this event is unknown, but the first permanent stationing of an army unit is not attested by inscription until the AD 70s.

For the Greek cities, with Roman land forces still distant and only sporadic protection from the navy, the early 1st century was a time of unease; the *Barbaricum* unstable, shifting round them like the winter ice floes against the Black Sea shore. This was the mood at the time of Ovid's arrival; and archaeology confirms his pessimism. Constantsa's modern overlay makes Tomis less easy to dig, but Histria, the next city northwards, has provided considerable evidence. In the 2nd century BC its size had doubled. Temples had been built. There were stone houses with upper stories. Its own coinage was issued. A period of contraction then followed; and construction of a stronger town wall indicates the coming of the Sarmatians and disorder in the Pontic region generally.

Regarding the character of the Sarmatians and the flavour of life in an outpost among them, Ovid's verse is our principal source. His *Poems of Exile* consist of two major compositions: *Tristia* (The Sorrows) and *Epistulae ex Ponto* (Letters from the Black Sea), together some 7,000 lines, which have survived almost entire. As literature and the testament of a personal ordeal these are works of unique interest. As history they must be treated with caution. Ovid loathed this thraldom and his poems are a plea for deliverance. To whomever they were addressed, their real target was the emperor, or those who might influence him favourably. It was not in his interest to paint Tomis and the Black Sea region in cheerful colours. On the other hand, neither archaeology, modern climatic data, nor the views of other ancient witnesses entirely refute his impressions.

We must also remember that Ovid's style, with its abundant echoes of other authors, sometimes puts his value as an observer in doubt. His description of the Black Sea's winter climate is, for example, embarrassingly close to a passage in Virgil's *Georgics*.[14] One Ovidian commentator rightly points to resemblances between his portrayal of the Pontic barbarians and those of the *Aeneid's* later books, in which Virgil visualizes the primitive tribes of Italy.[15] Where, then, do Ovid's descriptions end and his plagiarisms begin? After forty years weaving poetic spells, was he capable of straight reporting? Probably not. Certainly, allusion was indispensable to his compositional method. Ovid's motives were idiosyncratic and no one could call him an impartial witness. But he was not necessarily a perjured one.

As well as personal pleading there is also the more general bias of Roman against non-Roman. The steppe barbarians bequeathed few impressive remains and no written evidence. As ever, the reputation of the illiterate was in the hands of the literate, who had no reason to depict Rome's potential enemies with sympathy and understanding. Here Ovid is as culpable as other ancient authors. It did not occur to him that fate had placed him at a unique vantage point, a forward listening post from which the steppe could be monitored and a fascinating study written.[16] What he does give are glimpses of the grassland barbarians at their grimmest; strikingly perceived and expressed, but always subordinated to his own propaganda intention: that he should be allowed to return to Rome. In view of contemporary literary tastes, it is in any case barely conceivable that he would have placed the barbarian in the foreground of his work. As we have said, literature tended to feed on its own traditions and to be more intent on refining subject-matter than enlarging it in an ethnic or social sense. One may doubt whether *any* man of letters would have respected Sarmatian society sufficiently to be its ethnologist or lexicographer. Today, by contrast, we live in an age which professes to cherish less advanced peoples and their cultures; guilty perhaps that so few are left. Furthermore the modern Western nations are comfortingly distant from alien continents. Theirs were maritime empires, with oceans between themselves and their colonies. Even now, direct First World–Third World interfaces (as between South Africa and Mozambique, or the United States and Mexico) are surprisingly rare. Classical antiquity's sense of being adjacent to and surrounded by the envy of less happy lands was stronger; with fear and prejudice correspondingly more acute.

It is time to turn to the Roman side of the story. This was the eighth year of the Christian era and the thirty-ninth since the battle of Actium had brought peace to the Roman world and Octavian, generally known as Augustus, its first emperor, to unchallengeable power. Ovid, aged fifty-one, with his wife (whose name is unknown to us) was on vacation in the Isle of Elba. She was his third wife and the only one with whom he had found lasting happiness. By rank he was a member of the equestrian order,[17] entitling him to the white toga with a thin, purple stripe. He was proprietor of a fine estate, the Villa Ovidio at Sulmo, the family seat, ninety miles inland from Rome; and a comfortable town house close under the Capitoline Hill. As a young man he had studied law, indeed begun its practice and even held minor office. However, as he put it, 'no matter what I tried to write, it came out verse'.[18] The Muse beckoned and he followed, abandoning the substance and respectability of a public career. Not that poetry was without respect. Despite his father's

warning that 'even Homer died broke',[19] there was no more propitious moment at which to excel, especially for one who could
combine poetry with patriotism. It is a peculiarity of the Augustan
Age that its greatest artists were able to reconcile themselves to the
political background, matching stirring events with noble song. Here
Ovid was a misfit, whose destiny was to be the ancient world's
supreme poet of love. His counterpart is surely Byron, with echoes
of subject-matter, of attitude, even of place.[20] Both were associated
with scandal. Both would end in the loneliness of a Greek exile. And
for both, success came early and in a rush. 'I awoke one morning
to find myself famous',[21] said Byron of the publication of *Childe
Harold*; and Ovid's first work, the *Amores*, brought much the same
response. 'When pressed to give public recitations', he tells us, 'my
beard had been trimmed but twice.'[22] At a stroke he attracted distinguished patronage and the acclaim of dilettantist Rome. This early
reputation would be confirmed, indeed outshone, by the *Ars Amatoria* (Art of Love), published during his early forties: a sparkling essay
on seduction, sometimes compared to Pope's *Rape of the Lock* and,
it seems to us, as inoffensive. Be that as it may, Ovid would thencefor-
ward choose subjects more suited to his maturity: the less successful
and uncompleted *Fasti* (the Festivals), a poetical calendar of the
Roman year and its holy days. Then came his central work, the
Metamorphoses: a series of verse episodes, each concerning a super-
natural change; a thesaurus of transmogrification; a glittering amal-
gam of myth, magic and invention. In all Ovid enjoyed thirty years'
homage, first as the *enfant prodige* then as the literary lion of Rome.
And yet, during the last decade of this happy and productive time,
a cloud began to smudge his sky.

He had never sought the approval of officialdom. In this sense he
was the odd man out in the golden quartet of Augustan writers.
Livy's *History*, in 142 books, had Rome's greatness as its unswerving
theme. Virgil's *Aeneid*, a patriotic epic, climaxed in the birth of Rome
and its rebirth under Augustus. Even the hedonistic and satirical
Horace reflected, in his *Odes*, the great pageant of the Roman story.
These were, in the highest sense, the Augustan apologists. Rome's
mission had been their inspiration and they lifted Latin to parity
with Greek as the supreme language of civilized mankind. All three
were, however, older than Ovid. Theirs was the civil war generation,
which had longed for peace and prized the blessings it brought.
Ovid's was the post-war generation, which took peace for granted

and had heard enough of valiant deeds. Understandably he turned toward less patriotic themes, unrelated to public events. His commitment was total but it was to poetry itself, not to a regime, however glorious. It is of course clear to us that, far from being contrary to the glory of the Augustan Age, Ovid's achievement was a proud part of it; and that his deviations from orthodoxy were refreshing as well as harmless.

Not entirely harmless. The emperor had long been disturbed at the state of morals, behind which lay a genuine concern for the falling upper-class birthrate. Laws were passed to protect marriage and outlaw adultery. Though carrying stiff penalties, these were regarded as unenforceable and something of a joke, especially in view of gossip about Augustus' own peccadilloes and his ability to reconcile them with his position as *praefectus moribus* (corrector of morals). Nor was he exceptionally prolific himself, having produced only one child, Julia, despite four marriages. The birthrate remained low, the morals uncorrected.

Joke or not, Augustus took the matter seriously. Dio has left an account of his harangue, directed toward unmarried or childless knights during the year of Ovid's banishment. It was a long and scathing speech, of which a few sentences give a flavour:

> How should I address you? As Romans? You are heading toward the elimination of that name. The truth is you are on a collision course with our national future. What would be left of mankind if everyone behaved like you? You are murderers, in the sense of not giving life to those who should be your descendants; and traitors, in the sense of leaving your country bereft of heirs. For it is people who make a city, not empty houses or deserted squares. How can we preserve the state if we neither marry nor have children?[23]

Further laws were passed to penalize the unmarried, both fiscally and in matters of inheritance. These were called the *Papia-Poppaea* laws, after the consuls of that year. To the discomfort of some and the amusement of others, it was then realized that Papius and Poppaeus were bachelors.

Despite severity on this issue, Augustus could hardly be called a figure of fear. On the contrary, with middle age he had become increasingly relaxed and approachable. Unfortunately this was about to change. Events within the imperial family would trigger outbursts of that youthful ruthlessness which had won battles and eliminated opponents. Robert Graves,[24] not without support from Roman historians, would have us believe that Augustus' blood relatives were being disposed of through the bad offices of his fourth wife, Livia, in favour of her son (by her first husband) Tiberius. This is the woman called by Tacitus, 'a curse to the state as a mother; to the house of Caesar as a stepmother'.[25] Though there is no hard evidence, her alleged methods were either to poison her stepchildren and step-grandchildren, or to poison her husband's mind against them. True or not, public splendours were to be soured by a succession of private griefs. In AD 2 a scandal broke around the emperor's daughter, Julia, who was accused of adultery and exiled to a tiny and desolate island. Such harshness is explainable only in terms of her father's acute sensitivity to ridicule. Another source of amusement was that the adultery law was part of a code called the *Lex Julia*; named after Augustus' family, the Julians.

The appearance of Ovid's *Ars Amatoria*, only a year or so later, was an all-time publishing gaffe. Here was what appeared to be a philanderer's charter. It would have been less humiliating for the administration had the book flopped. But no, it sold like hot cakes! Ovid argues somewhat lamely that adultery had been far from his thoughts, that the poem was intended as a *divertissement* relating only to affairs with courtesans. In his favour was the fact that his own personal life was relatively blameless. 'No scandal ever attached itself to my name,'[26] he maintains. 'My muse was merrier than myself',[27] meaning he had been a playboy in poetry rather than practice. Whatever Augustus' feelings, there was no official rebuke and no action was taken. In any case, Ovid's pen now pursued more seemly subjects. However, to the government's and perhaps the author's embarrassment, that poem on illicit love refused to lie down. On the contrary, its popularity continued to soar.

In AD 8 there was another hammerstroke to the greying, imperial head: the arrest and banishment of his granddaughter, daughter of his already exiled daughter, also called Julia, again for adultery, complicated this time by an alleged conspiracy to replace Tiberius as heir. Livia, if Graves' theory is correct, was working overtime. It is probable that the same year also saw the death of Ovid's patron, M. V. Messalla Corvinus, distinguished general, statesman and honoured friend of Augustus. Without subscribing to the poet's indiscretions, Messalla's very presence would disarm retaliatory measures. With his passing, a trusty shield had fallen quietly away.

We return to Ovid, unaware of the gathering shadows, on his visit to Elba during this same year. If he had offended Augustus, surely he had by now redeemed himself? *Ars Amatoria* may have been an almighty *faux pas*, but seven years had elapsed since publication and no harm had come. At this juncture, out of the blue, a man (or probably men) appeared at the villa where the happy couple were guests. Perhaps they were plain-clothes officers of what later became known as the *frumentarii*[28] (military supply services), a cover-name for the secret police. The poet was staggered. Under arrest ... for writing a love poem! But that was not apparently the question. Ovid was party to some knowledge. He had seen something. Something he should have reported.

In the lonely years ahead, Ovid would brood interminably on this fateful moment. He had blundered. An indiscreet poem, certainly; that he would rue, long and deeply. He had erred too in the direction of his work: its disregard for all the age had accomplished. But of the other matter, the last straw which broke the imperial patience, Ovid would never speak. That is to say he would never mention it in his verse. Though the desire for self-justification was obsessional, to speak out clearly on the reason for his banishment could only rekindle the emperor's anger and damage his chance of reprieve. Doubtless the secret was fully discussed in his private correspondence and was common gossip in Rome. Nothing of either has survived; and hints in the *Tristia* are all we have:

> Two 'crimes', a poem and a *faux pas*
> Have brought me to this pass.
> On the latter I must hold my peace
> Lest insult to injury be added.
> For it is enough, O Caesar,
> That you should have been injured
> Once already.[29]

And again

> Why did I get my eyes into trouble?
> Why was I so stupid as to cover up
> That which I knew?[30]

He swears that what he saw was by accident:

> And I am punished because my blundering
> Eyes beheld a wrong, as if it were a
> Sin that I have eyes.[31]

Whatever he beheld, his implication in this 'wrong' seems not to have been deep:

> And yet the gods, who see through all
> Men do, know that I have
> Nothing done which could be called
> Great guilt.[32]

What was it, this wrong of which he dared not speak? Scholars have speculated endlessly. As the poet implies several times, *Ars Amatoria* was only a contributory cause. It has often been surmised that the true reason concerned the indiscretions of the younger Julia, for both his and her banishments occurred in the same year. Perhaps he knew of those indiscretions. Perhaps, in some peripheral way, he was accessory to them. It is unlikely we will ever know.

Ovid would, however, be let off lightly. Not even *exsilium* (exile): something milder; something called *relegatio* (demotion). He would keep his knighthood, estate and fortune. *Ars Amatoria*, now in all the public libraries, would have to go; but otherwise he could continue to work as he pleased, write as he pleased, correspond with whom he pleased. Only he must return immediately to Rome, pack his bags and take ship for somewhere in Greece; a place called Tomis.

Back in Rome he tried to steel himself for suicide. But there was little steel in Ovid. One thinks of Romans as martial, but here was a quiet man, a meek and on the whole a modest man; physically timid, frail and nervous. Even in boyhood he had shrunk from sport and the mandatory war games. He loved his wife, his home, his work and the adulation it brought. Virgil had died a generation earlier, Horace that very year, leaving Ovid as the language's greatest living poet. Above all he loved Rome herself; the sights, sounds, tastes, smells, talk and endless stimulus of this mother city; queen and crossroads of the world. Now the cup was snatched away. A sudden confrontation by nameless men; a verdict and a sentence pre-imposed.

And yet life among the Greeks might be bearable. Romans of his class saw Greece as a spiritual home. Indeed he had studied in Athens. Neither was this to be *relegatio in insulam*; banishment, like that of the tragic Julias, to some God-forsaken rock. Nor *in oasim*; expulsion to an oven-hot clump of datepalms on Egypt's fringe. At least he was bound for a city, long established, older even than Rome herself. Nevertheless, however packaged, the reality was exile: the destination to which he would be brought by the 'crooked axle' of his luck, 'the destiny, knitted at my birth from a black fleece'.[33] Nor was it a comfort to recall that until half a century earlier 'exile' had been the traditional grace-period during which a citizen condemned to death was allowed to flee Roman territory. This suggests that flight into the *Barbaricum* was scarcely preferable to execution: for where, in that lawless wilderness, might refuge be found? The view was that earth's most felicitous regions by now belonged to Rome and what she did not have was not worth having. Though Ovid was not being sent into barbarian territory (the Pontic cities were already under Roman protection) the point was a fine one, for as yet this protection was largely nominal and in a day-to-day sense the Tomitans were expected to defend themselves. It was a place of which he was soon to write:

> Only guarded wall and barred gate
> Shield us from the baleful Getans' hate.[34]

Ovid's fear of mutilation or violent death, though natural enough, was in his case morbidly acute. This would make exile to the Sarmatian steppe a singularly unpleasant experience, so much so that one might wonder whether it had been devised with his particular sensitivities in mind. We have compared Ovid to Byron, but there is also a resemblance to Wilde. Both were brilliant, witty men. Both defied the orthodoxies of their age. Both were early fêted and abruptly dropped. Both served spiteful, life-shortening sentences. And both produced two 'poems of exile',[35] works strikingly different from anything they had previously written.

By the spring of AD 9 Ovid was in Tomis and had begun work on the *Tristia*. Its opening book describes his last night in Rome; how he looked up toward the Capitol, flooded in moonlight; how, the next morning, his wife, hysterical, rolled in the hearth, clutching the household gods. Glimpses of the voyage follow: lying awake beneath the thwarts of a creaking ship, with seas so mountainous that the terrified helmsman abandoned the tiller and turned to prayer. Since he later mentions an exchange of letters as requiring a year, we may guess his journey was long, with various pauses, changes of vessel and overland stretches. Here is a characteristic passage about Tomis and its ambience:

> Would you like to know just how things are
> In Tomis town and how we live?
> Though Greek and Getan mingle on this coast
> It owes more to the Getan than the Greek.
> Great hordes of them and their Sarmatian
> Cousins canter to and fro along the rough roads,
> Everyone with bow and quiverful of
> Arrows, yellow-nibbed and vile with venom.
> Villainy of voice and face betray their thoughts;
> Hairiness of head and beard tell us they
> Have never seen a barber. Right hands itch
> To pull the universal knife. Such is, alas,
> The company your Bard must keep.[36]

The steppe peoples were formidable archers, using bows perhaps thirty inches long and shooting from the saddle at full gallop. A cavalry bow must of course be short, but strength was added by means of horn tips and plates, bound and glued to the wood. It is possible that the Sarmatians were the first in Europe to develop stirrups, in their original form of leather footloops, which steadied the mounted archer while riding hands-off and greatly increased his accuracy. To be ready to hand, the bow was carried strung, in a large holster attached to the belt, which served also as a quiver. The arrows were poisoned. Ovid's imagination brooded on the Getan arrow and he developed a special revulsion toward it. He described it as 'dealing double death': from the venom as well as the wound itself. The arrowhead was spliced around its base with a collar of thorns, to increase tearing power. The venom's recipe has been reconstructed from ancient references and with medical advice by a German scholar, C. J. Bucher.[37] Extracts from the rotted corpses of adders, including the venom sac, were steeped in putrefying human blood tainted, in its turn, with excrement. The intention was clearly to manufacture a blend of toxicity with gangrenous and tetanoid infections. If the wound failed the poison would succeed; and if the poison did not the diseases would. Herodotus confirms this ferocity in gruesome terms; though he is speaking of the Sarmatians' predecessors, the Scyths. On the matter of head-hunting, Ovid tells us that the Sarmatians continued Scythian practice.[38] Being related peoples we might expect this to be true of a number of customs.

A Scyth drinks his first victim's blood. He takes the heads of enemies to the king, for otherwise he will have no share in the booty. He then cuts around the ears and, gripping the scalp, shakes out the rest of the head. After cleaning it with a bone scraper, he works the skin by hand till supple and makes a kerchief of it. This he attaches to his horse's reins. The best man is the one with most trophies. Some even sew these scalps into coats. Others make quiver-covers from the skin of enemies' hands: human skin being brightest and finest for such use. Yet others flay the whole body and carry the skin splayed out on a wooden frame. Regarding their worst enemies: those able to afford it have the skull sheathed in leather and the inside gilded for use as a drinking cup. This may also be done with a kinsman slain in a feud. If visited by guests he will serve them with these heads as a token of honour. This they call courage![39]

Blood was drunk in brotherhood rituals: 'They bleed those involved, mixing blood with wine in a large pottery bowl into which is dipped a sword, axe, spear and arrows. Then, after solemn oaths, they and the witnesses drink.'[40]

Their source of wine was of course the Pontic cities. The Sarmatians' national drink was *koumis*, a fermentation of mare's milk. Hemp (in Greek *kannabis*) is native to the steppe. Sets of inhaling equipment, consisting of bronze cauldrons, trays to contain hot stones, clusters of short tentpoles four feet high, with leather seed bags and charred hemp seeds, were found in the Scythian tombs. Such was the apparatus rendered obsolete by the invention of pipe and cigarette. Herodotus describes hemp as a fumigant as well as an intoxicant, even a source of clothing.

They have cannabis in their country, like flax except thicker and taller. It is both wild and cultivated. The Thracians make cloth from it, hemp being very like linen. The Scyths take the hempseed and, crouching under blankets, throw it onto hot stones. The seed smoulders and gives off steam at which they emit cries of pleasure. This serves instead of bathing, for seldom do they wash in water.[41]

The practice of ritual divination is mentioned by more than one author. As Herodotus put it, 'there are many fortune-tellers, who divine by means of willow wands'.[42] The wand is still of course associated with magic, but here the method was to drop a bunch of osiers to the ground and consult the pattern which they formed. In this matter it can hardly be maintained that Roman practice was superior, for the latter included the examination of animal entrails, observations of birds and other 'omens from the sky',[43] such as lightning, the shape and movement of clouds and all natural or accidental occurrences, reading into them what they hoped or feared, 'constantly peering into the intestines of sacrificial victims and watching the flight of birds. Agonizing over vague and equivocal predictions'.[44] It has rightly been said that epoch-making Roman decisions hung on a chicken's innards.

The steppe had its own answer to diviners whose prophecies misdirected royal policy. 'Such fortune-tellers are bound and gagged inside a waggon laden with kindling wood, to which two oxen are harnessed. The wood is then fired and the terrified animals stampeded. Sometimes the oxen are roasted with the fortune-teller, sometimes the pole is burned through and they escape.'[45] Regarding religion, there are Euripides' references to the Crimea of the Scythian period, with its cult of Artemis.[46] We have only a single, specifically Sarmatian image, though a powerful one: worship of a naked sword thrust into the ground.[47] 'In their country is neither temple nor shrine, nor even thatched hut; only a naked sword stuck into the soil, which they worship with due reverence. Such is the war god who presides over the lands on which they wander.'[48]

The above quotations mention the absence of huts and presence of wagons. The latter were the standard dwelling of the Sarmatian tribes and an essential part of nomad equipment. Where might timber for these carts be found? Though the steppe was generally treeless, its river bottoms were often wooded. The so-called Iron Age was a period of major advance in wood working, not least in the construction of vehicles with strong, spoked wheels. Clay models, probably toys, from Scythian tombs show these as covered wagons, with skins stretched over (or bark nailed onto) hooped frames. Sometimes only the rearward half was enclosed, leaving an open-fronted driving compartment. Occasionally the covering was pyramidical, a sort of wigwam erected on the wagon's stern. The classic shape, however, resembled the American or Afrikaner covered wagon and was possibly a distant ancestor of the gypsy caravan.

The 4th-century historian Ammianus Marcellinus of Antioch has this to say about Sarmatian nomadism:

> Midway along the Black Sea's northern coast are numerous Sarmatian tribes whose lands have no known limit. They roam over vast solitudes: places ignorant of plough or seeds and knowing only disuse and frost. Here they forage like animals. Their families, homes and chattels they load onto bark-roofed wagons; and when the mood is on them they move off, without a second thought, rolling on toward the place which takes their fancy next.[49]

This is the means by which they and others like them had travelled along that great and grassy road whose beginning and end none knew. When they halted, the wagons would be formed into a *laager* or defensive ring. Though the able-bodied lived in the saddle, vehicles were essential for child-rearing and winter shelter.

> Indeed they are without even hovels and cannot be bothered with ploughshares, living on meat and milk, dwelling in wagons roofed with rounded canopies of bark and driving them over the wide solitudes. When they come to good grazing they arrange their carts in a circle, then gorge like beasts. And when foraging is finished they load their cities, so to speak, and off they go. In these same wagons the men lie with the women and the children are born and brought up. Such are their houses; and at whatever place they chance to arrive, that to them is home.[50]

The Greeks were amazed and amused by the nomad diet, calling the steppe peoples *hippemolgi* (horse milkers) and *galactophagi* (milk eaters). 'They live on meat, including horse meat; and mare's milk, the latter (prepared in a certain way) being especially enjoyed. Hence the poet[51] calls all the nomads *galactophagi*.'[52]

Other food products were nevertheless available, both from the north and the Crimea. The latter, in climate a mini-Mediterranean, had been famous for its grain from the late Bronze Age.[53] There is also evidence for millet cultivation in valleys on the steppe itself; and the Pontic cities had surrounded themselves with fields. All this the Sarmatian peoples regarded as their own. Having conquered the entire western steppe from the Scyths they believed it their right to charge for its use: 'They turn over their land to anyone who wishes to till it, requiring only that in return they receive the rent they have put on it.'[54]

Even so there were shortages. The trading colonies did not consider it their role to feed the Sarmatians but rather, with their help, to acquire grain for shipment to Greece in return for luxury goods. This could be a recipe for trouble. In winter the pasture disappeared under snow and the undernourished herds produced little milk. The Pontic colonies then faced starving tribes to their front and frozen seas at their back; for the freshwater of the great rivers reduced the freezing point of the coastal waters and induced the formation of fringe ice which in turn blocked the harbours and completed their isolation. As if this were not enough, the Danube and other rivers also froze, allowing easy passage for raiding parties. Even wagon columns could now cross. Herodotus' claim that the Sea of Asov freezes for eight months in the year was doubtless an exaggeration. It does, however, share the same January isotherm as the Gulf of Finland, though 850 miles further south. 'For eight months every year there is frost unbearable [. . .] the sea freezes [. . .] and the Scythians drive their wagons across to the land of the Sindi.'[55] Pliny the Younger adds that: 'When the Danube banks are joined by ice and it can carry great preparations for war upon its back, then its fierce tribes have both their arms and the cold to fight for them . . .'[56]

Did the Sarmatians incline to villainy only when pushed to starvation's brink, or were they habitual robbers and raiders? Though winter was the time of greatest danger, sources are unanimous in branding them as bad for all seasons. Ammian calls them 'a tribe highly experienced in brigandage'[57] and 'a people better suited to theft than war'.[58] Tacitus admitted their quality as fighters, though only when mounted: 'While they are useless on foot, on horseback it is another matter. The line of battle which can stand up to them hardly exists.'[59] He describes an incursion by one of their tribes into imperial territory higher up the Danube in AD 69 when the intruders were intercepted by Roman infantry on ground unfavourable to cavalry: 'The Rhoxolans, a Sarmatian tribe [. . .] 9,000 rampaging horsemen, seeking booty rather than battle [. . .] had scattered for plunder and [returning] loot-laden were unable, because of the slippery paths, to benefit from their horses' speed. They were delivered as lambs to the slaughter.'[60]

But once out on the open steppe there was little likelihood of catching them. 'Pursuing or pursued, they gallop great distances on fast horses, leading one or even two more so that by alternating mounts they can maintain speed.'[61]

Herodotus touched upon a universal military problem when he wrote: 'They who are without permanent towns or fortifications and live not by agriculture but by stock-raising, carrying dwellings in wagons: surely such people will be uncatchable and therefore unconquerable.'[62] The underlying point is that strength alone does not determine the outcome of war. Rome had often defeated the strong, whose weakness was that they possessed roads which could be marched on, granaries which could be commandeered and towns which could be knocked out. What of that other kind of enemy whose territory was trackless and townless, whose soil had never been ploughed? Conflict with backward peoples would prove less and less rewarding as Rome advanced and the Mediterranean fell behind.

On the other hand, steppe brigandage becomes more understandable, perhaps more excusable, as the empire takes shape. It has already been noted how the Sarmatian tribes migrated as far as the Black Sea and then stopped. Whatever the earlier reasons, by Ovid's time one is dominant: the growing presence of Roman arms in the Balkans. Like westbound wanderers generally, their path was now blocked. Particularly it meant they had ceased to be true nomads, exchanging the carefree, open-ended steppe for confinement to one area, with other tribes behind and the unattainable wealth and security of the Roman provinces in front. An obvious solution was to settle and practise farming. Like the American Indian, however, Sarmatian development had not attained this level. Nor did the north Pontic region, with its summerlong drought[63] and winterlong freeze, invite it. Even in the late Roman period offshoots of this same group of tribes would still be hanging around in the lower Danube region with nowhere to go. In the 4th century of our era, when Tomis had risen to respectability as the seat of the Bishop of Scythia, a Greek cleric called Grigoris was out on the steppe, preaching to the Sarmatian tribes. He admonished them to mend their ways, abandon rapine and follow the path of Jesus. When he concluded there was a puzzled silence. Then their leader spoke, asking the question which evidently troubled them all: 'But suppose we do as you say and obey the law of the Church; suppose we cease to rob and plunder the goods of others: on what then shall we live?'[64]

Returning to the subject of winter: this was the season Ovid most dreaded. The Dobruja is in fact transitional, between Russian and Mediterranean climates. Mamaia and the other beach resorts remind us that this is Romania's playground, where winter can be mild. But when the wind backs toward Russia, Ovid's comments become credible. Ancient geography had little understanding of the influence of landmass on climate. Cold was attributed to latitude and altitude, but not to distance from the ocean or the direction of its currents. That is why Ovid imagined himself much further north than he really was, locating Tomis as 'close to the shivering pole'! In fact Constantsa lies on the 0°C January isotherm, which also runs through New York and across the northern United States. In his tendency to dwell on the cold, Ovid may be compared with a Southern Californian writing home from Chicago. One must therefore allow for exaggeration and the expectations of a warm-climate readership. Shocking descriptions of cold were a literary convention. In the *Poems of Exile*, however, cold is inseparable from the dangers it provoked:

> While summer lasts the Danube is our friend:
> His war-preventing water between us
> And them. But when the spiteful season shows
> His sordid face and grim frost grips the ground,
> Then are those savage peoples by the quaking cold
> Driven toward the limit of endurance.[65]

Now comes the ill-wind from the steppe: the mounted raider and the singing arrow. These Getans, like their Sarmatian parent tribe and the Scyths before them, wore scale armour: overlapping plates of horn or iron, sewn onto a leather jerkin. Helmets were cone-shaped. They flew tubular standards, like wind socks, painted to resemble dragons or snakes.[66] From Scythian tombs we also know of brightly coloured saddles and embroidered horse trappings. As well as the shortbow, they used sword or axe, plus a vicious weapon of their own: the fighting whip, multi-thonged with a small, metal weight on each tip, used against the enemy's face to inflict blindness.

Accoutrement and ornament depended on social status. Burials suggest wide differences, not only in finery but in horse size and even human stature. To have defeated the lavishly equipped Scyths, the Sarmatians must have had an aristocratic, heavy cavalry, perhaps using horses of Ferghana (Uzbek) origin. Their underlings, more lightly and crudely outfitted, rode the usual steppe pony, controlled, as was normal in the ancient world, by means of the knees and bit alone. The upper mane was shortened to prevent fouling the bow, the withers left long for hanging onto.

We may suspect that the raiders described by Ovid were of the lower social order: a rabble, acting in defiance of their own chieftains; for it is doubtful whether Tomis could have withstood an organized attack by heavy cavalry. Even so, these ruffians would possess the usual skills of steppe horsemen: capable of wheeling with the oneness of a flock of starlings; brilliant archers, able to shoot backwards, in Parthian fashion; employing clever ruses, including the celebrated feigned retreat, which enticed the enemy to break ranks or abandon a defensive position.[67]

On the other side of the picture we have the treatise, by an anonymous physician, known as *Airs, Waters and Places*, once attributed to Hippocrates. He visited the Pontic region around the same time as Herodotus, examining a number of Scythian men and women. It portrays the steppe warrior as far from fit or strong. Hip and spinal problems are given as the commonest ailments, wages of a life on horseback. The men are described as short, with skin pink and clammy; the women as ugly and loathsomely fat. At any rate, so they seemed to a sophisticated Greek. The Sarmatians looked fit enough to Ovid. He writes of their forays, in the danger zone outside the walls, where the small city was obliged to support itself by farming:

> When bitter Boreas cements both stream and sea,
> When Danube by the north wind has been frozen flat:
> Then comes the enemy, riding to attack,
> Savaging the surroundings far and wide.
> Some flee, abandoning to plunder what little
> The country and the wretched peasant has.
> Others, dragged off with pinioned arms,
> Gaze helplessly behind toward families and farms.
> Yet others, shot with barbed shaft, fall writhing:

> For poison rides aboard the flying steel.
> The barbarian will break all things he cannot take,
> His hungry flame devouring harmless home.
> Even when peace returns the land is paralysed.
> Fallow and fruitless the fields. Frightful the
> Foe, in prospect as in presence.[68]

Barbarian portraits are common on Roman soldiers' tombstones; especially of cavalry troopers, who are shown overleaping sprawling enemies. Prisoners are featured on triumphal arches: usually tousled and muscular, dressed (when not naked) in shaggy skins and often trousers. Were they always of strapping build, or was this so that Roman courage would seem greater? To the Mediterranean nations, trousers were as much a symbol of savagery as today's clichés of war-paint or bones through noses. In fact they were simply the invention of horseriding peoples and a practical part of their lives.

> With stitched trousers and sewn skins covering all
> But face, the savage grapples with grim winter.
> Ice hangs from hoary hair and sparkling beard,
> Wine stands moulded to the vessel's shape,
> Streams stop dead. Ice is dug as drinking water.
> The very Danube (no less narrow than the Nile
> And mingling with the deep through many mouths)
> Stiffens under freezing wind and gropes its
> Seaward way beneath the ice. Now will men
> Walk where ships once sailed and ice becomes
> A drum for horses' hooves. Across the new-formed
> Bridge over the still-moving stream, there rumble
> The ox carts of the Sarmatian.[69]

Progressively the ice builds against the coast, sealing Tomis from the south; closing that last option of a beleaguered port: evacuation by sea.

> The *Euxine*, called the *Axine* in the past,
> Now holds me captive in its cold embrace.
> No softness shields these waters from the blast,
> No foreign shipping, safe in sheltered place.
> Ringed round with ravening tribes, which endless vigil keep,
> The land is no more docile than the deep.[70]

As winter advances, so does the hungry savage. Now arrows begin
to fall inside the city.

> I am a captive of the counterfeit Euxine,[71]
> That luckless land beside the Scythian shore,
> Hemmed in by numberless and tameless tribes
> Who recognize no way of life but plunder.
> All outside is danger. Just saved by skilful siting,
> Our little hill with little walls defended.
> The foe rises quickly as a cloud of birds:
> Scarce sighted, they are already on their loot-laden way.
> Though closed the gate we gather deadly missiles
> In mid-street.[72]

Now Ovid, though in his mid-fifties, must arm himself and
mount the town wall. Gentle Ovid, 'the soft philosopher of
love'.[73]

> I shrink from matters military.
> Even as a young man
> I never handled weapon but in jest.
> Now, in middle age, I buckle sword to side,
> Fit shield to arm and helmet to grey head;
> For when the lookout signals the attack
> I rush to arm myself with trembling hand.
> The foe, with bent bow and poison-pickled
> Arrow, wheels the wall on snorting steed;
> And as the sheep, which lacks the shelter of
> The fold, is dragged o'er field and forest by
> The ravening wolf, so he who reaches not
> The shelter of the gate can count himself
> A goner, with a rope around his throat,
> Or else a dead man, dropped by deadly dart.[74]

Weeks pass and the hit-and-run attacks upon the beleaguered town
become more hit and less run.

> Now are the frighted walls made dizzy by the mounted archer
> As stockaded sheep are giddied by the circling wolf.
> Now is the shortbow, strung with horse hair, never slack.

> Our housetops bristle with a feathered mist of arrows
> And the stoutly crossbarred gate scarce counters the attack.[75]

The barbarian is at the gate, yet there is little comfort inside it.

> The town's defences scarce defend; and even within
> The walls a tribal riff-raff mingles with the Greek.
> What safety when unbarbered barbarians
> In skins inhabit over half the houses?
> Even descendants of the Grecian mother-city
> Instead of patriotic dress wear Persian breeches.
> What conversation! They in local lingo, I in gestures.
> Here *I* am the barbarian, understood by none.
> At Latin words the Getans simply gape and giggle.[76]

This was a frontier town, a 'wild west' in the Greek east. Violence might erupt at any moment; even in the *agora*, close to where Ovid's statue now stands:

> Law has no force and force is all they know
> Since force replaces justice in their eyes . . .[77]
> Here sword is law and many is the wound
> Inflicted in the middle of the market place.[78]

Such then was the favour to which one of the Olympians of Latin verse had come.

> Pathetic, for one whose name was ever on
> Men's lips, to live among the Bessans and the Getans.
> Pathetic, to do one's stint at the gate
> And on the wall: a wall scarce strong enough
> To guard its guardians.[79]

Ovid was an amiable, companionable man; Tomis shrewdly selected to ensure his dejection. He broods constantly on the total absence of Latin-speaking company, indeed of kindred spirits of any kind. He feels his powers waning through disuse and the absence of stimulus or encouragement. He struggles with composition in surroundings deeply hostile to poetry.

Though clash of arms is ever near
I cheer myself with versifying as I may,
Albeit there is no one here to hear;
In this wise may I pass the dawdling day.[80]

And again

Poetry should be free from fear;
I cringe continually from the throat-slitting sword.
Poetry should spring from peace;
I am churned by suffering.
Poetry should flow from sweet solitude;
I am vexed by sea and storm.[81]

Even so, though he never stopped complaining, neither did he stop composing. Timid as a man, his toughness as an artist is beyond dispute. However monotonous his plea, the fact is that he found the strength to write and write well. If exile were a contest to break or preserve his spirit then, in the long view, we must judge Ovid, life's loser, the winner. At the time, however, he was a desperately lonely man. He even began to learn the despised Sarmatian tongue. Such was his need of an audience that he started to write in groping Getic:

While some have smatterings of Greek, made barbarous
By tribal twang, none knows a word of Latin.
A Roman poet (Muses forgive me!)
Here I have no option but Sarmatian;
And to my shame, from long desuetude,
Latin words come sluggishly. A man apart,
I talk to myself, seeking by practice
To keep bright the tarnished coinage of my art.[82]

I have become, to my embarrassment
Something of a Getic poet, having
Done a piece in Getic tongue, working their
Wild words to fit our metre. So the uncouth
Getans begin to call me 'bard'.[83]

Ovid's descriptions of his Getic essays are not without a rueful humour. Unfortunately none has been preserved. But would his

serious work now be read? With high hopes the winter's stanzas
were collected and sent to Rome on the first ship. Would they arrive?
And now that he was a non-person, would anyone spare his work
a second glance? Suppose only the copy kept in Tomis would survive,
one day to perplex some puzzled savage:

> Oft have I asked myself, 'For whom this
> Careful craftsmanship? Will Getan or
> Sarmatian read my verse?'[84]

Two things troubled him most. First, had his sentence a limit? Was
it to be loneliness and danger without relief and without end? Might
he at least be moved to some more peaceful place?

> Not just a climate cold,
> A soil shrunken under hoarfrost;
> Not even a Latinless land, or one of garbled Greek:
> But because of how I live, enclosèd by
> The thorny hedge of instant war, compared with
> Which our little wall gives grudging comfort.
> Though peace there sometimes is, belief in peace never.
> Such is this place: either under attack,
> Or in fear of it. Punishment I accept,
> But beg that I may suffer it in safety.[85]

Second, there was his dread that he would die in Tomis and his
troubled spirit find no rest.

> Often for death I pray, yet bite my tongue
> Lest death one day should come
> And to Sarmatian soil my bones belong.[86]

But spring comes even to Tomis, lifting the winter-long blockade of
the Sarmatian shore.

> Lucky who may love an unforbidden Rome.
> But joy to me is snow made soft by spring
> And water in the pond instead of ice.
> No longer is the sea fast frozen;
> No longer the Sarmatian ox-driver
> Coaxes creaking cart across the Danube.

> Soon ships will come, even as far as here!
> Soon a friendly sail will reach our shore:
> How I will run to meet and greet the skipper,
> Asking who he is and where he's from.[87]

Down at the harbour a stir of excitement, a whiff of the world outside. But on the inland side of town, reality was unchanged: rank fields which farmers feared to plough; and beyond, the dour steppe, with no trees to respond to the strengthening sun.

> Bare fields and leafless landscape without tree.[88]
> The sour steppe begets the dismal wormwood
> And from its bitter lesson do we learn
> The land's own bitterness.[89]

> The steppe sprouts wormwood,
> Aptest crop for bitterest place.
> And fear: the wall slammed by the enemy,
> The dart dipped in dripping death.[90]

We have said much of Tomis and its tense relationship with the surrounding Getans. What of the relationship of both to Rome? By now Greece and most of Asia Minor were in Roman hands. Nominally Tomis was imperial territory, not only through Rome's custody of the mother-city, Miletus, but more directly in that M. Licinius Lucullus had visited the area as early as 72 BC in support of his brother's campaign in Asia Minor; and had taken the north Pontic cities under the eagle's wing. Getica was regarded as a protectorate, ruled by its own chiefs and after its own customs but in allegiance to Rome. Indeed its king, Cotiso, had been Roman educated and Augustus may even have contemplated marriage with his family.[91] It is possible that Cotiso was still being held in Rome in polite captivity as a royal hostage: Ovid's situation in agreeable reverse. In practice, however, Rome's control over the untrustworthy Getans, like her protection of the insecure Pontic Greeks, was still tenuous. During Ovid's time at Tomis the nearest Danubian base was probably a naval station, Ratiaria, 375 miles upstream. Its name, meaning 'rafts', suggests a lighterage depot. What is more, only two legions were presently allocated to supervise the entire distance from Belgrade to the delta. The fact is that Rome was preoccupied with problems closer to home and Tomis must look after herself. More broadly, the lower Danube had been placed under the guardianship of Rome's ally, King Rhoemetalces of Thrace, whose territory began some 150 miles south-west of Tomis and whose capital was Viza, now a village just north of Istanbul. In the event of a crisis too big for Rhoemetalces to handle, Roman reinforcements would be sent down the Danube, assuming they could be spared, and naval units were available to move them, for no riverside road yet existed.

So, in Ovid, we have a Roman banished to a Greek city surrounded by Getan barbarians, all under nominal Roman rule but presently being looked after by Thracian allies, who were themselves the Getans' ethnic cousins. Doubtless the average Getan cared little for these complexities, continuing to rove and rob as steppe and season dictated.

> For thee, fair Rome, they nothing care,
> Belief in bow and quiver makes them brave.
> Inured to thirst and hunger,
> With tireless horses under them,
> They know an enemy will fall behind
> For want of water.[92]

In a propaganda sense Augustus' trump card was as peace-bringer to the Roman world. He had consecrated an altar[93] to the *pax Augusta*; and three times closed the door of Janus' temple, previously 'shut but twice since Rome's foundation . . . signifying peace by land and sea throughout the Roman realm'.[94] One of his admiring subjects wrote that the Augustan peace had reached the limits of the known world, 'preserving every corner of it free from fear of brigands'.[95] Even the careful Ovid cannot forgo a hint of sarcasm:

> . . . in the wide world, take my word,
> You will hardly find a land more lacking
> The Augustan peace.[96]

Of interest to all who study the Augustan period is the extent of the conviction that the world was Rome's oyster, to swallow as it suited her. This may have gone far beyond popular jingoism; invading top decision-making, colouring Augustus' view of the outside world and boosting his confidence in Rome's ability to take and hold central

Europe. Weighty literary sources, like Virgil at his most majestic,[97] can be quoted to support divine ordination as the source of Rome's right to rule. Even Ovid had written, from the safety of the capital:

> Gentibus est aliis tellus data limite certo:
> Romanae spatium est urbis et orbis idem.[98]
> (To other nations their allotted place:
> Only the globe restricts the Roman race.)

From Tomis he would see this matter differently:

> Along the Black Sea's northern shore
> The light of Roman day grows dim:
> From here begins Basternian and Sarmatian sway.
> Perched on the empire's very rim,
> This land comes last of all beneath thy law.[99]

The difference between these two statements implies Ovid's acceptance of a far-reaching truth: that world dominion was not granted by Rome's gods or decided by Rome's poets. It rested on her military arm, whose strength and length were not indefinite. Though we do not know the exact date of the second passage's composition, it is possible that events in Germany were bringing the emperor face to face with the same truth at the same moment. With the passing years Roman public opinion would also begin to recognize this reality, as seemingly endless campaigns beyond the Rhine reached no conclusion.

Reading Ovid's last work, the *Epistulae ex Ponto*, one is aware that something more than the usual steppe gangsterism was in progress. The Getans had stormed and taken two Thracian-manned outposts on the Danube: Aegisos and Troesmis, not far above the delta. In view of the steppe peoples' generally poor showing against fixed defences, it is not clear how they achieved this; but being already inside the lower Danube they were able to attack from the rear in an act of treachery against an ally of Rome. The two strongpoints were retaken by Roman forces, ferried downriver in AD 12 and 15, when, according to Ovid, the Danube was 'dyed with barbarian blood'. Though these events were only a hundred miles away, Ovid's anxiety was mollified by the Roman intervention and also by the pleasure of receiving the officers, Vestalis and Flaccus, who presumably visited Tomis in connection with the campaigns. It is, however, possible that Ovid visited *them*, for he writes of 'verses composed on the battlefield'.[100] Flaccus, the commander, was the younger brother of a friend. Here was an opportunity for Ovid to push his case. To Vestalis:[101]

> You see yourself the Black Sea white with ice.
> You see yourself the frozen wine stands stiff.
> You see yourself the ferocious Iazygian
> Steering laden wagon over mainstream Danube.
> You see how poison, flying on fast feathers,
> Delivers death twice over.[102]

To Graecinus, another brother of Flaccus, who was about to return to Rome after his tour of duty:

> Should you see Flaccus, recently commander
> Of this region . . .[103]
> Ask him of Scythia and its climate.
> How it is to live in fear of foes so near.
> Whether the slim shaft is dipped in snake venom.
> Whether the human head is used as gruesome talisman.
> Whether I lie when I say the sea freezes over
> Acres at a time.[104]

The years were passing, Ovid weakening. He complained of brackish water and poor food. He suffered stomach upsets, fever, sleeplessness and a constantly aching side. He was pallid, with hair prematurely white.

Augustus, too, was ageing. He had passed seventy-one when Ovid's exile began. What if the emperor should die first? Would his successor grant a reprieve? Augustus did in fact die first: at seventy-seven, during the sixth year of Ovid's absence. The poet wrote him an elegy, in Getic:

> You ask me what I wrote: a song for Ceasar,
> Telling of Augustus' earthbound body
> But his spirit soaring high in heaven
> And Tiberius holding now the reins.[105]

But no word from Tiberius; and there was little hope of reaching this increasingly reclusive and stone-hearted man. By now Ovid himself had less than three years to live. His sole consolation was an unexpected one. Latterly the city of his exile had begun to seem less hateful. He was touched by the simple kindness of its people. Though no one could read his verse, they honoured him. Perhaps the officers' visit enhanced his standing. He was exempted from taxes. At last Tomis was starting to seem like home!

> Dear as Latona[106] to the Isle of Delos
> Which alone gave haven to her wanderings,
> So dear to me is Tomis. From home far exiled
> It has become for me a faithful home-from-home.
> Would the gods had placed it nearer to some
> Promise of peace, further from the chilling pole![107]
> Tomitans, I have affection for you,
> But little for your land.[108]

Ovid died in AD 17 or soon after, aged sixty. Buried obscurely, this odd-man-out in the Augustan Parnassus ended as he dreaded most: in cold Sarmatian soil, somewhere between barred gate and bare steppe. So faded a comet, whose returning fire would be hailed in many an age to come. During the resurrection of Pompeii, when the spade uncovered the numerous wall-scrawls of the common man, the lines of poetry would be predominantly his. The cultural movement known as the Twelfth Century Renaissance would call itself *Aetas Ovidiana* (the Ovidian Age). His would be the poetry which most delighted Dante, who made him one of the 'four great men' encountered in Limbo. Ariosto and Tasso, Gower and Spenser were under his spell. Chaucer would call him 'Venus' clerke, who wonderfullie wyde hath spread that goddess's grete name'.[109] Meres would avow that 'the sweete and wittie soul of Ovid lives in honey-tongued Shakespeare'.[110] His work, especially concerning transformations, would be a treasury of plots and ideas for writers and painters, from the elder Brueghel[111] to Bernard Shaw.[112] He was the least awesome and most delightful of the great Romans; a poet to be loved as long as love is loved. 'Nor fire, nor cankering age, thy wit-fraught book shall once invade.'[113]

The steppe evoked little wit. Though never losing technical mastery, circumstances turned Ovid toward inwardness and darkness and away from the brilliance and brightness which had been his genius. The gain for history was a loss for literature, which fades markedly during the closing years of the Augustan Age. Regarding the *Poems of Exile*: it is a happy outcome that the fruits of so unpromising a place, shipped from so far, should have been preserved, despite official frost, to survive Rome's long life and painful death, to escape the Dark Ages, to be circulated among Meroving monasteries and Caroling libraries, finally to emerge into the safety of print and the daylight of dissemination. It is lucky, for those who study the edges of the ancient world, that such a man should have gone to such a place. Americans may still comprehend contemporaries like Henry James and Buffalo Bill[114] as contrasting aspects of the same national experience. British people, too, are just able to reconcile differences represented by the view from an empire's centre and from its edges, as in the work of opposites like Wilde and Kipling, Aubrey Beardsley and Robert Service. With Ovid the metropolitan and frontier experiences meet, though uneasily, in one man. It was an accident unlikely to be repeated. The fringes of the Roman world were the abode of backwoodsman, trader and soldier. Only occasionally and in flashes would they again be seen through the eyes of a supreme creative artist. The coincidence of voice and place which is Ovid in Tomis was unique and would not recur.

Banishment to the Black Sea was more than a way to be rid of someone, and the motive was more than plain punishment. Who devised this arrow, dealing double death to person and poetry alike? The style could be Livia's. Despite advice to her husband to treat dissidents leniently,[115] she herself was the last to be lenient in the event of a threat to her son's succession. She was motivated by what Tacitus called 'stepmotherly spite'.[116] If there is truth in the younger Julia's implication in a plot against Tiberius,[117] and if Ovid had knowledge of it, Livia's hate would be assured. All, of course, is guesswork. Only on the question of who gave the actual order are we on firm ground. As Ovid's wife puts it at the beginning of *Tristia*, 'It is Caesar's anger which commands you to quit your native land.'[118] Whoever devised the punishment, the order was the emperor's; and it diminishes his august name. State oppression of artists has many a resonance in the 20th century and it is comforting to be reminded that the outcome is the same. Art is in a curious way unpunishable and those who penalize poetry incur the penalty of its augmented power.

The Lawyer

In stirring pose the statue of Hermann, the German hero called by Roman authors Arminius, stands on the highest hill in a forested region of north-west Germany near the town of Detmold, a hundred miles east of the Rhine and fifty south-west of Hannover. The statue, known as the *Hermannsdenkmal* (Hermann's monument), is a celebrated landmark, commanding wide sweeps of country: westwards toward the Rhine, northwards to the plain and southwards over the tangle of wooded upland which will climax in the distant Alps. The summit on which it stands is called the Grotenburg, southern outlier of the Teutoburg Forest,[1] an arc of wooded hills which begins near Osnabrück, sweeping south-eastwards to join other ranges which mark the end of the flat, agricultural lands of Lower Saxony and the beginning of the wild and wooded Hessian hill country.

The statue depicts a youthful warrior, in winged helmet, sword held aloft with Wagnerian panache. On the twenty-one-foot blade is emblazoned in golden letters: *Deutsche Einigkeit meine Stärke, meine Stärke Deutschlands Macht* (German unity my strength, my strength Germany's power). Hermann's foot rests on a Roman eagle and a fallen *fasces*. The monument commemorates the greatest reverse suffered by Roman arms during the first two centuries of our era; an event know as the Varian Disaster, after the defeated commander P. Quintilius Varus.

The statue is 19th-century, its inspiration nationalism rather than exactitude. The battlefield's location was guesswork; its hero's appearance a product of the sculptor's imagination. Unlike Ovid's statue in Constantsa,[2] its creator had nothing to go on, except that a large Roman army was destroyed by a youthful German prince of zealous character and striking looks in the 'Teutoburg Forest'. Even his name is uncertain. Though Hermann is a possible equivalent of the Latinized *Arminius*, it is in fact a modern attempt to link the name with Herimannus, a Germanic god of war. We will compromise, using the name Armin. Finally, the location of the Teutoburg Forest is itself obscure. It appears in one ancient source as the *Teutoburgiensis Saltus*, a name not applied on the ground until the 17th century, when antiquarians based their suppositions on the accounts of four Roman historians who described the battle, none of whom was an eye-witness and only one a contemporary. The location chosen was the former Osning Range,[3] though this was without archaeological proof or even place-name and folkloric support. None of the Roman accounts is compatible with a hilltop. The Grotenburg was simply a striking place to put the monument. It is in fact the site of a hillfort[4] and the name *teuto burg* (Teutonic fort) appears to suggest a connection. On the other hand, Iron Age fortifications are numerous in this part of Germany. To compound the riddle, *saltus* is a word of vague and ambiguous meaning: woodland clearing or glade; pass, defile or valley. However, the translation 'forest' seemed best to match some Roman descriptions and, as we believe mistakenly, it has been accepted without question for the last 300 years.

Where was the battle fought? The fascination of this question can be imagined, especially for late 19th-century Germans, epitomizing as it did the clash between romantic and classical forces at a time of maximum interest in both: when Wagner was weaving his mighty tapestries of music and myth and Schliemann was unearthing Greek gold at Troy and Mycenae. Hundreds of sites were proposed, including at least thirty serious suggestions. For a time the Hildesheim Treasure was thought to provide a clue. In 1868 soldiers, building a rifle range into a hillside, uncovered a large hoard of Roman silver vessels of exceptional quality, still considered Germany's most important ancient trove.[5] Some speculated that this might have been the table service of Varus, the defeated commander, hidden as the Roman plight worsened; for the army was travelling with full baggage and Varus was a wealthy man. However, a few of the pieces have now been dated to the century following and it seems likely that the treasure was either the stock of a Roman merchant or a diplomatic consignment destined for what has been called the 'prestige goods zone' of Central Germany. The Teutoburg battlefield retained its secret till the late 1980s, when it was located nearly fifty miles from the statue. However, let us postpone that aspect of the detective story until the circumstances have been fully described.

Though without historical value, the Hermann Monument is of interest in its own right. It is the work of the sculptor Ernst von Bandel (1800–76) who, as a boy of six, on being told the story by his father, resolved to commemorate the Teutoburg battle in a style and on a scale appropriate to the sentiments it evoked in German hearts. It was to occupy his energies for thirty-seven years. The money was partly raised by public subscription, in part it came from his own pocket. The plinth, as high as the statue itself, is of sandstone blocks, some cut from masonry robbed from the dry-stone ramparts of the prehistoric hillfort. This was completed in 1846. There followed a decline in Bandel's fortunes and a sixteen-year hiatus while the statue lay in part-finished sections on the workshop floor. It was decided to sell it as scrap. But in 1871 German unification created a surge of patriotism. Armin was recognized as a powerful national symbol. The Reichstag voted funds. The statue was erected during the period 1873–5, when Bandel, now in his seventies, lived in a hut on the hilltop. By this time he was going blind and frequently bumped into trees.

The figure is eighty-eight feet (twenty-seven metres) to the sword-point. It is made from sections of beaten copper, attached to one another and to a steel framework by means of 31,000 rivets and bolts. The sword weighs 4 cwt. (203kg.). The idiom is 19th-century neo-classical and owes much to David, court painter to Napoleon.[6] David's heroic manner would influence other monuments, most notably the Statue of Liberty;[7] and Justice, on the Central Criminal Court (Old Bailey), London. Liberty is ten years younger and three-and-a-half times larger, though the higher pedestal and hilltop position of Bandel's statue make it seem almost as big. Both are identical in materials and construction. The Hermann Monument was dedicated in the presence of the Kaiser,[8] Wilhelm I, in 1875. It was Bandel's finest hour, though owing to almost total blindness he was unable to see the statue in place: a parallel with Beethoven which did not escape his admirers. He died a year later.

Today Armin's statue still stares eastwards over treetops and hilltops toward his country's interior; urging Germans to a unity they would fail to achieve for 1,862 years after the events of AD 9 which it commemorates. Following its gaze into Iron Age Germany, it may be possible – from the hints offered by terrain, texts, archaeology and guesswork – to assemble a setting in which to place the Battle of the Teutoburg Forest.

The settlement area of the Germanic peoples during the Roman period was far larger than that of modern Germany. It included Scandinavia, Holland, Western Poland and Czechoslovakia. On the other hand, today's England, Austria and Switzerland were all at that time what may loosely be called Celtic. Germany's approximate eastern limit was the Vistula, beyond which were the Balts and the *Veneri*. In German, *Wend* is still used to mean Slav; and we may assume that these were the westernmost Slavs of their day. Southwards, the Germans met the Sarmatians somewhere near the present Slovakian-Hungarian border. The Magyars had not yet arrived on the scene. The Sarmatian tribe nearest to the Germans was the Iazyges, moved north by the Roman army to fill a vacuum in what is now eastern Hungary. The western boundary of Germany was considered to be the Rhine, though this was a less precise dividing line than one might think. But before discussing the relationship between Gauls, Romans and Germans two reminders may be given.

First, neither Germany, Sarmatia nor Celtica resembled anything we might today describe as a country, an empire, or even a confederation. Rather, these were loose groupings of language and culture, within which individual tribes were often in rivalry or at war. Secondly, the main ethnic units (Italians and Greeks no less than Celts, Germans, Sarmatians and Slavs) were all cousins in the same Indo-European family; though 2,000 years of dispersion, wandering and varying arrival times in the West had led to major differences of life and language to the point of mutual incomprehensibility, as with their descendants today. This was especially true of the Sarmatians, whose steppe experience had given them a nomadic character distinct from the others. Thus Tacitus points to the contrast between 'Germans, having fixed abodes, carrying shields, walking and running quickly; and the Sarmatians, who live in wagons and on horseback'.[9] Similarly, of a southern Germanic tribe, the Basternians, he says that, 'by the sedentariness of their habits and their housebuilding they behave as Germans'.[10] In general, ancient sources portray the Germans as more advanced than the Sarmatians but less so than the Celts, who were by now building stone ramparts, minting coins and producing metalwork of finest artistry. Tacitus tells us that the

Germans were 'separated from the Sarmatians by mountains and mutual mistrust; and from the Gauls by the Rhine'.[11] On this point he was strongly influenced by Caesar's account.

In 55 BC, the same remarkable year as his visit to Britain, Caesar crossed the Rhine. Neither of these feats was necessary. Both were propaganda 'firsts'. Caesar describes the event as follows:

> To cross in boats would neither have befitted Caesar's own dignity nor that of Rome; even though building a bridge involved great difficulties because of the river's breadth, depth and current. Ten days after the first felling of timber the bridge was completed and the army marched over. [The Suebians, on the east bank] sent word throughout their tribal areas, telling people to abandon the *oppida*, take the women, children and valuables into the forest; then assemble all fighting men in an appointed place at their territory's centre, where they had decided to make a stand.[12]

However, Caesar's stay was short. He contented himself with laying waste the villages and crops near the bridgehead and declined a major confrontation.

> Then he crossed back into Gaul, slighting the bridge behind him. In total he had spent eighteen days across the river and considered he had done all which honour or interest required.[13]

In taking an army dryshod over the Rhine, where no Roman soldier had before set foot, Caesar's objectives were not dissimilar to John F. Kennedy's in placing an American on the moon. Both achievements beamed a warning of technical supremacy eastwards and a signal of pride and reassurance westwards. The bridge site, identified by the finding of steel-tipped timber piles in the river mud, is at Urmitz near Neuwied.[14] Caesar considered it important that the Rhine should be seen as a clear geographic and ethnic frontier; and he has been accused of exaggerating its significance to fit this view. Not only must he match the river's importance to the achievement of crossing, but he must also seek to justify intervention in Gaul in the first place. Ostensibly this had been to repel German invaders who could, he argued, have endangered Roman Provence: a nobler-sounding motive than personal ambition. By the same token he had reason to play up the differences between German and Gaul emphasizing the former's bellicosity. The bad press given to those east of the Rhine had begun.

Caesar's knowledge of Germany was in fact limited. Though German auxiliaries had served with him and he was sometimes drawn into Gallo-German politics, his reputation as an authority on German affairs is built on not much more than his Rhine crossings.[15] Two generations later Strabo was painting a somewhat different picture: 'The regions across the Rhine are occupied by the Germans who, though differing from the Celts in being wilder, taller and blonder, are in all ways similar; for in physique, habits and life-styles the two are very much the same.'[16]

Most ancient authors concur in regarding Gauls and Germans as similar. Indeed the two were often confused, both by writers and the Roman public. This may be surprising to the modern reader who, like Caesar, is keenly aware of the differences between the French and Germans. Archaeology helps explain the confusion by telling us that most of western Germany, between the Rhine and Weser and southwards to the Alps, had formerly been Celtic and strongly related to those successive cultural flowerings called Hallstatt and La Tène. This explains why many Celtic forts (like the one in which the *Hermannsdenkmal* stands) are found as far eastwards as the Weser; and indeed why that river belongs to a large group of Celtic river names.[17]

In fact the German heartland appears to have lain in the southern Baltic and north coastal areas of today's Germany. However, in the late 2nd century BC the Germans began to move southwards into the Rhineland and Belgium, setting in motion events which would shake Roman confidence and fuel her longstanding fear of the northern peoples. Two tribes migrated from Jutland, 'driven from their lands by a great flood-tide'.[18] One, the *Cimbri*, moved up the Elbe into Bohemia. Turning west through the Alps, they eventually reached the Rhone, where they joined the other tribe, the Teutons, who had arrived by a more direct route. The company included families, ox carts and herds of cattle. Both tribes were seeking land and a chance to settle, but with little notion where their trek might lead.

They defeated five Roman armies in succession, before veering west to plunder southern Gaul and Spain. Meanwhile, Caius Marius seized the respite to assemble and drill veterans who had fought with him in North Africa. At length the Teutons turned back toward Italy. Marius intercepted, defeating them decisively at the battle of *Aquae Sextae* (Aix-en-Provence) in 100 BC, fought on the plain beneath

Cezanne's Mont Sainte Victoire, where the local village is still called Pourrières[19] after the German corpses. The *Cimbri* were destroyed in the following year at Vercellae in Piedmont.

By Caesar's time the main body of German migration had reached the Alps. By that of Augustus the fringe areas of their latest settlements (eastern Gaul, the Alps and Bohemia) were still unstable, with incursions into Gaul remaining common. So, in the first decade of the Christian era, we have a picture of Germany in flux: with western Germany recently Celtic and a hybridized eastern Gaul (today's Belgium, Luxembourg and Alsace) where Celt and German mixed. Here was a Rhine far from the clear divide in which Caesar would have us believe.

To these influences must now be added the Roman. It is probable Caesar entrusted the eastward defence of Gaul to friendly Belgic tribes, paid and even placed for this purpose on the Rhine's western bank. The arrangement seems to have continued into Augustus' reign; the Gallic legions, numbering perhaps eight, remaining in the interior of their provinces. During this time, Roman relations with the German lands were largely confined to traders, as well as to markets on the Rhine bank and limited diplomatic contacts. These provide intriguing glimpses behind the Iron Age curtain.

Before plunging into the German forest it is worth a word on our principal source, for in the *Germania* of Tacitus we have a portrait of the prehistoric German people which is not only the sole survivor of its type but also the fullest account of an Iron Age society we possess. This is why, in recognition of its unique interest, renaissance scholars called it *libellus aureus* (the golden monograph).

Transmission was via a single medieval manuscript, uncovered in 1451 at the monastery of Hersfeld, southern Germany; demonstrating on what slender threads the bequests of ancient learning have sometimes hung. Its printing in Nürnberg, twenty years later, was a stimulus to national pride, leading ultimately to the first history of the German peoples in the 17th century. Enthusiasm must, however, be tempered on several grounds. In the first place it is unlikely that Tacitus visited Germany in person. On the other hand he did have access to sources since lost, including Livy's Book Nine and Pliny's twenty volumes on the German Wars. Perhaps he also drew on the reminiscences of his own father who, from the evidence of an inscription, is thought to have served as a senior official in *Gallia Belgica*, the province abutting the Rhine.

The ethnographic treatise was an established form, traceable to the Syrian-Greek Posidonius (135–51 BC), whose work on the Celts is known only through later authors. Despite the loss of almost all studies of this kind there are clues enough to know that the *genre* had its full share of truisms and that Tacitus was not always blameless in avoiding them. These included credulity (a tendency to parrot the same information from author to author) and the idea that barbarians were all the same. The latter, comparable to modern clichés about distant races,[20] resulted in a readiness to transfer information from one folk to another; so it is not always easy to know when Tacitus might be grafting Celtic characteristics onto Germans. Furthermore we must keep in mind the familiar prejudices of classical historians, where ingrained belief in the inferiority of barbarians is commonly contradicted by admiration for the 'noble savage'.[21] In obedience to this formula the German is praised for manliness, strength, hardihood, chastity, fidelity and other traits. While probably true, these were also devices by which Tacitus could castigate his fellow-Romans for addiction to soft living and loss of values which were considered to have belonged to the Republican period at its best.

There are yet other distorting features. History was seen as a form of literature, even of oratory; for it was read aloud to select groups, who expected artistry and polish. As with Ovid's, Tacitus' listeners would have yawned at the detail for which we yearn. Names, times, distances, instances, circumstances, all relating to places about which genteel Romans had only the haziest notion, were unpromising material for an author who wished to thrill literary audiences. What is more Tacitus was a supreme – at times extreme – prose stylist, who valued compression above explanation. It is this, among other characteristics, which makes it impossible to translate him adequately. English, though among the most telescopable of modern languages, is brought up by Tacitean Latin as sharply as a cat by a mousehole. Nor is he temperamentally simple. Had Tacitus been possessed of three feet it could be said that one was in history, one in literature and one in philosophy, for he was often more concerned with the moral than the actual. He was pessimistic and cynical, a curiously modern victim of his own conscience. Despite these difficulties, Tacitus is rightly regarded as the greatest of Roman historians and a vein of gold in the silver age of Latin letters. The *Germania*, dated to about AD 98, was probably his first published work and by no means his most accomplished, though students of late prehistoric Europe are lucky to have it.

Returning to the penetration of Germany by Roman traders, this was in three directions. The most obvious was from Gaul, simply by being rowed or rafted across the Rhine. A second door was opened by the conquest of the Alps and construction of a road through today's Switzerland. This was designed as a strategic short cut from Italy's north-west corner to the Upper Rhine, eliminating the detour via the Rhone. Symbolically, at either end of this route, were the towns named after Augustus: *Augusta Praetoria* (Aosta) and *Augusta Vindelicorum* (Augsburg). Like many roads built for the military, it soon became a commercial link. Thirdly, there was a back door into Germany, from Italy's north-east corner. This was the prehistoric commercial corridor, known today as the Amber Road. The yellow or honey-gold substance, familiar in Greece[22] from the Mycenean period, had been brought southwards on an organized basis since the 6th century BC. Amber is the fossilized gum of extinct pines, cast up on northern shores. Its principal source was and still is the Baltic's south-eastern corner, near today's Kaliningrad and the adjacent Gulf of Danzig (Gdansk). Tacitus tells us it was known to the Germans as *glesum*,[23] adding: 'one may guess it is the resin of trees, certain insects and even flies often being found embedded in it.'[24] He also grumbles at 'the peculiarly feminine extravagance by which hard currency is lost to foreign or unfriendly countries in return for precious stones'.[25] Nero, eager for a caesar's share, sent an expedition (under one Julianus, director of the gladiatorial games) to trace the 'stone' to its source. Pliny tells us that Julianus reached the Baltic coast and there found *commercia* (agencies) which dealt in the trade.[26] It had long been in Celtic hands, the road passing through a number of their *oppida*. In due course Roman merchants muscled in.[27]

The Amber Road is a figure of speech for what was in reality a series of tracks and waterways. These began sedately enough: up the lower Oder and Vistula and across the gently rising plain of southern Poland, via Lowicz, Lodz and Wroclaw. They then climbed the Sudeten Ranges, crossed the Bohemian Basin and rose again over the Bohemian Forest. Passing from German into Celtic territory, the Italian-bound branch made downhill toward the large *oppidum* at Linz. From here it dwindled into mountain paths through the Tauern,[28] across the middle of what is now Austria, before dropping down to Villach. Finally the steep but shorter Carnatic Alps were followed by the winding descent through today's Udine, entering the Italian road system at Aquileia.

This route, with its several variants, has been reconstructed from finds of amber and Roman coins on its course. The coins are commonest near the Baltic Shore and Vistula mouth, where Julianus reported that the wholesalers were established. Regarding the substance itself, we are speaking of more than a few droplets scattered along the way. In trading settlements in the Wroclaw area Polish archaeologists found three tons of raw amber![29]

Looking eastwards across the wide Rhine toward the German interior, one has two impressions. From Basle down to the Ruhr the view is largely of hill and forest, an impression not greatly altered since antiquity. From the Ruhr northwards the vista changes to one of flat fields and tall skies. Once the Rhine has emerged onto the North European Plain there seems no obstacle save the river itself. But this sector is deceptive. Since ancient times nature has been modified almost beyond recognition, not just in agricultural development but in the measures which made agriculture possible. Here the water of half Europe trickles and oozes northwards onto a plain with insufficient tilt to promote its run-off and with a dense layer of glacial clay to prevent its drainage. Modern ploughing has pierced this pan, while centuries of effort in ditch cutting and the embankment of rivers have redeemed huge tracts of peat bog for the farmer. Indeed, nearer the delta these efforts have created an entire country – the Netherlands – pushed into the North Sea where in Roman times there was a hollow, with mud banks, lagoons, reeds, silty streams and rivers shifting uneasily in their beds.

In short, whoever might wish to penetrate prehistoric Germany faced a painful choice: between groping through broken uplands clothed in forest or of floundering in a morass; the one usually beginning where the other left off. Tacitus puts a Roman's feelings toward this comfortless country into a five-word nutshell: 'While there is some variety of scenery it is typically a land of fearful forest and fetid bog (*silvis horrida aut paludibus foeda*); with the rain heaviest toward the west and the wind worst toward the south.'[30]

Though the northern marshes were relieved by sandy heath or deposits of gravel and the southern woodlands broken by clearings, especially in the river valleys, this verdict was substantially true. Foreigners, especially Mediterranean peoples, found the forest deeply depressing. Its extent was awesome. The largest tract, then called the Hercynian Forest, is mentioned by Caesar, who locates its western end between the Alps and the middle Rhine. From here it stretched eastwards in a broad band, from today's Baden-Württemberg, across Bavaria, Czechoslovakia and into western Russia, branching south-eastwards to cover much of the Balkans and Carpathians. This was part of Europe's primordial, broad-leaf forest belt, which once marched without interruption from the Atlantic to the Urals, beyond which rainfall becomes too light for dense growth. Gaul and the British Isles also belonged to this zone, though by the late Iron Age there seems to have been far more clearance in the Celtic world than the Germanic.

So Germany fronted the West with the double deterrent of forest and marsh. But there were chinks in each. The waterlogged plain could be penetrated by water. From the North Sea there were three rivers, the Ems, Weser and Elbe, which led into north-west Germany's heart. Rivers were the pass-key to the forest region also. The Rhine's eastern tributaries were corridors up which the traveller could march or row. This was something like entering darkest Amazonia and it probably inspired comparable sentiments. Both were rain forest, both had dangerous occupants and both presented formidable barriers to outsiders, as much psychological as real. Profit had, however, found a way.

Many thousand Roman coins have been discovered in Germany. Their spread was progressive. Of more than 400 hoards only thirty are of 1st-century origin and all were within 125 miles of the Rhine and Danube. However, by the century following, coinage penetrates far into Scandinavia and across eastern Europe to the Ukraine. As trade increased the German gaze became increasingly fixed westwards and southwards. Those closest would be eager visitors to the markets on the two great rivers. It is interesting to note the kind of Latin word then entering the German language: *kaufen* (to buy) from *cauponor* (to trade); Danish *øre* (gold) from *aureus*; *Münze* (coin) from *moneta* (mint); *billig* (cheap) from *vilis*, and so on. Traders exchanged metalware and household goods for skins, livestock and slaves. Though the Germans used coins for trade with the Romans, there is no evidence of their developing a money economy amongst themselves. 'Those nearest us value gold and silver for trading purposes and recognize and prefer certain types of Roman coin, while those further away continue to barter in the time-honoured way.

Our coins which they trust most are old and familiar ones. They try to get silver rather than gold, since silver change is more convenient for everyday transactions.'[31]

The author recalls youthful experience in the Aden Protectorates and the preference which tribesmen showed for the big, clinking, Maria Theresean silver dollars,[32] often wondering how an 18th-century coin from Austria-Hungary achieved such distant and enduring popularity. The ancient Germans were also fond of silver tableware. In addition to the Hildesheim Treasure, many of the best classical silver vessels have been found in Germany. Tacitus identified this with the diplomatic slush fund: 'One may see among them silver vases, given as presents to the chiefs and their henchmen. The strength and power of these kings rests on Roman authority. We occasionally give them armed assistance; but more often money, which does just as well.'[33]

Silver and coin were not the only tastes which Rome exploited. The early Germans were prodigious drinkers. Drinking-horns of two or three-gallon capacity have been unearthed.

> The tribes nearest the river bank are able to get wine in the market. [Their native drink, however, is] an extract of barley or wheat, which is fermented to make something not unlike wine. Their foods are simple: wild fruits, fresh game and sour milk. Though moderate in eating, drinking is quite another matter. Ply them with booze and you may win them more easily than by fighting them.[34]

Chemical examination of pottery vessels reveals traces of a fermented liquid of beer type, made from a mixture of malt and wild berries. Drinking and chewing the fat were evidently the main male pastimes, especially during the long winter. In this democracy of drunkenness weighty matters were discussed, with decisions emerging from an alcoholic haze.

> After breakfast (armed, of course) they get down to business; and often as not the business is drinking. When it comes to a binge there's no disgrace in making a day and a night of it. As you would expect among such devoted inebriates, rough-houses are common; and it's not just the bad language which pours out but usually the bad blood too. And yet everything gets an airing at

these carousals. Quarrels are patched up, alliances made, chiefs appointed and even questions of peace and war decided; as if this were a time to think straight on matters great or small!'[35]

Few modern historians would go as far as Gibbon in asserting (though perhaps tongue-in-cheek) that thirst motivated barbarian aggression: 'Strong beer, a liquor extracted with very little art from wheat or barley and corrupted into a semblance of wine was sufficient for the gross purposes of German debauchery. The intemperate thirst for strong liquors often urged the barbarian to invade the provinces on which art or nature had bestowed those much envied presents.'[36]

But not all Germans lost their heads at a sniff of the exotic or a sip of the alcoholic. As Caesar wrote of the Suebian tribe (said to be Germany's biggest and strongest): 'They allow traders to enter their territory as buyers of booty which they themselves have won in war, rather than as suppliers of outside goods. The import of wine they forbid absolutely, on the grounds that it makes men too soft and womanish to endure hardship.'[37]

Though Caesar described a largely animal diet this is probably truer of the north. Nevertheless many Iron Age fields have been traced in Schleswig-Holstein, southern Sweden and Jutland. Further south the Germans of the forest grew crops and tended animals in clearings. Both Caesar and Tacitus speak of shifting cultivation, but also of distaste for hard work or agricultural improvement. In view of the universal admiration for their size and strength it is, however, likely that most Germans had a good if boring diet and that farming standards were not greatly below those of the less developed parts of the empire. An interest in outside foods and Roman eating habits is suggested by the borrowing of a variety of Latin food words, as well as terms for utensils and even of cooking[38] itself.

The foremost male garment was a cloak, of high-quality woven and dyed cloth; or a short cape, worn perhaps in summer. Beneath they wore close-fitting but often crudely shaped shirts and trousers of fur, leather or sealskin. Women dressed in woollen skirts, or ankle-length costumes resembling a friar's habit, though of coloured wool or purple-striped linen.

Villages were open in layout, with rectangular huts of unfashioned timber, the walls filled in with wattle and daub. The loan-words *Fenster* (window) from *fenestra* and *Kamin* (chimney) from *caminus* (fireplace) suggest these features were copied from the Romans, huts being previously windowless and with only a central smoke-hole. Similarly *Mauer* (wall) from *murus* and (Dutch) *Tegel* (tile) from *tegula*, indicate that light, wooden construction was normal before the arrival of Rome. 'It is well known', wrote Tacitus, 'that none of the Germans lives in cities.'[39] They did, however, have forts, inherited from the Celts, plus mound-and-palisade or hedge-enclosed villages of their own. Roads were tracks, notoriously circuitous owing to bog or forest. Across parts of the northern quagmire there were also what the Romans called the *pontes longi*[40] (*Bohlenwege*), made of logs laid crosswise in the mud and padded with turf or brushwood to form causeways. These covered limited stretches, probably hundreds of yards rather than miles. No trace of prehistoric tracks or causeways survives.

Culturally Germany was, like Celtica, a preliterate society. The Runic alphabet, using heavily modified Greek and Roman characters, does not appear until the 2nd century. Its use would in any case be limited, especially to religion. Technical development was modest. In metallurgy the Germans lagged behind their Celtic neighbours. Ancient authors spoke of a scarcity of iron, which shows in the rarity of swords and the smallness of spearheads. There were, of course, large iron sources in Germany, such as the Ruhr and Silesia, but 'Iron Age' Germans did not seem overly zealous in exploiting them. Dagger and spear were the main weapons, the latter used both for throwing and thrusting. Horses were small; this and the terrain accounting for the dominance of infantry. The Germans were rated as formidable fighters whether mounted or on foot. Caesar described[41] how the infantry ran alongside the horses, clinging to their manes. Foot soldiers and horsemen fought together in wedge-shaped formations, each a hundred strong and composed of related families.

The finest Germanic technical achievement was in shipbuilding. Clinker[42]-built vessels, first and best in the ancient world, already appear in what is now Denmark and Schleswig-Holstein. Survivals include the forty-foot Hjortspring twenty-paddle boat[43] of the 2nd century BC and the seventy-foot Nydam boat of the 3rd century AD, with fifteen oars on each side: forerunners of the Viking longship.

Tacitus describes the Germans as monogamous and marrying for life; their existence one of chastity, without corrupting influences, with adultery rare and prostitution virtually unknown: 'No one treats vice lightly. None says that seduction is in fashion.[44] In every home one sees children, naked and apparently in impoverished circumstances; and yet they mature to a length of limb and stature of body at which Romans marvel.'[45]

He also describes a social and sexual condition of near equality. Slavery existed, but seems to have been confined to prisoners of war. Women were respected, even feared as possessing magical powers. Chiefs were elected and, as noted, tribal decisions were collectively if bibulously reached by all adult males. Military service was governed not by vassalage or compulsion but by honour. Loyalty was cemented by oath, freely sworn within family or tribe. Despite individual differences in wealth and prestige, this rude democracy, which Tacitus calls *libertas* (freedom), was recognized by him as their main strength and foremost weapon against Rome: 'Nowhere have we pricked our fingers more painfully. German liberty has proved thornier than Parthian monarchy.'[46]

Here Tacitus contrasts oriental absolutism, in which the subject has no voice, with the rough-and-ready egalitarianism of prehistoric Germany. In the former case, a tyrant's overthrow might be welcomed as a liberation, or at least as no more than a change of masters. But to those who had known freedom and shared the decision to defend it, defeat would be unthinkable. This was something Augustus and his stepsons had failed to grasp. Rome's experience was with oriental or African kingship and Celtic chieftainship, all more or less despotic and centralized; obedient to the rule that 'the more contracted power is, the more easily it is destroyed'.[47]

Nevertheless, the picture of prehistoric Germania as the home of beery liberty and fuddled democracy requires modification if we are to account for the high quality of German resistance. Differences between the accounts of Caesar and Tacitus imply that, during the intervening century-and-a-half, Germanic society was already moving away from family and tribal counsels toward more militarily efficient, supra-tribal groupings. Tacitus writes of retainers (*comites*):[48] young men who joined warrior bands outside their own localities, attracted by charismatic leadership and battlefield success. It is uncertain where or how these retinues lived, for villages at present excavated approximate to maxima of thirty-family size. He attributes private army formation to boredom, distaste for agricultural work and dissatisfied pride. Precedent may be sought in the migrations of the first two centuries BC, with their need for larger-than-local direction. It is a process which will end, in the late empire period, with the formation of powerful Germanic confederacies. Certainly Armin's success in conjuring so formidable an inter-tribal force is a memorable step on this same road, suggesting that the movement had been given a decisive push by the advent of Rome and the lessons in cohesion learned from her. So, at the time of Augustus, there existed a Germanic concept of liberty as a general notion, alongside the growing influence of supra-tribal warlords with a potential for resistance far greater than that emerging from village longhouses.

Surprisingly the concept of nationhood was unknown; the quality of 'Germanness' recognized by outsiders long before it occurred to the Germans themselves. In calling them by one name, *Germani*, it may be that the Romans mistook a tribal name, *Hermunduri*,[49] for a national one. Alternatively they perhaps confused *Herman*, or a similar expression, which could have been ancient German for 'brother', or 'fellow-countryman', with that of the people as a whole; for some such word was also taken into Latin as *germanitas* (brotherhood), surviving in the Spanish *hermano*. The Germans did not use a national name until the 11th century: *tiudisc*,[50] which became *deutsch*.

Regarding appearance and character, Tacitus summarizes: 'Their physique, as far as one can generalize, is the same: blue and wild of eye, red of hair,[51] tall of body; strong but inconstant in energy and not too fond of hard work; inured to cold and hunger but not to heat and thirst.'[52]

Josephus points to two other characteristics: 'First they are incapable of rational thought and ready to dash into danger, however hopeless. Secondly, they hate Rome, for they know that only the Romans have ever brought them to slavery.'[53] In the matter of impetuosity, Josephus is following Roman tradition, in which it was usual to attribute courage without prudence to northerners and prudence without courage to southerners, only those in between possessing both. German savagery was a stock Roman cliché. Their carrying of arms is described as compulsive, their behaviour as moodily aggressive: 'they do no business public or private, unarmed.'[54] They are one minute abject, the next menacing.'[55] Caesar suggests that no conflict existed in their minds between inter-tribal banditry and warfare proper. This may be taken as a general rule for the *Barbaricum*, where to bear arms was universal and to use them habitual. In the absence of an external enemy, brigandage was the next best thing. 'No shame is associated with banditry, providing it happens outside a tribe's own territory. Indeed they look on it as training for war, which keeps the young men active and alert. When a chieftain decides to lead a raid, those who volunteer to go with him are cheered by all.'[56] Tacitus also notes a peculiar restlessness, 'a temperamental paradox, by which they love to sleep but hate to be quiet'.[57]

Treachery, turbulence, bellicosity, dishonesty, lethargy and untrustworthiness were standard accusations against Celt, Sarmatian and German alike. In Germany's case they would prove, at least during the first two centuries of our era, an exaggeration. Though a period of migration had scarcely ended and Germany was still disturbed, she would remain a peaceful neighbour for most of the early imperial period. Contrasting the countless hillforts of Gaul, Spain and Britain with the open or lightly defended Germanic settlements, and considering the rudimentary development of tactics and weaponry, it is the Celtic character which seems the more quarrelsome. Germany's bad reputation may merely have reflected Roman priorities. Because the Celts were nearer, their turn had come first. With Gaul's teeth now drawn, Roman propaganda shifted toward a Germany whose teeth were still sharp.

If, however, one awards points for savagery between Celt and German the outcome might be close-run, especially in matters of ritual. The best hope for a Roman prisoner of war in German hands was slavery. Strabo gives this account of what jargon calls a 'worst-case scenario':

> The priestess greeted the captives, crowned them with wreaths and led them to a bronze cauldron of about 120 gallon capacity. Mounting a rostrum above the vessel, one priestess cut each prisoner's throat, making a prophecy based on the blood which ran into the receptacle. Another slit open the stomach, inspected the entrails and from them forecast a victory for their own tribal arms.[58]

Prisoners were also forced to fight duels with their captors, the outcome being taken as a prophecy of victory or defeat in battles to come. German priestesses were of fearsome aspect and regarded by Roman soldiers with superstitious loathing. Plutarch described how the Teutonic horde facing Marius at Aix-en-Provence was goaded on by such furies; and how they slaughtered all who retreated: 'Their priestesses were formidable and tall, with glaring eyes, in white robes and carrying a sacrificial knife. Marius took with his army a Syrian prophetess called Martha, to act as an antidote . . .'[59]

Germans worshipped and sacrificed *alfresco*, preferably in secret places, deep in the forest: 'consecrating groves and woods; and giving divine names to mysterious and invisible spirits'.[60] Clumps of oak, sometimes with perpetual fires burning, or islands in lakes, were favourite sanctuaries. Human sacrifice is amply attested archaeologically. More than four hundred corpses, some astonishingly preserved, have been recovered from pools and peat bogs in northern Germany and Scandinavia, often ritually drowned or buried; though it is difficult to distinguish these from victims of execution, for example for adultery or homosexual offences. The custom of consigning offerings to wells, rivers and marshes has provided the richest source of Germanic or imported artifacts and treasures, including jewellery, tableware, weapons and even ships.

Women were especially linked to divination. The prophecies of seeresses were sometimes based on the snorting and neighing of white horses, stabled in the sacred groves. The principal deities of the German pantheon are well known from legend, some even surviving into modern speech. Tiwaz, god of war (later Wodan) and Donar, god of thunder (later Thor) are among the most prominent. As elsewhere in the Roman orbit, local gods were often twinned with classical counterparts, resulting in common worship on both banks of the Rhine. The Saxons later carried the German gods to England. Thus, comparing with the French equivalents, we have Tuesday/*Mardi*, which shows the equating of Tiwaz and Mars; Wednesday/*Mercredi*, of Wodan and Mercury; and Thursday/*Jeudi* of Thor and Jupiter.[61]

What was the population of the German lands? The question of numbers, both inside and outside Roman territory, is a vexed one. Until the mid 1970s learned guesses were putting the Germans at below two million,[62] the Britons even less, the Gauls slightly more; as distinct from the longer-civilized eastern provinces; such as Egypt, at eight million. Over the last twenty years, however, the accelerating tempo of 'rescue archaeology', as well as the increasing frequency of aerial survey, combined with dry summers, have revealed settlement to be far commoner than formerly supposed. Opinion is moving toward a trebling of estimates for Iron Age North-West Europe.[63] Six million now seems feasible for Germany, not even including Scandinavia. As mentioned, Augustus' new, professional army was

about one third of a million, with the part normally available to
the German theatre numbering perhaps 95,000. Caesar estimated
Suebian fighting strength alone as 100,000.[64] Nevertheless, Roman
experience continued to teach that discipline, assisted by the usual
barbarian shortcomings, could prevail against limitless odds. After
all, the Gauls, more advanced and better equipped, had been demolished by nine legions in a few campaigning seasons. Why not the
Germans?

How might such a conquest benefit Rome? Germany's reputation
as a source of metals was low. 'The gods have denied them gold and
silver,' said Tacitus, 'though whether to spite them or protect them
I know not.'[65] Agricultural potential was considerable but presented
huge problems of development. Manpower, too, was valuable but
the people were intractable. From any practical standpoint the test
of worthwhileness would surely read negative. Yet strategically Germany *was* important. Possession would complete Rome's hold on
Central Europe. Eastern Europe would then lie open. On the other
hand, one must ask how well Romans understood the German
character or the practical problems which the country presented.
Had they grasped Germany's size? Did they appreciate the scale of
the lands beyond? These questions lead to an even more elementary
question: did they have maps of the scope and accuracy to offer an
overview on which strategic judgements could be based?

The entire question of Roman cartography is blurred by the survival of the wrong sort of map. First there is the *Tabula Peutingeri-
ana*, now in Vienna, named after one Conrad Peutinger (1465–
1547), town clerk of Augsburg, through whose hands it passed. This
is a medieval copy of a 2nd-century route map of the empire which,
together with surviving *itineraria* (road manuals), sees the Roman
world much as a traveller on the Underground might see London: a
series of destinations laid out in stylized pattern, with the character
of the earth's surface virtually ignored.

Secondly, there were the 'world maps', in the Greek tradition.
Relevant to our period was the *orbis terrarum*, commissioned by
Augustus and supervised by his minister, Marcus Agrippa. It was
displayed beneath a colonnade on the east side of what is today the
Via del Corso, Rome. This was the Portico of Marcellus, dedicated
by the emperor's sister, which the errant Ovid so tactlessly specified,
in his *Ars Amatoria*, as a first-class location for picking up girls! All
trace of the map is lost, but Pliny often quotes its data in his *Natural*

History. From this – and from the maps of Claudius Ptolemy, a century-and-a-half later – we may guess that Agrippa's depiction of north-eastern Europe was sketchy; and beyond the Vistula virtually non-existent. The main intention of the *orbis terrarum* was doubtless propagandist: to display the superimposition of Rome's works upon the face of geography rather than geography *per se*.

Thirdly, there were almost certainly military maps, based on the realistic appraisal of terrain. A variety of references[66] tell us not only that the army made maps, but that it was probably the main instrument of mapmaking, as it was of exploration. We also know of the excellence of Roman surveying, though much of it concerned property boundaries,[67] which required measurement for fiscal reasons. Surveyors were part of a legion's normal complement. Indeed the entire road system was a product of their skills; and the precision of its alignments over long distances suggests reference to accurate maps. Unfortunately none survives.

Regarding knowledge of Germany: if topographic maps were soldier-made and roadwork-based, these are two reasons why there would be no mapping of the roadless regions beyond the army's reach. At best there would be sketch-maps embodying merchants' accounts. Nevertheless, Augustus must have been aware of Germany's dimensions, since the empire was ranged along two of its sides; and the third was known through the Amber Road. On the other hand, there is no certainty that ambitions ended with Germany. His view of the lands beyond was presumably coloured by the universal error which judged nearer places as relatively bigger than places further away or lesser known. Pliny, for example, gives Europe as 42 per cent of the world, Asia as 32 per cent and Africa 22 per cent (the remaining 4 per cent being ocean!).[68] It would therefore hardly be surprising if the Augustans underestimated Eastern Europe. Above all, it is doubtful whether any Roman could have evaluated the northward turn of the Baltic coast beyond the Vistula's mouth, even had he known of it. This trivial-seeming feature is perhaps the most fateful in the entire relationship between geography and history. It means that the North European Plain, a mere thirty miles broad at Brussels and just 200 at Berlin, widens to 1,400 at Moscow. This progression is the true deterrent to an invasion of Eastern Europe and has defeated all who tried. However, realities only deter those who know of them. Almost certainly this generation of Romans was ignorant of the true extent of the eastern lands and did not have maps on which to base sound judgements regarding their potential for conquest.

What were the influences prompting Augustus toward wider ventures? The mood of the time, if correctly reflected in the early empire's literature, leans unmistakably toward expansion on the grounds of mission, destiny and divine will. For example Pliny (AD 23–79) on the role of Italy and the Latin language:

> A land chosen by divine providence to unify empires so disparate and races so manifold; to bring to a common concord so many rough, discordant voices; to give culture to mankind; to become, in short, the whole world's homeland.[69]

Vitruvius argues yet more firmly of a right earned by effort, with effort attributable to vigour, vigour to climate and climate to celestial guidance:

> So Italy, twixt north and south, combines the best of both with a superiority beyond dispute. She is by her wisdom able to defeat the courage of the northern and the cunning of the southern peoples. Surely then it was a divine intelligence which placed the city of Rome in so perfect and temperate a country, with the intention that she should win the right to rule the world.[70]

'The gods favour us,'[71] says Tacitus more tersely; while Virgil has Jupiter himself proclaim:

> On Romans I place bonds neither of time nor space.
> To them empire without limit do I grant.[72]

And again, in a celebrated expression of Roman dignity and destiny:

> Rome, be this
> Thy care: to hold the nations in dominion and
> Impose the law of peace; to spare the humble
> And to crush the proud.[73]

What were Augustus' own views on empire without limit? Suetonius tells us of the emperor's reverence for Alexander the Great and of his visit to Alexandria, where he crowned the mummified body with a golden diadem.[74] One of his seals of office also bore Alexander's likeness. His arrangements for the Forum of Augustus in Rome offer comparable hints:

> After the gods, Augustus most revered those who had uplifted Rome from her modest past to her glorious present. To these he caused statues to be erected in the two colonnades of his Forum, with the inscription: 'This have I done in order that my fellow citizens may expect that I while I live, and my successors after me, shall match the promise of these great ones of our history.'[75]

Reverence for Alexander was equalled by admiration for Caesar, whose heir Augustus claimed to be. Plutarch tells us[76] that Caesar's ambition, forestalled by his death in 44 BC, was to conquer Parthia, returning via the Caspian, southern Russia and Germany; so describing a vast arc which would settle all frontier problems to Rome's north-east: a concept of breathtaking optimism, displaying the haziest grasp of the true extent of those lands and the difficulties they presented. This was, nevertheless, the climate of thinking which the first emperor inherited.

Underestimation of space was matched by the under-rating of people. The Germans, docile in the army, affable on the Rhine bank, tolerant of mercantile penetration, seemed to promise light resistance. Beyond Germany, in today's eastern Poland and western Russia, lay races whose extreme backwardness rendered them of little military consequence. Tacitus describes the *Fenni* (Finns), then dwelling in the Moscow region, as: 'Living in astonishing barbarism and disgusting misery, eating wild plants, wearing skins and sleeping on the ground. Nor have their infants protection against wild beasts or weather, save a few crossed branches. Beyond, the rest is fable: the *Hellusii* and *Oxiones*, with men's faces but beasts' bodies . . .'[77]

Such then were the distortions of the early imperial view. If it is correct that Germany was seen as a military prospect no more daunting than Gaul, that the Eastern European peoples were considered of little account and that Asia was judged as a quarter of actuality, then a policy of indefinite expansion might have appeared less megalomanic than it does today. Viewed from Palatine Hill, conquest of the world (or at any rate the possession of all its useful lands) was a destiny which may have seemed both manifest and attainable. Nor need one doubt Augustus' intention to carry the empire a substantial step toward it.

The pretext for a German war was not difficult to find. In 16 BC, the twelfth year of Augustus' reign, a Roman legion commanded by Marcus Lollius had been wiped out in a foray into northern Gaul by the Sugambrian tribe, an event which became known as the Lollian Disaster. Some four years later – ostensibly in response to this affront – Roman forces in large numbers were streaming northwards from the Rhone and eastwards from the interior of Gaul toward forward positions on the Rhine where Drusus, Tiberius' younger brother, was soon to take command. These were the brothers, Livia's sons and Augustus' stepsons, who not long before had made short work of the Alpine tribes by engulfing them in a deadly succession of pincer movements: a two-season conquest recorded on the *tropaeum Alpium*, a still-standing memorial at La Turbie, behind Monte Carlo. Now duty divided their paths. That of Tiberius lay across the Julian Alps, where he was pushing through Illyricum toward the middle Danube; that of Drusus across the Rhine, with orders to carry Roman arms to the Elbe. First he must install his legions and many auxiliary units on the Rhine's west bank, then probe the routes to the German interior.

The historian Florus, writing a century later, tells us that Drusus built 'over fifty forts on the Rhine alone'.[78] Perhaps half that number has been found. These were earth-and-timber transit camps for outward-bound armies, which would also serve for overwintering and as supply bases. Almost all lie under later forts and are seldom easy to trace. Some are the progenitors of great cities like Basle, Strasbourg, Mainz, Cologne and Nijmegen, whose ancient centres and cathedrals stand where, in the last decade before our era, there were leather tents and crude timber buildings within palisaded mounds of turf or mud.

The biggest of these forts were placed opposite favoured invasion routes: the Rhine's eastern tributaries, whose valleys cut into the wooded hills of western Germany. In practice, though all exits from Germany must be guarded, few matched the cautious requirements of Roman entry. The Ruhr, Sieg and Lahn, for example, twist and turn, hemmed in tightly by hills. These were death-traps. The Neckar appears to lead eastwards but then betrays its early promise by snaking back toward the Alps. Throughout the southern half of the Rhine's course the Main alone fulfils the invader's expectations. Though winding, it leads the traveller to within twenty-five miles of today's Czech border. Accordingly, opposite its discharge into the Rhine, the two-legion base of Moguntiacum (Mainz) was founded.

In the northern sector only the Lippe offered comparable benefits. Its valley is straight and open. Furthermore it was navigable for at least three quarters of its 100-mile course. This was a far greater asset than it seems today. The Romans used every known device to bring supply vessels upriver (flat bottoms, inflatable skins to reduce draught, poling, towing, dredging, lighterage, portage and so on), for this reduced the need for pack animals who in turn required fodder. Another advantage of the Lippe is apparent from its wider setting. The northernmost tributary, it flows for most of its course along the line where plain and foothills meet, entering the Rhine 130 miles from the mouth. It could thus be employed as the southern prong of a forking movement to envelop the North German Plain, whose northern counterpart would be a seaborne attack from the North Sea itself.

Drusus gave special attention to what we would today call the Dutch sector: a land much drained since Roman times and whose river system is greatly altered. The Rhine, as we now know it, begins its deltaic phase just inside the Dutch border, dividing into Waal and Lower Rhine, of which the Waal is decisively the mainstream, heading west to enter the sea at The Hook (Hoek van Holland). The smaller, Lower Rhine heads north-west via Arnhem, dividing northwards again into an even smaller branch, the Old Rhine, crooked and silted. This passes through Utrecht and Leiden, entering the sea at Katwijk, a small resort twenty miles north of the Waal mouth. Two thousand years ago this pattern was reversed. The Lower Rhine-Old Rhine was then the major channel and the Waal a minor river. So Tacitus: 'On entering Batavian territory the Rhine divides into two: the one running without change of name or force of flow from Germany to the Ocean; and the other, on the side toward Gaul, becoming a wider but more placid stream, called the *Vahales* (Waal).'[79] The Waal stole the water during the Middle Ages. Had it not, then Katwijk-aan-Zee rather than Rotterdam might today be Europe's principal port.

Let us return to the Old Rhine, now the backwater, then the mighty Rhine itself. At Utrecht it is within twenty miles of the former Zuider Zee. This was a huge embayment[80] where the greedy sea had bitten sixty miles into the Netherlands. In the 1930s it was sealed by the construction of a causeway across its mouth, renamed the Ijsellmeer, and is now in large measure reclaimed.

Near Utrecht the River Vecht branches (northwards, yet again) from the Old Rhine into the Ijsellmeer. This is believed to have been the *Fossa Drusiana* (Drusus' Ditch), a fifteen-mile channel cut by the Roman Army to link the Rhine to the Zuider Zee and thence to the North Sea. This ingenious feat gave Drusus a short cut to Germany. It avoided the open sea entirely, connecting into the sheltered and shallow Waddenzee,[81] inside the Frisian Islands, whose long chain, bending back from the brow of Holland like a windswept plume, shields the entire coast as far as Jutland. From here the German rivers Ems, Weser and Elbe are of easy access.

The North Sea, surly but familiar, was, to the Romans, a place of dread; for it was part of *exterior Oceanus atque ignotum mare* (the Outer Ocean, with its seas unknown),[82] believed to encircle the three continents. Northwards from here was only Thule,[83] the 'Congealing Sea'[84] and the freezing pole. However Drusus' Ditch would allow him to avoid such perils, putting an army and its supplies deep inside Germany. An all-land invasion would have meant that the interior tribes were alerted from the moment of crossing the Rhine. Now the Lippe column could start first, drawing the Germans westwards, while a fresh force suddenly landed by river in their rear. Such, at any rate, was the theory; and the discovery of a sheltered passage persuaded Drusus that it could be done without a mutiny, brought on by the sight of the waves.[85]

The first summer was spent in coastal reconnaissance and also in clearing the Lippe and the tribes on either side of it. Depots were laid along its valley, as stepping stones on the landward invasion route. Of these, four show on aerial photographs and perhaps another four await discovery. The pattern suggests camps at twelve-and-a-half-mile intervals, each of two-legion size. A larger force could of course have used the same chain by operating a day or more apart. However the Lippe corridor is not totally trouble-free. Though it begins in open country it ends, from Paderborn eastwards, among steep, wooded hills, which eventually bring the route to a halt. The answer was to strike northwards from Paderborn, through about thirty miles of broken, forested country, until the Weser was reached near Hameln. This dangerous though short section seemed a small price to pay for an otherwise perfect route. It passed not far from the Grotenburg, on which von Bandel's mighty statue stands.

At the beginning of the second summer both columns advanced. It is known that Drusus reached the Weser by the land route, and presumed that one of his lieutenants led the seaborne arm. The campaign was successful. It is said, however, that Drusus met one of those frightful German priestesses, 'a woman of superhuman size',[86] who cursed him and prophesied doom. The army retired to winter behind the Rhine, Drusus being summoned to Rome to celebrate a Triumph. North Germany had, it seems, been conquered.

Attention now switched to the middle Rhine, where Drusus' third summer, of 9 BC, was one of mighty accomplishment. Striking eastwards from Mainz, he defeated the Suebians, then pressed on toward the upper Main. Branching left over the narrow ridge of the Thuringian Forest, he picked up the north-flowing Saale, following it down to the Elbe, near today's Magdeburg. It was a 300-mile advance, not counting the winding of waterways and twisting of tracks. Few generals of the imperial period would match it. But on the return a fall from a horse, a broken leg and gangrene claimed him; dying in some God-forsaken camp on a night of shooting stars to the howling of forest wolves. He was not yet thirty. Augustus sent Tiberius to bring back his brother's body. With full ceremonial and universal mourning the ashes were deposited in the mausoleum which his stepfather had already built for himself on the Tiber bank. Patriotic fervour was now attached to this German war.

The command passed to Tiberius. Finding a Germany already reeling from his brother's onslaught and determined to keep up the pressure, the new general sent his armies forward from their various bases, criss-crossing the ravaged country almost at will for two more summers. Truculent tribes were uprooted and resettled on the Gallic side of the Rhine. Augustus forbade crossing the Elbe so as not to provoke more tribes than Rome could presently handle. Their turn would come later. Meanwhile the new province of Germania, from the Rhine at least to the Weser, was ready for formation.

But Tiberius was discouraged: Drusus dead and all the work falling on his shoulders; Julia's sons growing up and tongues wagging that their grandfather's favour and the likelihood of succession were inclining toward them rather than him, a mere stepson. Germany had been exhausting. Like all Romans he detested the melancholy forest and stinking swamp. Nor, though a sound and systematic commander, did he share his younger brother's keenness for this conflict. It was said that Drusus, who set his heart on the *spolia opima*,[87] had horrified his staff by rushing through the thick of battle to get at the enemy's leader. Tiberius, sombre and introverted, was of less spectacular stuff. Perhaps the Germans had proved disappointing opponents. Certainly their showing had been indifferent, with range of weaponry narrow, tactics crude, commissariat a joke, grasp of siegecraft nil, leadership limited and loyalty localized. It seemed clear that conquest was now inevitable, if not achieved already. He decided to retire to a Greek island.

His successor L. Domitius Ahenobarbus, Augustus' nephew by marriage, continued the good work. We know principally of his operations in the south, based on the Roman province of Raetia (Bavaria). Meanwhile the Fates (or Livia) were again busy on Tiberius' behalf. The emperor's grandsons Lucius and Gaius died under mysterious circumstances. The third grandson, Agrippa Postumus (who would later be exiled to an island) was still a minor. Tiberius' services were suddenly at a premium. Augustus was notoriously nervous of putting military reins into non-family hands, making nepotism a corner-stone of his policy. This so narrowed the field that there was now no other first-class runner left. He coaxed Tiberius to return from Rhodes; and since nothing soothes the sulker more than the knowledge that he is needed, Tiberius allowed himself to be persuaded.

So, two years later, he was back, preparing a new offensive across the Rhine. Had something gone wrong? Surely the attack phase should by now be over? Surely they should already be inside Germany, organizing, building and teaching the Germans to be Romans. The fact was, however, that they had terrorized all western Germany but Romanized none of it. Sixteen years after Drusus had first taken command, the province was still being held by bullying enemies and bribing friends. Though the legions advanced at will the Roman hold on the interior was based on little substance. There were still no roads and few forts. According to Velleius[88] it was not until this first year of Tiberius' return (AD 4) that the whole army dared winter in Germany; and then no deeper than the Lippe Valley. Seasonal withdrawal meant that each winter Rome's enemies could dismantle last summer's work.

In fact events had revealed a blindspot. The high command was failing to grasp the difference between this conquest and others. Nations had normally passed into Roman receivership with assets intact and functional framework in place. The task had been to improve. Here it was to build from scratch. Even essential measures for the army's own security were incomplete. Germany needed a comprehensive fort network, strong points and signal towers linked by all-weather roads and bridges; with massive tree-felling to reduce concealment and extensive drainage and causeway building to assist movement; a strong naval presence on the internal rivers, fortified ports of entry, jetties, quays, arsenals and granaries; in short the infrastructure for a big garrison on a long stay. Tiberius' error was not in shirking responsibility but in continuing to see it as a fighting general rather than as a planner, builder and engineer. With hindsight it seems clear that the priority was not more victories and Triumphs, but a military highway linking Rhineland with interior. This was a project which must await Adolf Hitler.

In AD 5 the pincer movement was applied for a third time. Again the army marched up the valley, again the navy sailed up the rivers and north-west Germany was said to be subdued. It is probable that on this occasion Tiberius met the young prince, Armin of the Cherusci. Many German-speaking officers would soon be needed for the so-called 'Bohemian campaign', planned as stage two of the German War, with its simultaneous drives eastwards from the Rhine and northwards from Vienna. However, this was not to be. In the mountainous central Balkans, 200,000 men, outraged by the greed of Roman tax farmers, were suddenly in arms. Extirpation of the Illyrican Revolt would involve Tiberius for three years and draw in fifteen legions. As a commander of auxiliary cavalry, Armin served with distinction in this costly and unnecessary war. It was on its completion that he was posted back to Germany to assist the next governor, P. Quintilius Varus.

Varus was another of the emperor's relatives, in this instance the husband of a great-niece. A jurist by training, he had been consul with Tiberius in 13 BC. Since then he had governed Africa and Syria, two of the choicest provinces. In the latter he is mentioned by Josephus as intervening in one of the Jewish uprisings and crucifying two thousand insurgents. That he lined his pockets at those provinces' expense was seemingly kept from Augustus. It is from his governorship of Africa that we have the only known likeness. A coin issue from the mint of Carthage carries on its reverse a profile of Varus, whose weak and smirking face reveals no hint of a soldierly disposition.[89]

The colonel and senator C. Velleius Paterculus, who dashed off a potted *History of Rome* to celebrate his own consulship in AD 30, is the only contemporary chronicler. Ironically, where many an historical masterpiece sank without trace, his enthusiastic if naïve effort survived in its entirety. It is of no great value until the final third, which deals with the events of his own day. Velleius may be taken seriously in military matters, since he served nine years as commander of Tiberius' cavalry and of one of his legions, both in the German and Balkan theatres. He must have known both Varus and Armin personally and has left precious portraits, together with a brief account of the fateful circumstances of which his beloved army was to be the principal victim.

Varus was sent to govern Germania in the year of Ovid's exile, by an over-optimistic Augustus, who either saw the German conquest as a *fait accompli*, or had lost patience with his cautious generals and believed it should be. Now that the imperial stepsons had supposedly done their work it was time to implement the *lex provinciae*.[90] This was the system by which Roman law was adapted to the traditions of each new territory, the inauguration of a province being normally accompanied by the formulation of its particular code. Who better to send than a lawyer? It would also be Varus' task to introduce the reluctant but cowed Germans to the blessings of Roman taxation and a way of life in which the bearing of arms was superfluous. Of course, as governor, Varus would automatically be commander of the German legions. Because of the drain on manpower caused by the Illyrican Revolt these were presently reduced to three: XVII, XVIII and XIX. It was normal to phase down the military presence after a province had been won. However, for Germany at this stage, the establishment was dangerously low. On the other hand, these were legions Varus did not expect to use, except for policing and other peacetime work.

By now Ovid had arrived in Tomis and begun the composition of his *Tristia*. Six months from Rome in postal terms, he could only guess at events in Germany. Naturally he assumed a 'best-case scenario', the usual outcome when the legions marched:

> Already wild Germany may have followed
> All the rest in kneeling to the caesars . . .
> But I, obliged to live apart, see nothing
> Of such celebration; and can only
> Go by rumour's distant echoes.[91]

Turning to the actual scenario, Velleius writes as follows:

Quintilius Varus, of a well-known rather than aristocratic family, was of mild and quiet temperament, somewhat ponderous both in mind and body; and more at home in the camp than on the battlefield. During his spell as governor of Syria he had shown no aversion toward cash: for that episode began with a poor man's arrival in a rich province and ended with a rich man's departure from a poor one.

When given the German command he went out with the quaint preconception that here was a subhuman people which would somehow prove responsive to Roman law even where it had not responded to the Roman sword. He therefore breezed in – right into the heart of Germany – as if on a picnic, wasting a summer lording it on the magistrate's bench, where he insisted on the punctilious observance of every legal nicety.

Meanwhile the Germans, a race combining maximum ferocity with supreme guile (and being born liars besides) fawned upon Varus, making much of their lawsuits, marvelling at his jurisprudence and flattering him regarding his civilizing mission; until the poor fellow came to think he was still handing down verdicts from the judge's seat in the Roman forum; quite forgetting he was in fact field commander of an expeditionary force deep within darkest Germany.[92]

Vain, pedantic and gullible, Varus had spent years presiding over servile provinces which Rome had inherited from others. Now, over-confident and under-armed, incapable of comprehending that Drusus and Tiberius might have done their work with less than total thoroughness, he held court in the heart of Germany and spent a summer on the bench instead of building forts and roads. Tragically he allowed his army to be accompanied by a large number of women and children, with servants and a cumbrous baggage train; giving the impression of not being on a war footing or even in a state of preparedness at all.

Though Varus' force was less than half that of recent invasion armies it was enough for self-protection, amounting perhaps to 35,000 men, including auxiliaries. Among these he was doubtless comforted by the presence of a large German brigade, of proven loyalty to Rome. All around was evidence of a defeated people, cringing and eager to please. But, as in the Balkans three years earlier (and in Africa five years hence),[93] the danger would not be immediately after conquest but later, when the realities of taxation, disarmament and other restrictions had begun to sink in. As then, success or failure could depend on how tactfully these medicines were ministered. Unfortunately Varus tended to arrogance as well as self-deception.

Here was a difficult job and the wrong man to do it; a mismatch so total it reminds us in an odd way of Ovid. Both were directed, in that same year to places which suited their temperaments least. Both were sent from safety and comfort to an unstable and frightening frontier region. Was Augustus entirely unaware that Varus had acted so venally in Syria and Africa? Is it possible he had found out; and determined that his next governorship would be of a more bracing and less lucrative kind? Can one detect Livia's hand in this spiteful appointment?

Dio (the Greek historian Cassius Dio of Nicaea), writing in the early 3rd century, takes up the story:

> The Romans had by now established themselves in parts of Germany, wintering there and founding cities.[94] On their side the barbarians had begun to accept Roman ways: holding markets and peaceful meetings. But they had not forgotten their ancestral customs. Nor had they lost their sense of freedom, or of what may be accomplished by arms. When Varus became governor he tried to force the pace of change, dishing out orders as if to slaves and squeezing money as if from docile subjects. However, in view of powerful regiments on the Rhine and within their borders, the Germans bided their time, pretending obedience and drawing Varus far into Cheruscan territory, near the Weser; while always behaving peaceably and amiably. The outcome was that he failed to keep his legionaries together, detaching many to different duties.[95]

'Cheruscan territory': this was Armin's own tribe, thought to have occupied today's Minden-Hannover-Brunswick area, between Weser and Elbe. According to Roman accounts, they had been defeated at least twice during the previous twenty years. However, as the currents of conflict swirled more savagely about them, we may imagine the usual fragmentation into resistant and collaborationist factions; a process which was no respecter of families. Under circumstances of which we know little, Armin (following his father, Sigimer, the tribe's leader) had thrown in his lot with the invaders, become a Roman officer and received a knighthood from the emperor. This was clearly a sweetener, for the cultivation of German friends was a priority at that time. Now, covered in glory and with the highest possible commendations, Armin returned to his tribe as Varus' deputy and liaison officer. He was still only twenty-five years of age. Velleius resumes the narrative:

> Onto this stage now strode a young German nobleman of firm purpose and astute mind; a high-flier, far above the usual run of barbarian intelligence: Armin, a prince of the Cheruscan tribe, whose face and eyes seemed to shine with the light of some inner zeal. He had served with the Roman army for some years, earning Roman citizenship and a knighthood to boot. Here was the type of man who would be quick to spot in Varus the perfect dupe, for none is more credulous than the incautious; and a sense of security is the surest recipe for calamity.[96]

It now becomes clear that Armin's devotion to the Roman cause was only skin deep; and beneath that skin there festered earlier hatreds. Bending before Drusus' and Tiberius' onslaughts had been one thing; dancing attendance on this military ignoramus was another. As a teenager he had thought Rome invincible; yet later, in the Balkans, he had seen brave people make a bid for freedom and almost win. What is more, when it came to rebellion, Germania had a telling advantage over Illyricum. There the mountains could be surrounded and in time reduced. Here desperate men could, in the last resort, retreat indefinitely north or east, beyond even Rome's long reach.

None the less it needed nerve to take on a superpower. This must not be a rash rebellion which ignites from a riot, but one which was meticulously planned and stealthily fostered; in the event by one man's will. Despite Varus' ineptitude, the odds were daunting. How could the young Armin unite warring tribes when even his own family was divided? He had married a girl named Thusnelda against her father's will. His father-in-law, Segestes, hated him and was to warn Varus repeatedly that he could not be trusted. This was dismissed as jealousy; for how could Armin, whom the emperor himself had knighted, behave in so un-Roman a manner?

To consider the problem from another direction: empires are seldom as powerful as they seem. They are based on bluff, on making their subjects think them stronger than they are. Had Armin sensed this secret? Might an obscure German princeling puncture the imperial bubble, as Japan would one day prick the British balloon at Singapore?

Velleius continues:

> At first Armin confided in a few of his compatriots only, but as time passed the circle widened. He argued that Rome could be beaten. More to the point he gave substance to his words by organizing a plan of action and fixing a date for its execution. Segestes, Armin's father-in-law, warned Varus of what was afoot and urged him to have the plotters clapped in irons. But by now the Fates were taking a hand, controlling all Varus did and lulling his suspicions; as they often do to those whose fortunes they are about to topple.[97]

A plot was hatched along the following lines. As summer ended and the army began to fall back toward the Lippe, an 'uprising' would be invented to divert the column away from the established route with its lifeline of fortified camps and depots, with its bridges ready-built and trees ready-felled. When the Romans had been lured some distance into unfamiliar and unfavourable terrain, the German auxiliary brigade would abscond. Finally, at an advantageous moment, the deserters (shadowing at a distance) plus all other dissidents and malcontents who could be mustered, would close in on the Roman column and destroy it.

Dio:

> The plot's ringleaders were Armin and [his father] Sigimer, constant companions with whom Varus often feasted. As a result he became more and more confident and completely off his guard. Then came news of an uprising designed to inveigle him through ostensibly friendly territory toward the supposed trouble spot. At first Armin and Sigimer went with him, but subsequently excused themselves on the grounds that they were going to mobilize more assistance. When each district had butchered the soldiers in its vicinity they all closed in on Varus, by now in almost inextricable forest. Then, at the very moment of showing themselves as enemies, the conspirators struck a terrible blow.[98]

Dio now depicts the final phase of this *débâcle*: the three or four-day running fight known to posterity as the Battle of the Teutoburg Forest. Not only did Varus follow the course which treachery had devised but the Roman response was hindered by a catastrophic change in the weather, favouring an enemy to whom slithering mud and rough ground were familiar conditions.

The slopes were uneven and creased with gorges. Felling trees, clearing a trail and improvising bridges, the Roman column advanced. It included large numbers of carts and pack animals, as if this were a peacetime journey. There were, besides, numerous women and children, with a big retinue of servants behind them, all tending to make the column longer and more scattered. A hurricane began, bringing drenching rain. The tops of trees snapped off and fell among the marchers. The ground was slippery and treacherous.

Now the savages began to close in, appearing through the dense forest suddenly and from all sides at once. At first it was hit-and-run, with spears hurled from a distance; but when they could see that many were being wounded and there was no serious counter-attack, they began to press closer. By now the column was in chaos, with soldiers, wagons and civilians all jumbled up: impossible to organize into defensive formations and being whittled away piecemeal.

A halt was called and – insofar as a suitable place could be found on a forested hillside – camp was established for the night. Here they reorganized, burning most of the carts and abandoning inessential equipment.

On the second day things went better. Despite losses, they broke through to open country. But on the third morning the column plunged once more into forest and began to take the heaviest casualties yet. There was no room to deploy the cavalry among the trees, or use infantry and cavalry in unison.

On the fourth day the hurricane struck again and the rain returned in torrents. It was difficult even to stand. Wet bowstrings, slippery spears and sodden shields deprived them of effective use of their weapons; while the Germans, more lightly armed, fared better. As word spread that the Romans were weakening, the enemy's ranks began to be swelled by fence-sitters and plunder-seekers; his strength growing as the Roman bled away.[99]

The crisis was now at hand. Neither Dio nor Velleius makes clear its tactical character or reveals the place and circumstances, though *à propos* of the battle's finale Tacitus uses the words *in medio campo*; 'in midfield', as it was formerly translated. A more recent reading[100] proposes a specialized meaning for *campus*, as the space in the centre of a camp, normally used as a gathering place or parade ground. This could suggest that Varus' men spent the last night crouched within the shallow mounds of a temporary fortification and that an inner redoubt[101] was improvised in the muster-area to which the perimeter's defenders could retire to join the senior officers, fighting back to back in a final stand. Dio describes the end:

> By now Varus and all his senior officers were wounded. Fearing they were about to be taken alive or that slaughter was imminent, they steeled themselves to face the terrible alternative. When the soldiers heard that their commanders had taken their own lives, resistance collapsed, some killing themselves, others throwing away their arms and inviting anyone to kill them who wanted. Every man and animal was cut down without returning a blow.[102]

Some were in fact taken prisoner. Velleius summarizes:

> And so a Roman army, in bravery, discipline, dash and battle-worthiness the best we had bar none, was entrapped through its general's fecklessness, its enemy's trickery and its own wretched luck. Hemmed in by bog, bush and ambush it was exterminated almost to a man by the very enemy it was used to slaughtering like swine.
> Varus found more pluck to die than he did to fight. Following the example of his father and grandfather,[103] he ran himself through with his own sword. V. Numonius, the cavalry commander, deserted the field, leaving the infantry unprotected, and tried in vain to break through to the Rhine. The body of Varus, partially burned, was further mangled by the enemy; his head cut off and dispatched to Maraboduus, who sent it on to Augustus. Despite the ignominy it was honoured by burial in the family tomb.[104]

Here Velleius, one of Augustus' staunchest propagandists, is making Varus the scapegoat for the emperor's miscalculation. As for Armin's

cruder but shrewder propaganda sense: the head, sent to Maraboduus, King of German Bohemia, was a way of saying, 'See! It can
be done! Rome *can* be defeated! Join our resistance movement!'
Maraboduus, fearing resumption of the Bohemian plan, preferred to
keep his options open. Nevertheless, in forwarding the consignment
to Augustus he was doing Germany a service; for with the de-
composing head of Quintilius Varus the message from the Teutoburg
Forest reached its ultimate recipient.

This defeat would henceforth be known as *clades Variani*, the
Varian Disaster. It wiped out twenty years' effort east of the Rhine.
At a stroke it cost a province, its governor, his staff and perhaps
30,000 men, women and children; including three crack legions
and their eagles. All garrisons within Germania were massacred.
In all forts so far excavated on the Lippe, evidence of intensive
activity, with coins, abundant to AD 9, ends in the sardonic silence
of a layer of ashes. However, one of these, Aliso,[105] held out for a
short time. Haggard and wild-eyed, a few of Varus' survivors
stumbled in. Armin was not far behind. Soon the last fort in Germany
was surrounded by an exultant mob 'brandishing the impaled heads
of slain Romans on spears before the rampart'.[106] At night, when
perhaps the Germans were drunk, the garrison made a break for
freedom and fought its way back to the Rhine with the grievous
tidings.

The sombre dispatches burst on the emperor like a bomb; his
over-reaction resembling that of three years earlier, to the Illyrican
revolt,[107] when he foresaw the imminent invasion of Italy; confirming
him as a man of alarmist and emotional temperament, hardly in line
with the serene public image:

> On hearing of the disaster Augustus rent his clothes and mourned
> deeply, not just for the dead soldiers but also as an expression of
> fear for the endangered German[108] and Gallic provinces, and
> because he expected the enemy would march on Rome. No citizens
> of military age worth mentioning were left. Moreover there were
> many Gauls and Germans in Rome, both in his bodyguard and
> on other business. These he sent away: the bodyguard to certain
> islands, the civilians out of the city.[109]

A panic recruiting drive now followed, in Italy and the capital itself.
This was by lot, with draft-dodgers punished by confiscation of prop-

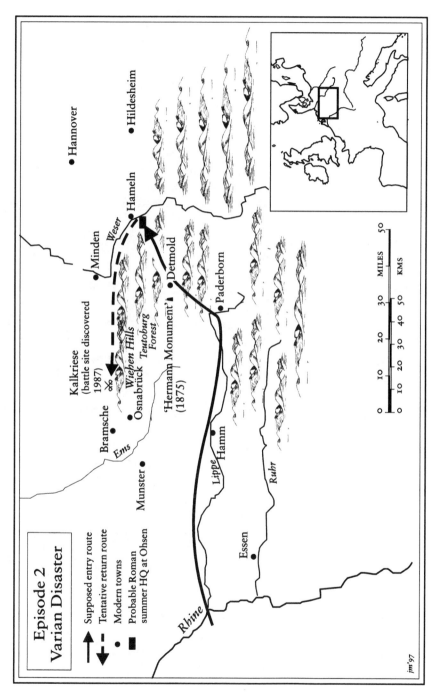

Episode 2
Varian Disaster

⬆ Supposed entry route
⬇ Tentative return route
● Modern towns
▪ Probable Roman summer HQ at Ohsen

erty and even death. Freed slaves were enrolled and veterans recalled. The new units were sent to stand between Italy and Germany. Nevertheless the three lost legions would not be replaced. Their numbers, henceforward considered unlucky, were omitted in perpetuity from the army list.

Suetonius allows us a more personal glimpse of the emperor's distress:

> When the news arrived Augustus had night watches posted throughout the city in case of disturbance and prolonged the terms of all provincial governors.[110] He was said to be so stricken he refused to cut his hair or shave for months and would often bang his head against doors, shouting: 'Quintilius Varus, give me back my legions!' Each year he observed the anniversary of the disaster as one of grief and mourning.[111]

Augustus was now seventy-two and had ruled for thirty-six years. Though he displayed private and public grief, the *débâcle* would not, as far as we know, be mentioned in official documents or pronouncements, least of all in his own *Accomplishments*.[112] Like the Balkan setback, this was a responsibility which could not be offloaded. Having stripped the senate of military powers and kept all decisions and appointments to himself, he could hardly complain of having been ill-advised. As Tacitus would put it, 'Augustus so arranged it that the emperor must bear the blame or praise for Rome's distant wars alone.'[113] He had sent a civilian into a savage land; a governor with neither tactics nor tact, a commander who had never commanded and a judge incapable of judging men. Nepotism and distrust of career generals had cost Augustus dear.

Armin did not march on Italy. It is probable that his coalition fell apart the moment Rome's presence was removed. Far from uniting a nation, he could not even resolve his private feuds; and it was owing to them, twelve years later, that he was murdered. In view of Roman prejudice, Tacitus' tribute is remarkable:

> Without doubt the liberator of Germany. A man who took on the Roman nation, not in her infancy but at the summit of her sovereignty. In war without defeat, he lived thirty-seven years, twelve in power. Even now[114] his fame is sung in barbarian ballads. He fell by the treachery of his own kinsmen.[115]

Armin's power did not spread far. Nor does his name survive in German folklore. It would remain for 17th-century learning to restore it to memory and for 19th-century nationalism to equate it with unity. Armin became Kaiser Wilhelm's answer to Napoleon III's glorification of Vercingetorix and the Victorian cult of the misspelt 'Boadicea'.[116] So earnestly did such rivalries seek Roman precedent that Clemenceau would argue Gaul's boundaries in support of French claims at Versailles.

It would be time to leave this remarkable young man who, at twenty-five years of age, defied and defeated Augustus; except that a group of events, six years later, offers a final glimpse. The postscript is by courtesy of Tacitus who, in his latest work, the *Annals*, deals with Rome's vengeance. In the last year of Augustus' life a war of revenge was unleashed on Germany. In command was Drusus' son, Germanicus; Tiberius' nephew and father of Caligula, next emperor but one. Here was a young man with his father's feverish zeal, buoyed up and urged on by popular expectation that he would restore Rome's tarnished honour. 'He was', as Tacitus reminds us, 'great-nephew of Augustus and the grandson of Antony; and in his imagination there resided the whole great picture of triumph and tragedy.'[117]

Nothing in this resumption of the German War could be closer to Germanicus' heart than revival of the amphibious strategy by which his father had first led the eagles into northern Germany. This would also be the perfect pincer to nip the Cheruscans, prime target of revenge, though it seemed likely that Armin himself would by now have fled eastwards or into Scandinavia. In Tacitus' view the objective was 'rather to expiate the shame of Quintilius Varus than extend the empire',[118] but the inferences of Germanicus' dispatches and conduct are that he saw the restitution of a lapsed province as his sacred duty.

Like his father, he would spend three summers in Germany. It is the second of these, AD 15, which is of special interest: for not only did he rediscover the site of the Teutoburg battle, but also there are vivid descriptions both of the sea passage and the bog war, which compensate in some measure for the sources' silence on similar aspects of his father's and uncle's campaigns.

So, with Germanicus, the North German War returns to its starting place; what are now the Netherlands; and particularly to that part of them which the Romans called the Batavian Island, the largest piece of relatively dry land, between the Old Rhine and the Waal.

The rest of the huge delta was water or reedy fen, though with ridges left by former river courses and the natural levees of existing ones, along which ran prehistoric paths and tracks. Native settlement was mainly on mounds (in Dutch, *Terpen*) elevated and enlarged by centuries of tipping. Here were small plots, a few animals, plus a living to be made from fishing and fowling; for this vast wetland must have been a bird haven whose like northern Europe has long forgotten. The Romans copied the local method of mound-making, or founded their buildings on wooden stakes, hammered into the mud. Place names with the syllable *wijk*,[119] Latin *vicus*[120] (village), show how numerous Roman settlements were eventually to become.

Now, throughout the winter, scores of small shipyards sprang up along the muddy shores of the Batavian Island. With timber floated down from the German forest, thousands of soldiers instructed by hundreds of sailors laboured to cobble together the shallow-draught troopships and supply vessels for the coming campaign. We have statistics for the year following, when eight legions, their auxiliaries, horses and supplies embarked in a thousand newly built ships. The scale suggests how terrible Rome's revenge would be. Why, one may ask, were new ships built before each season? The answer must be that Germanicus had no option but to use green timber, which warps rapidly, rendering ships useless within a few months. Tacitus' celebrated narrative of the seaborne operation concerns the return journey only. His account of the overland arm of the expedition, which deals with both the outward and inward journey, is no less sensational. Here a vanguard detachment, partway up the Lippe Valley, encountered a group of Bructer,[121] perhaps thirty miles south of the Teutoburg region. They engaged and the Germans fled. To the Romans' surprise and intense excitement, a search of the captured *impedimenta* revealed the eagle of *Legio XIX*, lost with Varus. Led by survivors of the disaster, who were acting as guides, they pressed on:

> Now they were approaching the Teutoburg *saltus* where the remains of Varus and his legions were said still to be lying unburied. On they marched across the gloomy plain, chilling both to look at and to think about. Varus' first camp was wide in extent, with its tent plots marked out for men and officers, suited to the size of three legions. Then a half-ruined dyke and shallow ditch showed where the last remnant had taken cover. In the

parade ground area were bleaching bones, scattered where men had fallen individually, or in heaps where they had made a stand. Splintered spears and horses' legs lay around. Human skulls were nailed to tree trunks. In nearby groves were savage altars at which they had sacrificed the young lieutenants and warrant officers. Some among the relieving force, who had survived the battle or given their captors the slip, recounted where the commanders had fallen, where the eagles were seized, where Varus was first wounded and where he died by his own tragic hand. They told of the platform from which Armin had harangued his fellow victors, of the arrogance with which he had insulted the standards and the eagles; and of the gibbets and torture pits for the prisoners.

Following the main army's arrival the battlefield was tidied and a memorial service held: 'And so, six years after the disaster, a Roman army buried three legions' bones, while Germanicus laid the first sod upon the funeral mound.'[122]

Little is known of the season's retribution which followed. One can only guess at the extent of atrocity committed in the name of *Mars Ultor* ('Mars, who has the last word'). At the end of it, in September or early October, Germanicus began the usual retirement toward the Rhine. His army now regrouped into two columns, one returning by land the other making for a pick-up point on one of the rivers, where the fleet waited.

The landward army, under the veteran commander V. Severus Caecina, was crossing stretches of log causeway, improved during previous campaigns but now badly deteriorated. The route was seemingly along the line where the wooded hills and the plain met; a place of danger and difficulty owing to the excessive run-off from the adjacent high ground and the concealment which its trees afforded. 'All around was vile, heaving bog and clinging mud, veined with small streams.' The legionaries struggled to repair the causeways. At this worst of moments the worst happened. Not only did a large force of Germans appear through the trees above, but their leader – it could clearly be seen – was none other than Armin himself: not skulking beyond the Oder or a refugee across the Skagerrak, but here in person, uncomfortably close to the scene of the Varian Disaster and under circumstances which looked painfully similar. As his main force rushed downhill to attack, others diverted streams, flooding the area where the Romans were already stuck. Not just the place and season, but also Armin's instinct for the psychological moment, were frighteningly familiar. The only improvement, from a Roman viewpoint, was that Caecina was no lawyer but an able and experienced soldier.

> The subsiding ground made it too soft to stand still and too slippery to move. They were in heavy armour and could not balance themselves to throw their javelins effectively. To the Cheruscans, however, such conditions were normal. The legions were close to breaking point when nightfall saved them. But this would be a night of little ease.

In Tacitus' description of the nocturnal ordeal, strongly reminiscent of the night before Agincourt,[123] the predicament of the two armies is suggested by contrasting sounds. However, in the apparition of Varus, Tacitus plays an even more horrific card.

> As the Germans revelled, the valleys and forests echoed with their savage shoutings and jubilant chants; while in the Roman lines men huddled round fitful fires, speaking in snatches, lying down behind their improvised dykes or wandering among the tents in a sleepless daze. That night, too, the general had a most horrible dream in which he beheld Quintilius Varus, drenched in blood, rising from the morass and beckoning him.
> In the morning Armin resumed the onslaught, shouting: 'Here is Varus and his legions, trapped by fate in the same way!' Luckily the enemy's greed worked in our favour, for many stopped killing and started looting.

The Romans were now able to regain firm ground and dig in before the onset of the second dusk:

> Without spades or turf-cutters an earthwork was somehow thrown up. The units were without tents, the wounded without dressings. As the mudcaked, bloodstained rations were passed round the men groused at the funereal dark and the end which the next day would bring to thousands.

But fortunes were about to turn. The ground was drying fast and when, next morning, Armin stormed the camp on one side, the

Romans rushed out from the others and fell upon the German flanks and rear, shouting:

> 'Where are your woods and swamps now? This is good ground and the odds are even!' The enemy, who had looked for a quick kill, proved as panicky in defeat as he had been rash in success. Armin slipped away unhurt. The massacre went on as long as daylight lasted.[124]

Tacitus next described the no less hazardous progress of the sea-borne column, led by one Vitellius. Here two legions were marching along the coast toward their embarkation when a great northerly began both to back up the tidewater from the sea and impede the escape of freshwater from the land, increasing the flood level by the minute.

> Now the entire landscape began to liquefy: wave, shore and plain merging into one so that the fluid and the firm, the shallow and the sea, became indistinguishable. Men were dragged under. Drowned packhorses, their loads and human corpses began bobbing back through the ranks. Units became muddled up, men one moment chest, the next chin deep. Here was death without glory.[125]

Disaster was averted by the timely arrival of the fleet. In the season following, however, a storm caught the same operation a stage later, soon after embarkation. This time it was a southerly, driving the leaky and overladen vessels onto the East Frisian Islands.

> Germanicus guided them down the Ems and out into the North Sea, that last and landless deep. At first its calm was troubled only by the whispering sails and creaking oars of a thousand ships. But soon black clouds massed in the sky, unloading hail. The wind, rising from every quarter, stirred the sea, blurred the view and plagued the steering. Then all heaven broke loose. The south wind, drawing its strength from Germany's drenched land, deep rivers and unending clouds, caught and scattered the vessels to the open sea or onto islands made savage by sunken shoals. Horses, pack animals, baggage, even weapons were thrown overboard to lighten the leaking ships as the sea overrode their gunwales. Some went

down. Others were thrown ashore on remote islands where (apart from a few who ate the horse carcasses washed up with them) they starved to death.[126]

It was during this third campaigning season of AD 16 that Tacitus offers a last, sardonic snapshot of Armin. On one occasion Roman and Cheruscan forces were separated by the Weser, with neither having the superior strength to cross. Armin's brother Flavus, still a serving Roman officer, was brought forward to parley across the water. The two brothers faced each other from opposite banks. Flavus had lost an eye fighting under Tiberius in the Balkans. Noting his scarred face, Armin asked how he had come by the wound. Flavus explained. And what had he received in compensation? 'A pay-rise and some decorations,' said Flavus. 'The wages of slavery are low,' was Armin's sneering retort. The conversation then degenerated into abuse and threats; and the two brothers had to be restrained from floundering across the river at each other's throats.

Germanicus could never quite trap Armin, but he did succeed in catching his wife Thusnelda and their infant son. They were taken to Rome and paraded in Germanicus' Triumph, while her father, Segestes, watched the show from the VIP seats. So Rome sundered tribe and tribe, brother and brother, father and daughter; and through these sad vignettes[127] one glimpses the other side of the coin of conquest.

The German War was twenty-eight years old, outlasting by two years the emperor who began it. With Augustus' death in AD 14 Rome's imperial ambitions reached a watershed; for his testament, read to the Senate after the funeral, signalled a memorable downturn. This was Augustus' 'advice': a posthumous thunderclap described, in Tacitus' famous phrase, as *consilium coercendi intra terminos imperii*[128] (advice that the empire should be kept within its existing boundaries) and amplified by Dio as, 'the opinion that we should be content with what we now possessed. Under no circumstances should we seek to expand the empire. It would be difficult to defend and we might lose what we already had.'[129] This pronouncement may be variously interpreted. *Prima facie* it was simply an assertion that the empire had achieved its natural limits. More broadly it was a veiled admission that the German War was lost. Most broadly of all it proposed a changed relationship with the outside world; a renunciation of the military adventurism which had made Rome great; a turnabout so total that even Augustus had not dared make it in his lifetime. Only the distress and disappointment of the Varian Disaster, playing on a tired and ageing mind, can explain it. Of course, it need not be binding on future emperors. Each would insist on his own foreign policy. Nevertheless, one of Rome's most influential imperialists had recanted; and the effect on future thinking would be considerable.

The advice was principally intended for Tiberius who, as Augustus' successor, inherited his commitments. There may even have been a secret protocol: that the old emperor would make his posthumous declaration in order to let the new emperor off the hook. True or not, it suited Tiberius to respect his predecessor's last wish. He too was tired. He had served nine times in Germany: enough to recognize the futility of seeking out those capable of infinite concealment and chasing those capable of indefinite retreat, through a land where every handful of grain had to be carried. Surely three more seasons' campaigning had sufficed to avenge the loss of three legions.

Accordingly, when Germanicus wrote to Rome requesting a fourth summer, in which German resistance would be crushed for ever, Tiberius replied, 'There have been successes enough already.'[130] With this weary comment the German venture and the dream of endless empire ended. A line was drawn under the Varian Disaster, soon to be translated into the physical line of Rhine and Danube, which would divide Roman from barbarian for more than four centuries. Not all emperors would respect it. Indeed the next two Episodes concern major excursions beyond it. Nevertheless, non-aggression now becomes the imperial norm.

Soon Tiberius would retire again, this time finally: to Capri and pastimes which would earn that charming island the nickname *Caprineum*[131] (goatery). Small wonder, writing of this reign, that Tacitus would lament: 'My theme is narrow and inglorious: an emperor unconcerned with enlarging the empire . . .'[132] It is in this change, from a foreign policy of breadth and glamour to one of narrowness and inglory, that the significance of the Teutoburg catastrophe lies. In purely military terms Rome had survived far worse. Despite Augustus' alarm it had not been a Second Punic War, with Hannibal at the gate and every Roman woman in mourning. None the less, the Teutoburg was more than a battle. Time would show it as the moment when the caesars first recognized unlimited goals as a fantasy and limitless miles as the reality. Of course this meant the simultaneous birth of a contrary idea: that the empire would have formal frontiers; for if expansion were to halt there must be halt lines.

All in all it is hardly surprising that when retired generals write about history's decisive battles, the clash in the Teutoburg Forest is almost always given an airing. Without this defeat, argues Major-General Fuller, Germany would have been a Roman province. It follows therefore that:

> Had Germany been for four centuries thoroughly Romanised, one culture, not two would have dominated the western world. There would have been no Franco-German problem, no Charlemagne, no Louis XIV, no Napoleon, no Kaiser Wilhelm II and no Hitler.[133]

Even more fundamentally: had an emperor's niece married a soldier rather than a lawyer; had the German tribes been progressively defeated and recruited to the Roman side, the empire would have disarmed what were in the long term to be its worst enemies and might therefore still exist. The imaginary consequences run on and on.

Returning to more realistic speculations: of the many theories regarding the Teutoburg battle site, that proposed by the eminent 19th-century Romanist, Theodor Mommsen, always seemed the likeliest. He reasoned that to pay for services and bribe chieftains, Varus' column must have carried substantial sums in gold and silver coin; and that this would be the most detectable and dateable element of the looted baggage. He therefore plotted all Augustan coin-finds in north-western Germany to determine whether a significant number appeared to radiate from a central spot. On these grounds Mommsen pointed to the Wiehengebirge as the probable location, at the northern extremity of the upland area designated the Teutoburg Forest by 17th-century antiquarians.

On flat ground, a little to the north of these Wiehen Hills, was an area between the villages of Bramsche and Venne, known since the 17th century to be rich in Roman coins. Most of the finds had been accumulated by the local landowning family, the von Bars of Barenaue Castle, whose collection consisted of one *aureus* (gold), 179 *denarii* (silver) and two *asses* (copper). Mommsen examined it and was struck by the fact that all the coins were dateable to between 194 BC and the first decade of our era. This seemed to verify proximity to the battlefield. However, since the two villages are in the

1. Left: statue of Ovid, Constantsa, Romania; by E. Ferrari (1887).

2. Centre: detail, gold necklace, 4th century BC; nomads curing sheepskin.

3. Lower left: steppe art. Gold lion, Peter the Great's steppe collection.

4. Lower right: mounted archer. Greek coin of 4th century BC.

5. The *Hermannsdenkmal*, near Detmold, north-west Germany: erected 1873–5, to Armin the Cheruscan, victor of the Varus Battle.

6. The monument takes shape in von Bandel's studio.

7. A field at Niewed, near Bramsche, Germany: richest source of finds to date. The earthwork narrowed the gap, squeezing the Roman column. Waterlogged ground begins ten yards to rear of camera position.

8. Portrait of P. Quintilius Varus from a coin minted in Africa sixteen years earlier.

9. Augustan penny (*as*) counterstamped with monogram VAR.

10. Roman temporary camp on ploughland, foreground. Proposed battlefield on rising ground in middle distance. Bennachie, thought to be *Mons Graupius*, background.

11. Celtic shield of characteristic design and artistry, recovered from the Thames at Battersea.

12. The antagonists: King Decebal of Dacia (L) and the
Emperor Trajan. Details from Trajan's Column.

13. Trajan's Column: inauguration of the Danube bridge.

14/15. The *Tropaeum Traiani*, Adamclisi, Romania. *In situ* reconstruction, completed 1977, encasing the original core.

16. In Transylvania, a local hero: modern rendering of
    Decebal at entrance to the Orashtie Mountains.

17. The road to royal Sarmizegetusa, ultimate Dacian
    stronghold, on background hilltop.

18. Trajan's Column: suicide of Decebal.

19. Ulpia Traiana Sarmizegetusa, capital of Roman Dacia: Forum

adjacent plain and Dio's descriptions favoured densely forested upland, Mommsen stuck to his choice of the Wiehen Hills, only three or four miles to the south.[134]

Mommsen's theory soon came under attack. It was argued that he had been wrong to base his findings on gold and silver coins, which could be evidence of a diplomatic mission or a merchant's purse. The quantity of copper coins was insignificant. These were the soldier's everyday spending money; and a battlefield, with thousands of Roman casualties, should be expected to yield them in large numbers. Further, the von Bar collection had been gathered sporadically, without record of provenance; and was therefore challengeable. Part had been sold to a dealer in 1884 and dispersed without trace; the remainder reportedly looted by Allied soldiers, occupying the property in 1945. Even more damaging was the complete absence of military accoutrement. It will, of course, be obvious that, while gold and silver have always found favour with the accidental finder, small, scattered, scarcely visible objects of baser metal have often awaited the coming of the metal detector.

In 1991 press reports, promising some resolution to the long search, were followed by publication of a more substantive account by a group of North German scholars, behind whose guarded opinions exciting conclusions seem to lie.[135] It concerned the first phase of an investigation into the same part of Lower Saxony, some ten miles north-north-east of Osnabrück, which began in 1987. Earlier that year Major J. A. S. Clunn, a British officer in the Osnabrück garrison, had begun to conduct solo searches in the vicinity of the Barenaue estate, uncovering a hoard of 160 Roman coins. Though this was not proof of military presence, his second discovery (in the spring of 1988) of three pieces of lead slingshot, provoked further attention and provided the starting point for a large-scale effort. A systematic survey yielded 162 silver coins, plus three glass beads of a type associated with Roman children's games. The dating of the last coin, though disputed, is probably AD 4. All this was intriguing but still inconclusive. During the next two years, however, the evidence sharpened dramatically. Over a hundred copper coins were discovered, many minted at Lyons between 8 and 3 BC. Two silver coins could be dated with certainty to AD 9, the year of the Varian Disaster. Most thrilling of all, some copper pennies were counterstamped with the letters *VAR*. Provincial countermarking with the monogram of a governor is well attested for this period and almost always associated with monies issued as bonuses or soldiers' pay. *VAR* points unerringly to the German governship of P. Quintilius Varus, AD 7–9.

A convincing series of military finds now accompanied the coinage. Especially noteworthy were two bronze hauberk clasps of serpentine design, one scratched and the other punched on the back with the inscriptions: 'the Century of Terentius Romanus' (or 'Romanus, of the Century of Terentius') and 'M. Aius of the 1st Cohort, Century of Fabricius'. Besides this there was a silver-dipped, iron face mask, of considerable individuality and realism, part of a ceremonial helmet. In addition a rein-guide was identified, thought to be from a yoke joining draught animals. Other finds included a spear tip, a Roman pickaxe head, rings, buckles, pins and many small metal components from uniforms or equipment. But it is the first four items, plus the beads, which must be stressed; for the clasps are of legionary, the sling shots of auxiliary, the face mask of cavalry and the rein-guide of wagon-train origins, while the beads suggest families and civilians; all verifying Dio's picture of a large, combined, cumbrous army or its remnant, perhaps still partially burdened with baggage and dependents.

The objects were found scattered over an area of three-and-three-quarter miles from east to west by 1,000 yards from north to south, randomly and in what had been the topsoil, as if lost or trampled into the surface vegetation. Because so many clues were won from relatively few archaeological incisions, and despite the likelihood that the battlefield was picked clean by the victors, the presence of thousands of people may be inferred. Abundant coins of the later Republic, peaking during Augustus' reign and ending abruptly at AD 9, debar the earlier campaigns of Drusus and Tiberius, and cast strong doubt on the revenge expeditions of Germanicus (AD 14–16) as sources of the lost articles.

Geography adds comparable weight. Kalkriese Hill, northern outlier of the Wiehen Range, on the extreme edge of the Teutoburg Forest, descends some 350 feet to the North German Plain, where it meets a marsh still called *Grosses Moor* (big fen). Between this last slope and first bog a sandy strip affords dry passage for east-west traffic, doubtless the location of a prehistoric pathway and carrying today's B218 between Engter and Venne. It is by now beyond question that this was the Roman line of march. In the Middle Ages soil from drainage ditches, cut into the morass, was laid down on much of the sandy strip to promote cultivation, further concealing but also preserving the battlefield's secrets.

Here, then, was a natural ambush corridor between densely forested hill and quaking fen. At its narrowest, adjacent to Niewed Manor, the dry passage is 120 yards wide; with only the modern road, a fringe of trees and the width of a small field separating slope from quagmire. Below the imported topsoil is yellow sand and in it archaeological investigation has revealed the substantial remains of a sandy, sod-capped ridge, perhaps four feet high; running parallel to the foot of the hill for several hundred yards, believed to have been thrown up by the Germans, both for their own protection and to retard the Romans by reducing the bottleneck to a mere sixty yards. Numerous coins and fragments of military equipment have been found on and around this improvised dyke, suggesting a desperate struggle across it. Though not yet certain what stage of the attritional process this represented, it was already difficult to deny the Niewed Field as the focal point of a brilliantly executed ambush. However, in 1994, another vital piece was added to the puzzle. Near the adjacent foot of the Kalkrieser Berg, Professor W. Schlüter discovered a mass grave, with bones placed in a pit and turves laid over them, resembling convincingly the Tacitean description of Germanicus' visit to the battlefield; so pointing to this vicinity either as the battle's climax, as one of its peaks, or as the place where, in Major Clunn's view,[136] the remnant of an already depleted Roman force was finally annihilated.

The findings could point to the following scenario, generally compatible with the written sources. In the autumn of AD 9 Varus was tricked into a westward march in the general direction of today's Osnabrück in order to quell a fictitious disturbance, instead of the usual south-westward journey back to the Lippe. This took his column along a natural route, following the northern front of the foothills where they meet the plain. A trap was prepared at the narrowest part of this corridor where the army would be squeezed between upland and wetland by a convergence of tribes and German deserters.

The surprise of these findings is their incompatibility with Dio, whose setting is decidedly forest: an army caught 'in almost inextricable woods', 'unable to deploy the cavalry because of trees', and so on. Tacitus (a century after the event but a century before Dio) is our sole source for the expression *Teutoburgiensis saltus*;[137] and it is possible that the discrepancy originated from his peculiar use of *saltus.* It now seems unlikely that Tacitus intended it in its usual sense of 'clearing in the forest'. Livy had employed the word quite differently in relation to Thermopylae: *Thermopylarum saltum ubi angustae fauces coartant iter*[138] (the pass of Thermopylae, where a narrow gap constricts the road). Was Tacitus echoing this usage? Had propaganda sought to ennoble the Varian Disaster by choosing a loaded word, associated in historical writing with the Spartans' defence at Thermopylae, an event of legendary heroism; and was Tacitus simply repeating what had become the standard description? In either case the parallel with doomed heroes and the topographic resemblances are clear, for both battles were fought in constricted terrain or natural gaps. In this event – and in view of the recent discoveries – a more correct reading of Tacitus might not be Teutoburg Forest but Teutoburg Corridor; meaning the sandy, east-west passage where the line of foothills met the North German Plain. By contrast Dio seems to have lighted on the meaning of *saltus* as a glade, leading to his enhancement of the forest aspect, adding to the theatricality of his account and helping to excuse defeat. His description led successively to mistranslation by the humanists, the renaming of the Osning Range as the *Teutoburgerwald*, the placing of Bandel's statue in its midst (some forty-seven miles from the newly discovered site) and the misdirection of all battlefield theories southwards, into wooded hill country.

By contrast, the recent findings point to a setting where sloping forest met open marshland, strongly reminiscent of the place where Caecina was ambushed by the remontant Armin, seven years after the Teutoburg battle. Why (if Tacitus is to be believed) did the German leader then cry out, 'Behold, Varus and his legions, trapped in the same way!'? This too suggests a similarity of predicament and terrain. Velleius Paterculus, author of the only contemporary account, was seemingly accurate in describing Varus as 'hemmed in by bog, bush and ambush'.

Such is the strengthening evidence for locating the Varian Disaster in the Osnabrück rather than the Detmold vicinity; and indeed, Germany's learned have already largely abandoned using the expression, 'Battle of the Teutoburg Forest', in favour of the less tendentious 'Varus Battle'.

The Varian Disaster, which cost Rome Germany, also cost Germany Rome; or at least the benefits of Mediterranean civilization. Both sides had much to learn from the encounter, but as the Germans returned to the forest it was not Roman ideas on urbanization, road-building, the peaceful arts or the rule of law that they took with them. Despite Quintilius Varus' season on the bench, German enthusiasm for the practice and principles of Roman law was totally feigned. In fact absence of the appropriate loan words from Latin into German suggests a disinterest in theoretical or abstract concepts of any kind. Fascination was with Roman tactics and weaponry. In due course it would go further. As time passed the Germans would recognize that the empire's secret lay in diplomacy and the ability to make common cause. These gifts they would one day mimic: not to the extent of achieving nationhood, but sufficiently to win wars. In this sense the exhortation to unity emblazoned on Armin's sword at the *Hermannsdenkmal* was not many centuries from realization. Small wonder that a 4th-century Roman continues to call them '*Germanos hostes truces et assiduos formidantes*' (the Germans, our ferocious and implacable foe).[139]

The Soldiers

THE RECITAL SEEMED INTERMINABLE, ITS prolongation assured by an enraptured audience and Nero's eagerness to bask in its rapture. Nor was there likelihood of escape from the cycle of applause and encore till the emperor tired; and being scarcely beyond his teens and endlessly hungry for adulation, that was unlikely to be soon. Of all places which appreciated artistry, recognition in Greece, the land of artists, was doubly sweet. So it was that, as Nero struck the lyre yet again, a pin could have been heard to drop; while he sang they sat spellbound; and when he stopped they exploded, with shouts of 'Blessed are they that hear thee!', 'Apollo, thou art with us!' and 'Surely it is Phoebus himself who sings!' And yet in truth the playing was plain, the voice thin, the theatricality forced and the whole occasion acutely embarrassing.

Irksome as this was for the audience of Greek notables, it was doubly so for the emperor's Italian entourage, who had no choice but to endure these unendurably boring exhibitions at each stop on the long itinerary. Performances had been known to last from early morning till late evening and some Greeks had hit on the idea of swooning with ecstasy, so they could be carried out as if dead: the only way of escape. For those in the imperial suite, on the other hand, endurance was perhaps a price worth paying for an otherwise pleasant and leisurely progress around the hospitable cities of Hellas, a country regarded by Romans with an affection similar to the Englishman's view of Italy in the age of the Grand Tour. Besides, Greece flattered the emperor and moderated his moods, which made things easier as well as safer for his travelling companions. The catastrophe was for the host country, owing to the endless attainders and confiscations which Nero was currently devising to pay for his Corinth Canal project. It was said that the roads were busy with messengers carrying news of condemnations or confirmation of murders performed.[1]

Among the Italians present on that fateful evening, quite distinct from the usual run of officials and hangers-on, was a senator, already in his forties, on whom the mantle of pretended pleasure sat uneasily. T. Flavius Vespasianus was not only a soldier among senators, he was even a rough diamond among soldiers, being of bourgeois rather than aristocratic background and rustic rather than metropolitan origin. Not that social handicaps mattered greatly. The awkwardness was in the man, here emphasized by the extreme contrast between caesar and soldier: Nero, last of the lines of Augustus and Livia, rouged, ringed and ringleted; and Vespasian, inelegant, gruff and practical. A portrait bust in Naples[2] shows him as bald, with vestiges of coarse and crinkly hair, the features clenched and determined, the expression searching, the mouth stingy but redeemed by an ironic smile. Though the eyes are blank marble, the sculptor has contrived to suggest a twinkle. Homely in looks and rough of tongue, short on social graces and long on common sense: such was the man designated by a jest of fortune to be Nero's successor.

Why should the emperor invite so unlikely a companion on a fine arts tour of Greece? The answer can only have been that Nero liked him. He was also a national hero. When scarcely in his mid-twenties, he had done singularly well against the Britons. It seems Nero distrusted the commander of that campaign, Aulus Plautius, whose murder he would in due course arrange. Perhaps it was to spite Plautius that Nero now favoured his former lieutenant. Whatever the reason, Vespasian's star was rising. He had come far since the ridicule to which he had been subjected as the youthful official in charge of the Roman street sweepers, when (if the expression may be excused) he had fallen foul of the then emperor: 'Caligula, spotting a pile of mud in an alleyway, ordered it to be thrown onto Vespasian's toga; he being at that time the official responsible for street cleaning.'[3] Vespasian was obliged to offer up his white toga, with its senator's broad purple stripe, much as a girl might hold her apron in gathering flowers, while guardsmen trowelled the ordure, doubtless with full measure of donkey droppings, into his lap. Suetonius enjoys the irony: 'Accordingly the soldiers shovelled the dirt into a fold of his senatorial gown, filling it to capacity. This was later seen as an omen, that Vespasian would one day take the soil of Italy into his care.'[4]

Under Claudius had come a brighter turn. A contact in high places brought command of a legion. It was a job that would fit like a glove. 'Vespasian was a born soldier: marching at the head of his men,[5] choosing where they should camp,[6] harrying the enemy day and night by his leadership and where necessary by personal combat; content with whatever was going in the way of food and dressing much like a private soldier.[7]'

His reward for a brilliantly fought campaign in Britain was the governorship of Africa. Straight as a die, he declined all bribes and in consequence was ruined by the grievous expense of this post. 'He governed Africa with great justice – and with dignity – save once when the people of Hadrumentum[8] pelted him with turnips. That he came back no richer than he went out is proven by his having to mortgage the family land and invest in the mule-breeding business, from which he got the nickname "muleteer".'[9]

After Claudius came Nero and a return to better days. Perhaps the boyish caesar found Vespasian's directness and jocularity refreshing. At any rate, it was highly unlikely that a 'muleteer' would ever grow too big for his boots. So Vespasian's reward, both for his achievement and his modesty, was the honour of accompanying the emperor on this pleasantest of tours, plus a front seat at a long succession of imperial lyre recitals. We may assume that he was sitting near the front since Nero, in mid song, now spotted something which came close to costing Vespasian his life: Vespasian had fallen asleep!

How could a man of such sense allow himself so dangerous a lapse? We must suppose that disinclination toward the artistic, distaste for the pseudo-artistic, the excruciating tedium of the occasion, combined with the balminess of the evening, allowed his attention to wander further than usual, so that reverie slid into sleep, causing his head to nod under circumstances which, had he been less popular, would certainly have cost him it. We next hear of him dismissed from court, fleeing Greece and hiding in the Italian countryside; self-exiled to a life of total and indefinite obscurity. However, before pursuing this strange story, it may be rewarding to look back at those events in Britain which had brought Vespasian to prominence, indeed to consider that remote island generally.

Augustus' advice to his successors, not to expand the empire further, had stood for almost thirty years until Claudius repudiated it by the British invasion of AD 43. This was a misguided enterprise, the decision to embark upon it taken against the weight of evidence. Certainly Rome's northern frontier could hardly have been more clearly defined or better protected than by the Channel. 'What wall', Josephus asks, 'could be stronger than the sea which is Britain's bulwark?'[10] Equally it was Rome's. This Augustus recognized; and though he called himself Caesar's heir, he had rejected the option of invasion:

> Though Rome could have taken Britain she declined to do so. In the first place the Britons are no threat, having insufficient strength to cross over and attack us. In the second, there would be little to gain. It seems that we presently get more out of them in duty on their exports than we would by direct taxation, especially if the costs of an occupation army and of tax collecting be discounted. The same goes even more for the islands round about Britain.[11]

For Claudius the temptation of Britain lay not in strategic or fiscal advantage but in newsworthiness and the stir which would be created by extending the empire across 'outer ocean', seen by Romans as a symbolic barrier. But though Britain possessed the potential for a quick propaganda *coup*, it was less easy to predict events in the long term, to foresee that the problem would not be crossing perilous water or landing on a hostile shore, but deciding how far to go and where to stop. This search for a stopping place would be long and vexatious, with no comfort in the knowledge that the Channel had been best in the first place. It would, alas, be characteristic of policy toward this island that practical arguments were overruled by emotional. Fame awaited the conqueror of Britannia. Conversely, infamy awaited whoever might relinquish her. So, once started, the line of action would be difficult to retract. Indeed, within ten years Nero was already wishing he could ditch the enterprise but found it politically prudent to stay, since 'not to do so would have belittled the glory won by Claudius'.[12]

Glory was what Claudius most needed. Claudius the family fool; the coward who, during the desperate hours following Caligula's assassination, had been found cringing behind a curtain in the palace. Claudius the insecure, who had bribed his way to the throne with payments of 3,750 *denarii* to each Praetorian guardsman, equivalent to sixteen years' pay for a legionary private. Now he would show them. Subjugation of the 'Celtic world' had taken centuries and was still incomplete. Claudius would strike the culminating blow.

Ninety-seven years earlier Caesar had charted a comparable course. He too had recognized Britain's power to stir the imagination. His visits may be connected with sensation-seeking and rivalry with Pompey, rather than with practical benefit. In the military sense they were reckless in the extreme. Gaul was not yet fully subdued and he had no business leaving her in his rear. But as the lion-tamer crowns his act by turning his back upon the lions, so it was Caesar's *pièce de résistance* to leave the Gauls lightly guarded while turning with seeming nonchalance to the Britons.

In 55 BC Caesar had set sail with the bulk of his force in order to test the problems of crossing and the British reaction, anticipating a more ambitious operation in the summer following. He landed in East Kent, traditionally on the shingle at Walmer or, if his estimate of seven miles beyond the end of the cliffs is taken strictly, at Deal.

> They embarked around midnight and Caesar, with the leading ships, reached the British Coast at about nine the following morning. He could see the enemy armed and in large numbers on all the hills. Hereabouts are steep cliffs, so close to the sea that missiles may be thrown from cliff top to beach. This seemed no place to land, so they pressed on for about seven miles to where the ships could be beached on a level and open shore.[13]

The sensation created by Caesar's despatches, as well as the Roman view of the hazards of crossing, may be guessed from the Senate's vote of a twenty-day thanksgiving on the army's safe return.

On his second visit Caesar crossed by the same route. His army forded a river, doubtless the Stour, and took a hillfort, probably Bigbury near Canterbury. They then marched west, perhaps along the North Downs, and swung north to wade neck-deep across the Thames in the vicinity of future London, despite sharpened stakes hidden below the water's surface. From here they penetrated the forest[14] ringing north London, of which Epping is a remnant. After defeating a tribal confederation, said to have included 4,000 war chariots, they stormed and occupied the stronghold of Cassivelaunus, the British leader and paramount chief of south-eastern England,[15] probably at Wheathampstead, north of present-day St Albans. But Caesar was soon obliged to retire to the coast, where his base camp was under attack; finally re-embarking before the autumn gales jeopardized safe passage.

This profitless adventure instigated a deception which could not fail to influence those who followed. It inferred that by seizing a major *oppidum* in tamest Hertfordshire the keys to Britain had somehow been secured. Geography seems to vindicate this view. Britain smiles toward the Continent, concealing troubles which will be revealed only gradually. In terms of terrain, climate and fertility, barely a third of the island lives up to its promise. What appears from the south to be an extension of France would, if seen from the north, be more like an extension of Norway. Even so, we must not leave the impression that antiquity was entirely ignorant of Britain's physical and human geography. Evidence existed, some of it from Caesar's own pen, on which a more realistic assessment might have been based.

In the passage following, Caesar refers to the 'coastal' and the 'interior' regions. By the former he meant the south-east, whose areas of recent Belgic settlement included Kent, the counties north of London and the Sussex coast. Here the wealthiest tribes lived. By the 'interior' he especially meant upland Britain; in modern terms the North, Scotland, Wales and the South-West. He contrasts the two ways of life, considering the interior peoples to be less advanced. Caesar also thought Britain's axis lay north-west-south-east instead of north-south, so that the west coast faced toward Spain and the east coast in a more northerly direction.

> The coastal regions are inhabited by Belgic invaders who came for plunder and stayed. The Belgians are numerous, with many cattle and farms, similar to those in Gaul. Like Gaul, too, there is ample timber, though without beech and fir. The climate is more temperate, with winter's less severe than Gaul.
>
> The island is triangular. One side, some 500 miles long, faces Gaul. A second faces westward, toward Spain. In this direction lies Ireland, thought to be half Britain's size. Between Ireland and Britain is the Isle of Man; and it is believed there are also a number of smaller islands where some writers have described a total winter darkness lasting thirty days. This western side, according to the natives, is 700 miles long. The third faces north. There is no land

opposite this, though its eastern corner faces Germany. Its length is reckoned as 800 miles.

By far the most civilized of the Britons live in Kent,[16] where life resembles that of Gaul. Most interior tribes do not grow cereals but live on meat and milk and wear skins. All Britons dye themselves with woad, giving a blue colour and a savage appearance in battle. Hair is worn long; the entire body shaven except the moustache. Wives are held in common among groups of ten or twelve men, usually the males of the same family.[17]

This island had also fascinated Claudius' predecessor, Caligula. Suetonius described the farcical events of AD 40, when the legions mutinied rather than embark. In a bizarre ceremony on the beach near Boulogne, Caligula declared Britain annexed, as it were, *in absentia*. The campaign would be sold to the Roman public as a victory against Ocean.

He deployed the army in line of battle facing the sea, with the artillery in readiness. Everyone was wondering what it all meant when suddenly Caligula shouted 'Gather sea-shells!' By this he meant 'spoils of ocean', as an offering at the Roman Capitol. So the soldiers had to fill their helmets and kilts with shells. Then he promised a bounty of four gold pieces per man. The triremes used in the Channel on this occasion were transported to Rome, largely overland; and he wrote ahead, ordering a Triumph more spectacular than any yet seen.[18]

There can be no doubt that seasoned soldiers quailed at the sight of open sea. It was not that the Channel is rougher than the Mediterranean or Black Seas. The fear arose from a world picture consisting of three continents moated by a dark and savage deep, within which were sea monsters and beyond which was nothing. There were also superstitions regarding Britain herself: for example, the eerie story that she was the abode of the dead and that souls were rowed across in unmanned boats, which left the coast of Gaul at nightfall and returned before dawn. Thanet,[19] the name of Kent's north-eastern extremity, may originate in this legend.

It is therefore not surprising that the Claudian version of the same project should have started in much the same way. Again there was near mutiny when the soldiers realized they were to go 'beyond the known world'.[20] On this occasion there was present one Narcissus, an imperial civil servant and former slave of the punctilious type Claudius liked to employ as his secretaries. This man, who we may suspect was empowered to offer an inducement, now mounted the general's rostrum and attempted to calm the lads. Some wag then shouted '*Io Saturnalia!*' (hurrah for the feast of Saturn) a greeting roughly equivalent to 'merry Christmas'. For just as it is some armies' custom that on Christmas Day the officers wait on the men, so for the holiday period beginning on 17 December, Roman masters and slaves traditionally swapped roles. The shout was thus a sarcastic reference to the indignity that an ex-slave should address the army in the emperor's place. Taken up by others the whole parade was soon convulsed with laughter, easing the tension to such an extent that the soldiers forgot their fear and obeyed the order to embark.

For the campaign which followed, our principal source is Cassius Dio, writing 130 years later. By contrast Suetonius is brief and dismissive: 'Claudius' only campaign was of little importance. The Senate had already voted him an honorary Triumph but this he refused, lighting on Britain as the place to seek the real thing. Her conquest was a project which had lain dormant since Caesar's day.'[21]

Four legions were mustered, one from the Danube and three from the Rhine, which had fallen unexpectedly quiet since the Varian Disaster. Aulus Plautius, 'a distinguished senator'[22] was appointed to command, with the youthful Vespasian leading the legion II *Augusta*. In essence the thrust would follow that of Caesar. Dio specifies embarkation in three groups, at least one of which sailed westwards from Boulogne,[23] raising the possibility that a diversionary force beached in Chichester Harbour. Nevertheless, it remains likely that the main force landed unopposed at Richborough, Kent. Plautius then advanced to a river, too wide to be bridged, presumably the lower Medway. Here the crossing was strongly contested. In an action, probably near the future Rochester, Vespasian sprang to prominence, both because of his spirited attack and as the first senior officer across. The Britons fell back on the Thames and Plautius advanced to a position facing one of the fords: at Southwark, Westminster, or Battersea. Here, in temporary camps somewhere under today's South London, the army settled to a long wait while a pre-arranged plan was set in motion. Claudius sailed from the Tiber to Marseilles, then probably up the Rhone and overland to the Channel, arriving in Britain with a large entourage of VIPs, guardsmen and elephants. All this involved a delay of six to eight weeks. The weather had been bad and on three occasions the imperial flotilla was almost shipwrecked.

At last Claudius joined the legions waiting by the Thames. Assuming command, he crossed the river, 'defeated the barbarians' and took the capital of the late king, Cynobellinus (Shakespeare's Cymbeline) at Colchester. However, the real leader, Prince Caratacus, a stout fighter and clever tactician, fled to south Wales, where he would live to lead again. It seems unlikely that Claudius met much resistance. Suetonius states bluntly that 'he fought no battles and took no casualties'.[24] Nothing is heard of the elephants. Doubtless their main contribution was in Claudius' victory parade where their effect would be stunning, lumbering through the streets of a Colchester only days removed from prehistory.

Elsewhere elephants had proved a dubious asset. Their trial against the Celtiberians at Numantia[25] had been a *débâcle*, when the drivers lost control and the trumpeting animals ran amok. It is strange that while we spend hours in zoos or make expensive trips to Africa to look at elephants, the ancients tended to regard them with revulsion. In warfare there was a real risk that they would frighten the enemy less than the side which was using them. Thus Ammian: 'With them came a striking sight: ponderous lines of soldier-laden elephants, bodies repulsively wrinkled; the most hideous of all forms of horror, as I have always maintained.'[26]

Having cracked champagne against the hull of the new province, the emperor returned the command to Plautius with instructions 'to subjugate the remaining districts', and retired to Rome. In all he had spent sixteen days in Britain. So much for the victory. What of the territory? What to take and what reject, where to terminate the conquest and how to round it off? These were quite other matters and Claudius may have been content to leave them to his generals.

We do not know at what point Vespasian's legion was detached from the main force and sent on the separate mission which would win him fame as perhaps the greatest gunnery officer the ancient world produced.[27] Suetonius mentions that officers decorated in Britain marched in the Triumph, suggesting Vespasian returned to Rome for this purpose and the conquest was not resumed till the following spring. Then, as the ponderous Plautius moved north, Vespasian swung west. For his part in the war one must be content with a single sentence in Suetonius, though a good one: 'He went to Britain, where he fought thirty battles, subjugated two tribes and took more than twenty *oppida*, the Isle of Wight besides.'[28] In fact Vespasian overran the south and south-west of England at least as far as Exeter, ending perhaps with a sweep to the lower Severn. His offensive resembles that of 1944 when Patton, pivoting on the slower-moving Montgomery, sped across France. Vespasian does not lose from the comparison, for here was a commander who seized three quarters of the ground with a quarter of the army. What is more, he faced, in Wessex,[29] one of the most formidable concentrations of forts in the ancient world. His answer to these citadels of soil was artillery.

Roman guns were based on the idea of twisting a rope until tension was created, then releasing it; which is why they are sometimes known as 'torsion artillery'. Hemp, horse, even women's hair was used, but animal sinew had the greatest elasticity, though there was a problem in keeping it dry.[30] Guns were of two basic models. The *scorpio* (whose firing arm resembled the upreared tail of the scorpion) was based on a grounded chassis of heavy timber, across which was strung a thick skein of sinew into which the slinging arm was rooted. This was pulled back and the ropes wound by handles until the required tension was created. When released and the arm had reached the near-vertical, its rush was stopped by a padded beam, creating a jerk which projected the missile. The *scorpio* was later known by other names, illustrating the inventiveness of army slang: 'The machine is called *tormentum* (the rack) as the tension is created by twisting; and *scorpio* because of the raised sting. More recently it has been called *onager* (jackass) since, when wild donkeys flee from pursuers they kick stones backwards, so cracking skulls or shattering ribcages.'[31] A crew of five is given for this machine (four winders and a loader-firer), a missile weighing fifty pounds and a range of 450 yards,[32] though 700 yards is also recorded. Unlike modern pieces, designed so that parts will interchange and with calibre matched precisely to ammunition, the *scorpio* could be made to almost any specification; so it is not surprising that various missile sizes, ranges, mounting and haulage arrangements are claimed.

The *ballista* had a different appearance. It was in effect a large, stand-mounted crossbow, except that the bow consisted of two halves, each embedded in a sinew coil. This was a highly effective weapon at a hundred yards. Again, larger versions were available.

A 4th-century source tells of a *ballista* able to shoot across the Danube.[33]

Both *scorpiones* and *ballistae* could be adapted to stone shot or iron bolt. Ammian describes fire-darts, with reeds bound around a hollow, wooden centre into which glowing embers were placed.[34] All had devices for sighting, tilting and traversing, so that a target could be pounded once its range had been found. Accuracy called for standard missiles, though random rocks were best for anti-personnel bombardment, since the sound of a jagged object in flight is more terrifying. Various grades of ammunition must therefore have been carried on campaign. Added to this was the weight of the guns themselves. A full-scale *scorpio* model has been found to weigh over two tons.

It cannot be argued that artillery was a decisive arm in warfare generally. It was cumbersome, weather dependent, of little value in rough country and useless in forest. None the less it was highly effective in sieges. Stone walls could be shaken loose. Defenders could be driven from palisades, opening the way for infantry attack. Though ineffectual against the mighty hillforts, stones and firedarts could be lobbed across their outer mounds and ditches to fall among the thatched huts within. From wooden towers erected outside the defensive ring, observers could guide the shotfall onto selected targets; subjecting the defenders to an ordeal of whirring missiles crashing among them from guns they could not see.

Vespasian was quick to grasp artillery's strengths and Wessex's weaknesses and to see that these were complementary. Mighty earth-works were being used to protect flimsy, fire-prone villages, without internal shelters or warproofing of any kind. Furthermore the forts had become overblown. As with nuclear stockpiling, the rivalries which promoted their proliferation had become obsessional and scale had outrun ability to defend.

It is difficult to guess the number of artillery pieces allocated to Vespasian. Vegetius, a late-period writer, describes fifty-five *ballistae* and ten *onagri* per legion, drawn by mules or oxen and having crews of seven. As well as ammunition, Vespasian would be moving with equipment of other kinds: prefabricated towers and battering rams, as well as boats and planks for river crossing. Naval squadrons must have been operating in support up rivers like the Test, Wiltshire Avon and Frome, as well as in the assault on the Isle of Wight. With logistics like these we cannot assume lightning war. Indeed

Vespasian's temperament inclined him to the more deliberate school of generalship which, though for a time eclipsed by the showier styles of Caesar and Pompey, was in fact the Roman norm. Nevertheless the siege operations, once begun, were probably concluded with a speed which paralysed the enemy. The sudden surrender of 'impregnable' positions can have grave consequences for morale and when they crashed so quickly in the face of this unprecedented weapon it must have seemed, to tribes which awaited their turn, like the knock of doom. The remains of several Roman artillery pieces have been found and reconstructed versions may be seen at the Saalburg Museum, ten miles north-west of Frankfurt, and a half-scale *scorpio* at the Lunt Fort, Baginton, near Coventry, England.

Before pursuing Vespasian's campaign, some account should be given of late Iron Age Britain as distinct from 'Celtica' generally. Terms like the latter are seldom used lest they imply unity in the Celtic camp. Of this there was little. Nor was there ever a Celtic empire. Separatism is, it seems, the enduring characteristic of a cultural group at loggerheads from that day to this; from whose differences the English would so frequently profit. In Britain's case, the accepted picture of envelopment in a wider Celtic world must be qualified by a stark (and, to many, an unpalatable) fact. Except in the extreme south-east (and an enclave to the north of the Humber) archaeology has failed to reveal changes of sufficient magnitude to demonstrate migration into the British Isles.[35] This puts a rock into the river of prehistoric studies around which emotional currents are certain to swirl; for it implies that most of Britain was not peopled by incomers at all, but by a miscellany of native tribes surviving from the Bronze Age. Hence it would follow that British Celticism is a fraud; indeed that a pan-Celtic ancestry, knitting Europe's Atlantic fringes into a cultural whole, is a modern idea, invented as a counterweight to the dominance of the English language and Anglo-Saxon institutions. It is of course true that no classical author used the word 'Celt' in a British context. Nor does 'Celtic' become familiar in this sense till the 18th century. However, a solitary word is not the sole issue. Opponents of a Celtic Britain must answer major questions posed by languages like Gaelic, Irish, Welsh, Cornish and Manx, related both to each other and to what we know of ancient Celtic. For instance, in his monumental *The Celtic Place-names of Scotland* (Edinburgh and London, 1926) W. J. Watson offers some 50,000 examples from that quarter alone. More broadly there is a common background of names for places and natural features, of which every-one will be aware: from Boulogne to Bologna, Trent to Trento, Severn to Seine, Ouse to Oise, Shannon to Saône, Mersey to Meuse, Don to Danube, Arun to Arno and Irun. From the Pennines of North-umbria to the Appennines of north Umbria, Western Europe is bound by eloquent strains of remembrance. Of what do they tell? Of Celtic invasions or merely of Celtic influences? Might this onomastic lug-gage have travelled without the passengers? It is a likelihood many will question. On the other hand, indigenous building methods, pot-tery and, to some extent, artistic styles, are among the evidence which continues to deny invasion. The controversy is complex and unresolved. It may nevertheless be accepted that the description 'Celtic' – albeit with modified meaning – retains at least partial valid-ity and will continue to be employed by students of ancient Britain, if only because no untarnished alternative presents itself. Pro-Celtic propaganda (if such it is) has handed a resplendent past to north-western Europe's peripheral peoples. They will be reluctant to hand it back.

What is the difference between the terms Celtic and Gallic? Names like Gaul, *Galle*,[36] Galatia, Galicia, Gaelic, Galway, Galloway, Don-egal, Portugal and so on, remind us how the Celtic peoples, then as now, described themselves. As we have said, the two words are largely interchangeable,[37] except that in Latin, Gaul became associ-ated with what is now France and posterity tends to honour the distinction. All were, however, one loose grouping which by late prehistory had colonized, absorbed or suffused western Europe from the Atlantic to Germany and from the north of Scotland to northern Italy, with an offshoot through the Alps into the Balkans and even an outlying pocket in Asia Minor.[38] Nevertheless, varying degrees of Celtic and pre-Celtic mixture, as well as centuries in various terrains and climates, created a wide range of development.

How did Celtic attainment compare with Roman? The traditional criterion of literacy as the difference between historic and prehistoric societies applies in this case. Though the arrival of Mediterranean influences had recently begun to provoke writing, using Greek and Roman alphabets, an illiterate majority may still be assumed and nothing resembling a Celtic literature had yet appeared. More recently the test of comparative technology has found favour; and in this sense achievement was close to Roman. Even so, common sense requires other insights; for Rome, after all, prevailed. At least one prehistorian suggests the real differences lay in social structure, civil order and organization: 'between stability and the complex conduct of affairs of state, on the one hand, and the impermanence and emotion-charged atmosphere of the clan or tribe on the other'.[39] This seems closer to the truth, owing partly to developmental level but also to the 'Celtic temperament'. In references to the lost account of Posidonius, in other classical authors, in the surviving Irish epics, even in echoes from the 18th-century Scottish Highlands, one has an impression of touchy pride, feud, argumentativeness and bombast, plus a life dominated by hunting, feasting and war. The sobriquet of the Irish hero, *Conn of the Hundred Battles*,[40] suggests this mood. Many such battles were doubtless mere cattle rustling. Others were over land and water claims, booty, revenge, or to repay some slight. Strabo went so far as to assert that 'the whole Celtic world is war-mad'. This emphasis on warriorship would have tragic consequences in the prolonged clash with Rome, when honour would oblige the Gallic people to stand and fight where harrying tactics, on German lines, would often have served better. Celtic thinking on matters like peace and war, law and order, taxation and absorption into an alien regime was incompatible with Roman. Most of all, an aristocracy based on privilege and military prowess felt compelled to answer a challenge to either. These entrenched differences meant that incorporation into the empire would be painfully accomplished.

The pain was not entirely one-sided. We have spoken of the Romans as boreaphobic or fearful of the north, especially in connection with the Cimbric and Teutonic migrations of 100 BC. A far deeper scar had been left by the sack, almost two centuries earlier, of Rome herself. This followed an overspill from the Celtic movement into the Balkans. Seventy thousand rampaging Gauls looted and burned all Rome except the Capitol; but after a seven-month siege this too was taken. The Romans were obliged to buy off the raiders with a humiliating ransom. A result of this shock was the building of the Servian wall, so-called because its 19th-century discoverers assumed it to be that of King Servius Tullus.[41] This was in huge blocks of dressed tufa, to a width of ten-and-a-half feet and a circuit of seven miles, the impressive relics of which may be seen outside Rome's terminal railway station. A second result was the Celtic settlement of northern Italy which, despite Roman annexation and some colonization, was still in essence Gaulish. So Virgil, from Mantua, was perhaps an ethnic Gaul. Romans would not feel secure until the land beyond the Po – and ultimately most of Celtica – was under total control.

This would take time. Meanwhile, as with other eager consumers on Rome's rim, Greek and Roman merchants were hustling the Gauls toward that 'prestige goods dependence', in which chieftainship is synonymous with showmanship. It was the same pattern as the later trinkets-and-gunpowder trade on the Gold and Ivory Coasts: luxuries, slaves to pay for them and war to get the slaves. We know the huge size of wine shipments but can only guess at the ills which this prolonged inflow of luxuries and outflow of slaves was inflicting upon the Celtic world.

What of the Britons? *Et penitus toto divisos orbe Britannos*[42] (and the Britons, wholly sundered from the world) as Virgil put it. This was an isolation more romantic than real. Despite the mystery and metaphor, the less-than-poetic activities of the Roman merchant had already gained a firm hold in southern Britain. The main port appears to have been Hengistbury,[43] but commercial control soon passed to the south-east, where the adoption of the wheat symbol on pre-Roman coins[44] suggests a grain-based export drive, probably to supply Rome's Rhine armies.

On the question of food production: opinion continues to revise this upwards. Strabo said of Gaul that 'nowhere is untilled except where swamp and forest prevail'.[45] It is not of course known how much swamp and forest there was; but relative to today perhaps more swamp than forest. Mastery of iron had increased the tempo of man's war on woods, with a far tamer terrain than that of prehistoric Germany as the probable result. Agriculture was in a state of revolution. In Britain productive wheat strains such as emmet allowed yields more abundant than was previously imagined.[46] Excavation of Roman forts in bleak, northern locations has in some instances revealed ploughmarks beneath their earliest levels. Though the north and west were still largely pastoral, these final decades of prehistory were a time of transition between grazing and planting. In the Celtic world generally this tendency was reducing the instability feared by Rome, though there was still the occasional migration. Another result of sedentary agriculture was abandonment of the native forts and the realization that wealth could better be pursued through activity in valleys than passivity on hilltops.

Europe's face is as pocked by defensive works as the moon's by craters. Most impressive of all are the earthen citadels (frequently though not invariably sited on dominant summits); Celtica's quintessential landmark. Collectively they represent one of the biggest constructional feats in the human story, though their earlier origins and their presence in other parts of the world denies that they were Celtic only. Even within the Celtic lands there were major differences of style and scale. Near the Mediterranean, mimicking the town walls of Greek colonies, the forts had developed as dry-stone citadels, their walls ambitiously provided with towers, usually square; defending paved streets and stone houses. Prominent examples include Entremont, near Aix-en-Provence, where the bastioned stone walls enclose nine acres; Puig de Sant Andreu (near Empuries,[47] at the northern end of the Costa Brava); also in Catalonia, Castellet de Banyoles (Tivissa, twenty-eight miles west of Tarragona), with mudbrick towers on a stone base; and Citania (Portugal).

In Gaul proper another technique, which Caesar called *murus Gallicus*[48] (Gaulish walling) had emerged in reply to the approach of Rome. The defenders grasped that perpendicular walls make stiffer obstacles than sloping mounds. They experimented with dry-stonework but soon found that it was brittle to the battering ram and breachable under bombardment. Accordingly they devised double masonry facings, up to forty feet apart, the gap bridged by joists and cross-braced. This framework of nailed timber packed with rubble and backed by an earthern ramp, was resistant to shot and ram; but not to the slumping and sliding which follow woodrot. Though great metalworkers, good carpenters and moderate masons, the Celts never mastered the simple process of firing chalk or limestone to produce quicklime. Its full exploitation, though not its invention, was the work of Rome and crucial to almost all architectural advance during this period. Without lime there could be no mortar or concrete; and without mortar to grip or concrete to back its stone facings, the *murus Gallicus* remains a cul-de-sac in defensive building. None the less impressive results were produced. Excavation of the Bibracte *oppidum* (near Autun) and that of Manching (Bavaria) revealed three and four-mile circuits of Gaulish walling respectively.

However, these advances were never to reach the Britons, who were in all respects more conservative. In the south and west of England traditional construction continued, with billions of basketfuls of soil, hand-dumped in ant-like operations. Size and imposing position are characteristic, but the forts are also numerous.

Herefordshire and Shropshire are their heartland, the seventy miles from Ross-on-Wye north to Oswestry containing some fifty major specimens, sometimes only a mile or two apart. Wessex too is rich in spectacular examples, including Maiden Castle (Dorset) of forty-five acres, capital of the Durotriges, a tribe opposed to Rome. Though less frequent, there are big hillforts in most parts of Britain. An impressive tribal capital is Eildon (near Melrose, Roxburghshire) of forty acres[49] and containing 300 roundhouses. North Wales, where rock is often more available than soil, developed its own style. Tre'r Ceiri, in a rugged and inaccessible situation near the north coast of the Lleyn Peninsula, is among Britain's most romantic, with a stone wall surviving to rampart walk and internal buildings visible. There are some 200 British hillforts of more than fifteen acres. They grew considerably during the last four centuries BC, doubling and trebling their rampart rings and developing elaborate gateways with interned entrances and flanking guard chambers. Within were villages of 300–500 souls; but occasionally much larger, up to the 5,000 size.

Smaller works are almost uncountable. Fortified farms and defended villages are typical of the North and West, with clusters in central-south Scotland and Pembrokeshire densest of all. In general there was a wide variety in size, from capital 'cities' to single dwellings; and in function, from tribal strongholds, local refuges and communal animal pens, to markets, industrial centres and chieftains' castles; sometimes all of these combined. In essence Iron Age forts were prototype towns and the Romans called them such. The very existence of this scale of structure suggests power, dictatorially held. Strabo states that Gaulish government was 'normally autocratic'.[50] He adds that in Gaul 'a single leader was chosen annually. In emergencies too, one man was elected by popular acclaim.' These were late developments, in imitation of Roman practice and unlikely to be found in traditionalist Wessex and western Britain, where reoccupation of hillforts suggests increasing lawlessness. Smaller forts were being abandoned and the larger made stronger, perhaps in response to slave trafficking.

By contrast, what is now called south-eastern England was a separate world. Belgic invaders, arriving only a half century before Caesar, had brought new fashions and more advanced ideas. These did not, however, include non-violence. Their takeover of all southern England was probably forestalled only by the arrival of Claudius. Mighty men, painted and tattooed, with copious moustaches; glorious in war, with dashing chariots and flashing helmets of gilt and bronze; they carried shields of superb artistry, wore hauberks of iron rings[51] and wielded long sword and spear. The Belgic settlers also led the descent to the plains. Though other areas were slow to follow, this process was now almost complete in south-eastern Britain, where topography was in any case less suited to hillfort building. Their *oppida* were nevertheless strong and guarded, presumably against chariot assault, by long dyke-and-ditch systems. These did not always form continuous circuits, but were often in straight lines, having some resemblance to a noughts-and-crosses layout, with settlement in the central square. Sometimes there are gaps, presumably where patches of woodland, thickened with thorn and felled tree trunks, made earthwork unnecessary. Caesar said that 'the Britons call any fortified place in the thick forest which they have defended with dykes and ditches an *oppidum* (town) and use it as a refuge in time of trouble'.[52]

Among these were the biggest British strongholds and the most sophisticated settlements. Wheathampstead (Herts), close to the Lea, encloses twice the space of Maiden Castle. Camelodunum (Colchester), scene of Claudius' durbar, was biggest of all: twelve square miles, including pasture and fields. At its heart was a thriving urban centre and seat of kings, with a mint, plus commercial and industrial facilities. Though in time superseded by London (which did not yet exist) this would be Roman Britain's first capital. Thus the process by which people congregate for safety, leading by degrees to formation of towns and so to social and cultural consequences unforeseen, was well under way by the eve of conquest. As an index of development, at least seventeen native coin types are known. These were adapted versions of classical originals, some with portraits of British kings and their names in Roman characters. They suggest an openness to Mediterranean influence and also the widening of a rudimentary reading ability, previously confined to the Druids. There were roads, unmetalled but serviceable, especially in summer. More broadly, here was a market economy able to produce food surpluses and to collect, transport and store them: factors which increased the risk of invasion, since Britain's potential for feeding and moving armies can hardly have escaped the notice of Roman intelligence. By contrast there is no sign of native coinage and no trace of pre-conquest Roman money or trade goods north and west of a line from Bristol to the Humber.

Regarding population, the once accepted figure of two million may now be trebled. For example, the capacity of the Welsh border hillforts points to about sixteen persons per square mile, suggesting that the more populous areas of the late Iron Age were similar to the quieter regions of Britain today. Though farm had cut deep into forest, landscapes were far from treeless. The natural climax-vegetation of southern England is oak, elm, alder, lime and hazel, with holly, yew and bramble underbrush; mix and density depending on local conditions. Large forests persisted. The Fenlands and many smaller areas were still waterlogged. The notion that Britain's moors and mountains remain unspoilt, while the lowlands have been transformed beyond recognition is, alas, a hiker's view of history. On the contrary, while pockets of near-native woodland survive in the South, almost the entirety of upland Britain has, in relatively recent times, been laid bare by felling and kept bare by sheep; with poisonous or inedible plants like heather, bracken and gorse unnaturally dominant. Wales and the North were once cloaked in oak, elm, alder and Scots pine (*pinus sylvestris*). The glens of northern Scotland are thought to have been thicketed in stunted oak, thinning to birch on the lower slopes, with pine up to 2,000 feet. Ancient sources refer to northern woodland, including the great Caledonian Forest,[53] probably covering the entire central Highlands.

The Celts were among antiquity's greatest artists. Content was primarily abstract, consisting in the main of curving and twirling lines. These have been traced to Greek and other sources, selectively imitated in a peculiar way. In effect the Celts copied detail such as decorative surrounds, of incidental importance to Mediterranean art, ignoring the representational part which was its true point. Marginal devices, like flowers, fronds, vine stems, abstract patterns and flourishes, were lifted so to speak from the edges of the originals and placed at the centre of Celtic expression. It is as if one were excited about the mouldings on a frame and ignored the picture, or bought a house because of its wallpaper. But the La Tène[54] artist was not a student of trivia. The borrowed bits-and-bobs were stylized and developed till the source was forgotten and the original excelled. Soon this school, fusing art with finest craftsmanship and metallurgy, developed a fluid beauty and a curious mystery of its own; simpler than later abstractions, like Arabesque, but bolder and more haunting also. Alongside these masterpieces, Roman provincial work, especially in the western provinces (where it lacked the hand of

Greece) seems lustreless. The art of the Roman army too is generally childish without childhood's charm. Unfortunately the imported would tend to replace the native, for La Tène modes of expression withered at the touch of Rome, not through deliberate discouragement but because they hung upon an aristocratic patronage which did not survive the conquest. On the other hand we must not be too hard on the Roman provincials, who make amends for miserliness in the fine by prodigality in the useful arts. Many have admired the profusion of instruments and practical objects to be seen in the most modest Roman museum. The Celts had style; but it was doubtless less unpleasant to have a dental abscess or a splinter in the eye on the Roman side of the frontier.

Artistic flair appears also to distinguish Gaul from German, an opinion to which Frenchmen still subscribe. Nevertheless Roman authors showed scant interest in Celtic creativity or capability, confining their comment to foibles. Caesar speaks of the Gaulish temperament as inconstant and untrustworthy.[55] Tacitus uses the expression *inertia Gallorum*[56] (the good-for-nothingness of the Gauls). Dio wrote of the Britons that 'their boldness is rashness'.[57] As we have noted, recklessness, fecklessness and untrustworthiness were standard Roman views of the northern European. Tacitus adds that the British tribes 'were once ruled by kings. Now the ambitions of petty chieftains pull them apart.'[58] This is substantially untrue. Kingly power was growing. Nevertheless in Britain, as in Gaul and Germany, there would be no coherent reply to the Roman threat. If a tendency can be recognized it is that the weaker tribes sided with Rome against the stronger. In Britain the east coast peoples, less confident of the terrain's ability to protect them, generally accepted the invader more readily.

Hints from ancient authors suggest that Romans, who had viewed pre-conquest Britain with awe, tended to speak slightingly or mockingly thereafter. Hence Appian (2nd century): 'The Romans already have the best half of Britain and do not need the rest, for even the part they have profits them nothing.'[59] There is also Dio's tongue-in-cheek reference to an officer who had been severely disciplined: 'Lucius Verus did not put him to death, but merely sent him to Britain!'[60]

What was the Celtic view of Rome? Though some chose to resist and others to acquiesce, it is not difficult to imagine that all feared and hated her. What was *imperium* (Roman rule) but greed? Despite lack of nationhood there were doubtless pan-Gallic sympathies, fed by rumour and refugees. Even the remotest Britons must have been aware of Rome's long progress through Spain and Gaul toward their shores, generating deep dread and resentment against a seeming conspiracy to expunge Celtic independence.

Turning to Celtic and in particular to British society: what we have said about style and swagger applies only to the upper class. That this was an aristocratic culture can be seen from social differences in burial. The majority was poor, ill accoutred and with little occasion for feasting and bombast. This underclass would not have much to lose and perhaps something to gain from a Roman occupation. A third estate was the Druids, a name which may have meant 'brotherhood of the oak':[61] a priestly class in which religious knowledge, learning and literacy resided. Their presence is attested in Gaul and Britain only, with Britain as their heart and Mona (Anglesey) at the heart of Druid Britain. Anglesey, a fair island beyond wildest Wales, its legacy of magic stretching back to the Stone Age, was southern Britain's ultimate refuge. This was doubtless a place apart, a northern Mount Athos, though we must not press that parallel, since human sacrifice was conducted there and observances included the burning of gargantuan effigies of straw and wood, with live humans or sacrificial animals inside. Because of these practices and because the Romans saw it as a focus of resistance, Druidism had been outlawed since earliest contact. This was a tactical error for it would give a desperate edge to resistance in places where the cult was most entrenched.

The Druids worshipped natural spirits, including trees, and believed in reincarnation. They were an intellectual élite, dedicated to philosophic enquiry and the pursuit of nature's secrets, ancestors perhaps of the medieval alchemists: 'In intellect lofty and united in brotherly societies, they scorned matters mortal and preached the eternity of the soul; prophesying the eventual ending of the world in a deluge of water and fire.'[62] They were also society's arbiters and peacemakers: doves made hawks by the knowledge that Roman victory would mean their dissolution. No major religious ceremony was possible without them. Though the Britons, like the Germans, worshipped in woods, a number of pre-Roman temples have been found: usually small and rectangular, like the one under Heathrow Airport. A custom which preserved some of their best metalwork was the throwing of votive objects into rivers and lakes. In addition there were sacred springs and wells containing human and animal bones, the deepest of which, at 140 feet, was found in Bavaria. There was also a cult of the severed head. Skulls, real or carved, adorned lintels of houses as well as gates and stockades of forts, though whether to glorify defenders or horrify attackers is not known.

Round houses, based on wooden uprights, leaning inwards, were the prehistoric norm, since this is the easiest way to make a shelter. The roof structure of an oblong or square building is more difficult, though once mastered there are advantages when it comes to division into rooms or fitting into rows to make streets. Rectangular buildings had long been standard in the Mediterranean. The Celts were now in transition between the two styles, though in Britain circular huts were dominant still: thatched and either all-timber or timber on low, dry-stone walls.

Another symptom of British conservatism was the use of war chariots, already obsolete on the Continent and long abandoned by the Romans (though still used for ceremony and racing). The idea of driving them through city streets, or of chariot-mounted generals leading the legions, is cinematic licence. The British chariots fascinated Caesar and he gave a detailed description of their tactics and the drivers' acrobatics.[63] Obviously they were worthless against forts and other substantial defences. Furthermore, they represented a fighting method based on individual prowess and difficult to subordinate to a battle plan. Their real value had been as a shock weapon, but by now they had become something of an heroic cliché; except in south-eastern Britain, where echoes of the Celtic dream-world still resounded and chariots were an aspect of its *bravura*.

Strabo, geographer of the Augustan period, draws together several impressions in the following passage:

In Rome I have myself seen British youths, six inches taller than the city's tallest, though bowlegged and of a displeasing appearance generally. In habits they are not unlike Gauls, but simpler and more barbaric. In warfare they use chariots. Their cities are the forest, for they enclose large areas of it by felling trees, building huts and keeping cattle within. The climate is rainy rather than snowy. Sometimes, on days otherwise fine, the fog hangs about so long that the sun comes through only for three or four hours around noon. The deified Caesar visited the island twice but did not stay long and accomplished little.[64]

Such was southern Britain in the last years of her prehistory: defiant in isolation; in some ways advanced yet stranded psychologically in the heroic age; an apple ripe apparently for biting, though one which would prove unexpectedly sour.

Let us return to the young Colonel Vespasian, now in the heart of Thomas Hardy country, where resistance was most resolute, tradition longest and forts strongest. There is, of course, a limit to what we may make of one sentence in Suetonius. But archaeology assists with the exciting concordance between ancient pen and modern spade which emerged from Mortimer Wheeler's 1930s excavation at Maiden Castle. Twenty-eight war graves were discovered near the east gate, containing skeletons with severe wounds of sword-thrust type, one with the head of a Roman *ballista* bolt lodged in the spine. The gateways had been slighted, the site evacuated and the inhabitants moved, perhaps to become the first residents of nearby Dorchester. Further, in the 1950s, Ian Richmond's excavation inside the fort of Hod Hill (near Blandford Forum) found fifteen bolts in a cluster round the largest house. The rampart's height, plus the hilltop situation, mean that fire must have been directed from a tall observation tower outside. After surrender the circumvallation was partially lowered and a Roman fort built into the north-west corner. A third hillfort thought to have received the artilleryman's attention is Cadbury Castle, Somerset.

Two of Vespasian's methods are now clear. The first was to drive the defenders away from an entrance with artillery fire, climaxing in an infantry rush. The timber gates would then yield to burning. Alternatively bombardment could be conclusive on its own, especially if observation of shot-fall were feasible and where defended areas were small enough to be within the field of fire, as in the case of Hod Hill. The *oppidum* would soon become a place of panic, with people and animals rushing about; and wherever they ran the guns could be directed to follow. So, of the 'more than twenty *oppida*' said to have fallen to Vespasian, we have evidence for two and the likelihood of three; a fair score when one considers the odds against finding a few pieces of roundshot or boltheads buried in those vast and numerous earthworks. It is also likely that Vespasian directed a sizeable resettlement operation: demolishing the stockades, with which the forts were crowned, reducing the ramparts and allocating lowland sites. It has been estimated that some 30,000 hilltop dwellers were in due course displaced in Hereford and Shropshire alone.[65]

It is probable that Vespasian found, in Exeter, a suitable site for a legionary base and cornerpost for his flank of the advance; as had Plautius, in Lincoln, for its eastern end. Joining them was the Fosse Way, later name for a prehistoric track following a discontinuous limestone ridge for over 200 miles from Devon to Lincolnshire. This would be the approximate halt-line of the Claudian invasion. It is not clear whether the location was preselected or the offensive ran out of steam; whether Claudius thought he could hold southern Britain and ignore the rest; or whether he had no diagnostic insight and simply left his field commanders to amputate as best they could.

Here we leave the army of Britain, about to deploy along its overstretched and not overstrong frontier, while Vespasian returned to Rome, a hero's welcome and the governorship of Africa. Claudius died in AD 54, reputedly poisoned by his wife. No matter, Vespasian continued to enjoy favour under Nero; that is until the calamitous lyre recital, when a career of promise was shattered in the winking of an eye. Suetonius develops the story:

> In Greece, as a member of the imperial entourage, he committed the most appalling *faux pas*, falling asleep during one of Nero's recitals. The upshot was total disfavour and dismissal from court. He then fled to some obscure country town, where he went into hiding for fear of his life. But in the end he was offered a province and an army command.[66]

The province was Judaea. The command to crush the Jewish rebellion of AD 67. 'In the end' meant at the age of fifty-eight, twenty-three years after he had last seen service in Britain. Why this sudden recall; this amnesty, so seldom offered by the spiteful Nero; this reinstatement of which Ovid had vainly dreamed? It was because the Jews had gone on the rampage, murdered their *procurator* and destroyed a legion. Now, bold behind strong city walls, they defied Nero and all his works. Artillery was needed; a general who understood guns and knew how to use them against great fortresses. Then someone thought of that fellow, long rusticated, who bred mules; the one who had done so well against the Britons.

In Judaea, Vespasian's first task was to reduce the Galilean stronghold of Jotapata.[67] Here the Romans faced skilful and desperate defenders, led by the historian Josephus, one of the few eyewitnesses

of the Roman army in action, whose descriptions throw light on the
effects of artillery as a terror weapon:

> Placing his 160 pieces in a ring facing the wall's defenders,
> Vespasian commanded the bombardment to begin. A salvo fol-
> lowed, the scorpions shooting bolts, the *ballistae* hurling stones
> weighing over 100 lbs, plus flaming torches and a hail of arrows.
> All this not only cleared our men off the wall but also from a
> broad zone where the missiles were landing within; for the Arab
> archers, the javelin throwers, the slingers and the guns were all
> firing in unison.[68] Such was the artillery's power that a single bolt
> transfixed a row of men. The stones removed battlements, even
> dislodging the corners of towers. The formation does not exist
> that can stand against rocks like this which carve through rank
> after rank. A man beside me on the wall was decapitated, his head
> rolling three furlongs. Most frightening of all was the rushing
> sound as the missiles flew through the air and the sickening thump
> of impact. Added to this was the thud of bodies as they fell from
> the wall. Soon the sentry-walk could be reached simply by scram-
> bling up the corpses. Inside was the wailing of women, outside
> the groans of the dying.[69]

The master had not lost his touch. Of the siege of Jerusalem, at
which Vespasian's elder son Titus later commanded, Josephus
described how lookouts, seeing the *ballista*-shot on its way, shouted
warnings in time for the defenders to take cover. In response, the
gunners blackened the stones, making their flight almost invisible.
Reminiscent of Hod Hill, though using larger ordnance, catapult
balls up to eighteen inches across have been found beneath the con-
vent of the Sisters of Zion and at other Jerusalem locations.

The siege of Jotapata ended with the city's fall and Josephus'
capture. Hearing his prisoner had the gift of prophecy, Vespasian
requested that his own fortune be told. Anticipating Macbeth's
witches, the Jew assured the Roman that he would be emperor thereafter. The superstitious Vespasian was greatly impressed. Josephus
was held under gentle duress and persuaded to act as interpreter
and mediator, in which role he witnessed the six-month agony of
Jerusalem from the Roman side. He would later become Vespasian's
friend, living as a pensioner in Rome and writing his history of the
war.

Now Vespasian's fortunes were about to take another extraordinary turn. The year after Jotapata, events in Rome caused the rebellion to be shelved, forgotten almost, and the rebels at least temporarily reprieved. Nero had been toppled. The Delphic oracle is said to have told Nero to beware the age of seventy-three. Only thirty-one, the emperor congratulated himself on having forty-two years to live. But already Galba, governor of Spain, aged seventy-three, was marching on Rome.[70] Deserted by the Praetorians, disowned by the army, reviled by the Senate: time was running out for the Julio-Claudian dynasty. Hiding in a servant's house on the city's edge, Nero stabbed himself in the throat and expired, crying, 'Jupiter, what an artist dies in me!' This was June, AD 68. The following year, known as the Year of the Four Emperors, was one of Rome's worst. 'The vacancy of the throne', as Gibbon commented darkly, 'is a moment big with danger and mischief.'[71]

So it was that Vespasian, a highly successful and popular general, whose rocklike character had immense appeal after the caprices of Nero and Caligula, happened, at that perilous moment, to be far from the dangers of Rome and close to the protection of armies. The prefect of Egypt broke the ice by declaring in Vespasian's favour. Emerging one morning from his tent, soldiers began to greet him as emperor, soon followed by the entire Judaean expeditionary force. Finally Syria, jewel of the eastern provinces, came out on his side. Now he could wait while the western claimants killed each other. When the time was right he would intervene as *restitutor orbis*, putter-to-rights of a Roman world gone wrong.

Toga muddied by Caligula, pelted with turnips in Africa, caught napping by Nero, hiding in hick towns, breeding mules: such was the improbable path to power of T. Flavius Vespasianus who, in the ten years remaining him, would do more than any emperor until that time to caulk Rome's leaky frontiers and bring Rome's insulation from the outside world a step closer to completion.

Four characters now enter the picture. First Vespasian's sons, Titus and Domitian. Mindful of the Year of the Four Emperors, Vespasian insisted that the Senate accept them as his heirs. The elder, Titus, who completed his father's work in Judaea, succeeded him in AD 79. His reign is memorable for the eruption of Vesuvius and the inauguration of the Colosseum. He was dashing, generous and popular. However, at the age of forty-two his health gave way and he died after little more than two years on the throne.

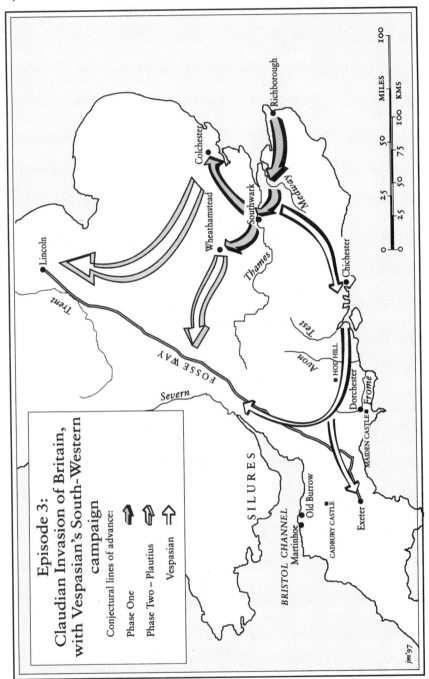

Episode 3:
Claudian Invasion of Britain,
with Vespasian's South-Western
campaign

Conjectural lines of advance:

Phase One

Phase Two – Plautius

Vespasian

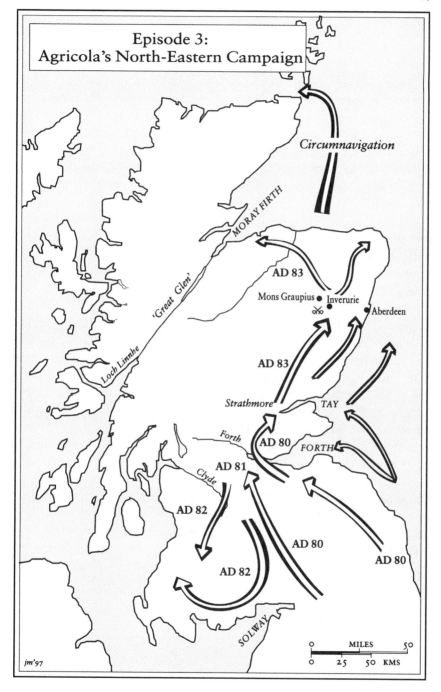

Episode 3:
Agricola's North-Eastern Campaign

Circumnavigation

MORAY FIRTH

'Great Glen'

Loch Linnhe

AD 83

Mons Graupius ● ● Inverurie
        ⚔
                    ● Aberdeen

AD 83

Strathmore   TAY

Forth

AD 80   FORTH

AD 81

Clyde

AD 82

AD 80   AD 80

AD 82

SOLWAY

MILES   50
0   25   50 KMS

jm'97

He was succeeded by Domitian, the shy and quiet younger brother, soon to reveal himself as a tyrant of Stalinesque suspicion, whose jealous eye lighted on all successful people. During his sixteen-year misrule, especially its sinister second half, the Roman state would be paralysed, its servants daring neither to fail nor succeed.

Then there is our principal recorder of events: the historian, Cornelius Tacitus, whose tortured personality may be understood as a product of terror, for his boyhood was passed under Nero and his manhood, from the ages of twenty-six to forty-one, under Domitian. He published nothing. Not only was he in danger of writing something which could give offence, it might be fatal just to write well.

Finally there is Julius Agricola, second soldier of this Episode, who served three times in Britain and whose name is forever associated with the country now called Scotland. Vespasian had been a genial, approachable and sound emperor, whose policies were of peaceful consolidation and thrift. Britain was the exception. There he had won his spurs and it pained him to see the enterprise languish. Accordingly he dispatched a series of Rome's best men. With Agricola, history is helped by a remarkable coincidence in which Tacitus is linked to the battle for Britain. The connection was the youthful historian's marriage to Agricola's daughter. In due course the son-in-law would be the father-in-law's biographer. Roman historical writing, fascinated by events at the centre, rarely mentions the margins, let alone the barbarian lands; and we are grateful to scavenge a sentence or two. In Tacitus' *Life of Julius Agricola* we have an entire book about the empire's edge. It is also a book about personalities and problems, in which a general's duty is played against an emperor's envy. Its subject is a province without a frontier, unable to find a territorial balance or to strike a durable bargain with the outsider; its context an empire no longer decisive about whether to take territory or to leave it. Though not an eyewitness account with the intense involvement of Ovid, it is the next best thing; casting a powerful beam into Europe's farthest corner, where we would otherwise grope by archaeological candlelight.

Agricola was born in *Forum Julii* (Fréjus, Côte d'Azur) and educated in Marseilles. When Claudius invaded Britain he was three. At eighteen his first posting was as tribune (second lieutenant) attached to the staff of Britain's fifth governor, G. Suetonius Paulinus.[72] By now the Fosse Way had failed at its western end, largely because of the Welsh wasps' nest, prodded by the fugitive prince, Caratacus, and buzzing still.

The second governor, P. Ostorius Scapula, had advanced his left to Gloucester and probably then to Chester. This was a crucial position, commanding the approach to North Wales and severing a possible alliance between Welsh and Pennine tribes. According to Tacitus, Scapula died of stress and exhaustion. Nevertheless he defeated and captured Caratacus, though the latter lived to ask his famous question of imperialism, whose artlessness disguised a sarcastic comment on Roman greed: 'And what do you, who have so much, want with *our* wretched tents?'[73]

Moving on to Paulinus (with the young Agricola on his staff): here was a general who had earned himself a reputation for mountain warfare in Morocco as first to lead Roman soldiers across the Atlas. He now spent two years on the reduction of North Wales, finally isolating Anglesey, heart of nationalist hopes and Druidical dreams. Its capture would be an achievement to equal that of Nero's general, Domitius Corbulo, in Armenia:

Britain's new governor was Suetonius Paulinus, Corbulo's rival both as a strategist and for public esteem. Could he produce victories to match the retaking of Armenia? He now decided on the capture of *Mona* (Anglesey) which had been a refuge for so many. Flat-bottomed boats were built to take the infantry across the treacherous shallows. The cavalry used fords, some troopers swimming beside their mounts. The armed enemy crowded the opposite shore. Among them were women, robed in black, hair wild like Furies, waving flaming firebrands. Nearby the Druid priests, with hands raised, called down terrible curses from heaven. This awful spectacle brought our soldiers up short. They stood as if frozen, until the general broke the spell by shouting how shameful it would be if they were halted by a gang of lunatic women. So the eagles surged forward, hemming in the enemy who was burned by his own torches. Paulinus occupied the island, felling the sacred groves dedicated to Anglesey's vile rites; for it was among their beliefs that altars should run with captives' blood and that prophecies should be made by examining human entrails.[74]

But Britain, a reluctant yielder of laurels, was not yet ready to let Paulinus win his. At this juncture there came news of rebellion,

250 miles to the rear. It involved the Icenians of Norfolk and the Trinovantians of Essex and Suffolk who had, for more than a decade, been simmering with resentment at the granting of their lands to Roman veterans. The late Icenian King, in the hope of saving some family influence, had willed his territory in part to his daughters and in part to Rome. It was like asking a pig to leave half the trough. When his widow Boudicca (Boadicea) protested, she is reported to have been flogged by Roman officials and her daughters raped. Such was the flashpoint for the last great attempt to reverse the conquest of the Celtic world. Dio describes the queen as:

> Boudouika [*sic*] a British woman of royal blood, with more brain than women usually have; tall, terrifying, with flashing eyes, menacing voice and a wild mass of yellowish hair falling to her waist; wearing a great, golden neck-torque, a many-coloured dress and thick cloak, fastened with a clasp. Spear in hand she harangued a gathering of armed men 120,000 strong.[75]

One should interpolate that what leaders said to armies, when no Roman was in earshot, was largely conjecture. Indeed it was an ancient convention to put speeches into the mouths of commanders; following Thucydides, who confessed that, since verbatim reporting was seldom possible, he would write what he thought the occasion demanded! Nevertheless such speeches rarely lack information. Here Dio makes the interesting logistical comment through Boudicca (already quoted): 'While we are able to subsist on wild plants and water, they depend on bread, wine and olive oil; and if one of these should fail them, they are finished.'[76] Grain was indeed essential; and while it was an exaggeration to claim that the eagle would not fly without wine and oil, sour wine in which to dip the bread and oil as the universal cooking medium were the soldiers' normal expectation.

Much of Boudicca's tirade is of course predictable: northern liberty contrasted with oriental servitude, British hardihood versus Roman decadence:

> I am queen not of toiling Egyptians or money-grovelling Assyrians.[77] I beseech heaven for victory against these insolent and insatiable men – if those who take warm baths, eat sweetmeats, drink wine unwatered, smear themselves with scent and lie with

boys on soft couches, deserve the name of men! They who are lackeys to a lyre player – and a bloody awful one at that![78]

Boudicca now struck swiftly at the lightly guarded towns of an already Romanized South-East. 'Avoiding fort and strong-point, the rebels headed for where the booty was richest and protection poorest; itching to chop heads, stretch necks, burn and crucify; as if taking revenge now for the retribution which would come later. The Roman provincial dead were put at 70,000.'[79] Colchester, St Albans and London were destroyed and their Roman or pro-Roman populations butchered before Boudicca was defeated, perhaps in Northampton-shire or elsewhere in the West Midlands. The queen and her family took poison. Such were Agricola's experiences at twenty years of age and his first taste of service in Britain.

In due course there followed the Year of the Four Emperors, with the heavy drafting of British troops to fight in the civil war. Those who stayed held steady; perhaps too busy with Wales to become involved in continental politics. None the less, reduction of the army's numbers would have dangerous repercussions in the North. The Brigantians were, according to Tacitus, the biggest British tribe, whose territory covered almost the entirety of what is now northern England, from Peak to Solway and from coast to coast. They were shepherds and stock rearers, ruled by a rich nobility. Their forts were few but impressive, like that on the summit of Ingleborough; or the sprawling, lowland complex of Stanwick, in North Yorkshire, seemingly enlarged in panic at Rome's advent to 730 acres! From here, or perhaps from Almondbury, near Halifax, Queen Cartiman-dua ruled in friendly alliance with Claudius and Nero. However, Brigantian politics included the usual anti-Roman faction and AD 69, Rome's hour of weakness, saw a successful *coup*, led by Venutius, the queen's ex-husband. Again one senses the stress set up by Rome's proximity; sundering husband and wife as it had Armin and his brother. Venutius now thought to assume the mantle of Boudicca as leader of British resistance. He might have been less eager had he reflected that this same year, which brought him to power, also called to the purple the master-gunner, whose Wessex campaign of a generation earlier had consigned so many British strongholds to oblivion. Vespasian did not return to Britain in person but would field his strongest side in order to quicken a conquest begun twenty-six years earlier and whose termination was exasperatingly overdue.

Accordingly he appointed three successive soldier-governors of unusual capability: Cerialis, Frontinus and Agricola, who would respectively take in hand the North of England, Wales and most of Scotland.

Petilius Cerialis was the emperor's son-in-law, a dashing general in the Caesarian mould, whose success in AD 49 had beaten Vespasian a path to the throne. He was first sent to put down a revolt on the lower Rhine. Tacitus describes his raffish and unorthodox character, careless of the trappings of discipline and a brilliant improviser. There had been a whiff of scandal. The enemy attacked while Cerialis was out of camp spending the night with a local woman. However 'luck always covered his lapses'. It was in a speech to the Germans that Tacitus attributed to him that crisp appraisal of the Roman system: 'no peace without armies, no armies without pay, no pay without taxes.'[80]

Cerialis took Agricola to Britain as one of his legionary commanders. It was his second tour and he was now thirty-one. We know little of the campaign, doubtless because Tacitus wished to underplay this part of the biography, keeping his best cards till its hero would himself be governor. We do, however, know that Cerialis sealed off Wales then headed north, defeating Venutius on some unrecorded field.[81] On the dreary Stainmore Pass is a legion-size, twenty-acre marching camp, cut in two by the modern road (A66), whose square shape and eleven gateways suggests this advance. With two similar camps in the upper Eden and Petteril Valleys, these point straight toward Carlisle, where Cerialis' drive is thought to have ended. The IXth *Hispana* legion now moved up from Lincoln to York, though there is no evidence for a widespread occupation of the North at this date.

Next came Roman Britain's tenth governor, Julius Frontinus, author of two books on the art of war: *De Rei Militari* (Matters Military) and *Strategematon* (Stratagems). The former and more important is lost. The latter, its supplement, gives examples of military ruses said to illustrate the principles of the earlier book. These are, in our view, largely nonsense. Nevertheless there was nothing nonsensical about his struggle in South Wales, where the resurgent Silurians had drawn the conclusion, from Vespasian's campaign of vivid memory, that Rome was better fought by taking to the hills than by waiting in the hillforts. It was this adoption of guerrilla tactics, plus Rome's preoccupation with civil war, which lengthened the Welsh involvement to thirty years and thirteen known offensives.

Pacification of Snowdonia, followed by the second invasion of Anglesey, was left until Agricola's first year as governor. His Welsh conquest employed the network method, in which successive mountain blocks were isolated by building roads in the surrounding valleys and placing forts at key intersections.[82] Agricola would also apply this to southern Scotland; which helps explain the large number of forts and immense road mileages with which he is credited. First, however, Wales and its borders received over 700 miles of road and thirty-eight forts or fortlets, plus strategic supervision from *Legio XX Valeria Victrix* at Chester and *II Augusta* at Caerleon-on-Usk (near Newport, Gwent); though all would be held in sketchy fashion during the subsequent offensive into north Britain.

Let us back-track for a moment, to include a happier interlude. While Frontinus was struggling in South Wales, Agricola enjoyed the governorship of Aquitania (south-western France) followed by the consulship. It was toward the end of this period that his daughter (whose name, like that of Ovid's wife, is not mentioned in her husband's work) married Tacitus:

After less than three years as Governor of Aquitania he was recalled with the consulship in view. It was while he was consul that I was betrothed to his daughter: a girl of exceptional promise – and I still in my youth. On the expiry of his year of office he placed her hand in mine just before he was given the governorship of Britain.[83]

So Agricola, now thirty-eight, returned to Britain as eleventh governor and commanding general of her four legions, with clear instructions from Vespasian to finish off Wales and then proceed to the subjugation of Britain *in toto*. In practice it meant the conquest of what is now Scotland, which would occupy most of the seven-year term of governorship and is the main subject of Tacitus' biography. This was written some eight years after Agricola's death, a postponement caused by the long wait for Domitian to die in turn. Nevertheless, some time after AD 96, with Domitian replaced by a humane successor, Tacitus was able to affirm: 'At last Nerva has united the two things we had ceased to believe compatible: rule by an emperor and freedom. Meanwhile fifteen years have been erased from our lives, during which time the young became middle aged and the elderly old, all without daring to say a word.'[84]

As long as Domitian lived, Tacitus, like Ovid, could be described as a literary exile, though of an opposite kind: the one able to write but condemned to live in Tomis, the other able to live where he wished but condemned to silence. Now, past forty, he was free to begin and the *Agricola* would be his first effort, published just before the *Germania*. Both are preserved in their entirety.[85] The earliest known reference to an *Agricola* manuscript is from the monastery of Monte Casino, around the time of the Norman conquest of England. It then disappeared and was presumed lost. In 1431 the Florentine scholar Niccoli discovered a 9th-century version at the Hersfeld Monastery in southern Germany. Pope Nicholas V, an avid collector, ordered his agent Enoch of Ascoli, who scoured northern Europe for this purpose, to acquire it; and receipt was recorded by the Papal Secretary Decembrio in 1455. It was printed in Milan, *c.* 1475; and it is perhaps from this version that the spelling mistake *Mons Grampius* for *Graupius* first arose, beginning the tradition which saddled Scotland with the erroneous name Grampian to this day.

Why should Vespasian favour the total conquest of Britain, irrespective of the island's value? Unlike Spain, whose promise revived as the gold-rich, north-west corner came closer, Britain's dwindles as one moves in that direction, in all senses except the scenic. However, in Spain's case the completion of conquest had brought savings as well as profit. Victory allowed defence cuts. With time these increased to the extent almost of demilitarizing the Iberian peninsula. This was a formula which could be applied to a Britain grossly over-garrisoned in relation to her worth. A supreme effort now could save indefinite occupation costs, inescapable as long as Rome sat in one part of the island with enemies at large in the other. So, 134 years after Caesar and thirty-six after Claudius disembarked in Kent, Rome's eyes turned toward the far north at last.

Though we use it for convenience, the name Scotland is strictly speaking incorrect until the Scots' arrival from Ireland in the post-Roman period. Pre-Roman Scotland (if we may so call it) was more populous than is often thought. There were some thousands of hillforts of less than one acre. In what are now known as Northumberland and southern Scotland almost every hill was utilized, the densest clusters being on the upper Tweed (near Peebles) and upper Teviot (near Hawick). Defended settlements in valley situations were also numerous: farms or small villages of round, timber-and-thatch huts, encircled by mound and ditch. In the Border region there were a few larger strongholds resembling those of southern England, such as the already-mentioned Eildon Hill (near Melrose), the Selgovian capital, an *oppidum* with perhaps 2,000 inhabitants. Even the Highlands were moderately peopled. Here were the small, stone-walled forts known as duns, most frequent in Argyll and on Skye. Further north still were the brochs: round, dry-stone towers as high as forty feet, with a staircase between double walls, especially common in Sutherland, the Western and Northern Isles. All tribes were pastoral with some cultivation. Tillage was more developed and forest clearance more extensive than once supposed. These amounts of settlement and development would have been less surprising to someone living only 150 years ago, for the emptying of the rural north is relatively recent.

The existence of so many separate communities, plus an obsession with defence, suggests Iron Age Scotland as a particularly peaceless place. It is clear from Roman sources that a Highland-Lowland distinction already existed and, as in later ages, these will doubtless have been at loggerheads. Pliny gives the expression *Caledonia Silva* (the Caledonian Forest) and Ptolemy places the Caledonian tribe right across the central Highlands, south of the Great Glen; a tract without a single large fort or town. He locates another, the *Vacomagi*, in north-eastern Scotland. By the 1st century AD these were probably one confederation. Tacitus speaks of a distinct Highland type, 'whose red hair and long legs betray German origins'.[86] Red hair perhaps, but German origins are unlikely. Despite this and other hints of racial differences which today might be seen as evidence of the earlier-than-Celtic origins of the British peoples, Tacitus concludes that the generality of Britons came from Gaul, a view disputed by modern archaeology:

> You will find there Gallic customs and beliefs. Nor is the language dissimilar. Temperamentally there is the same rashness: dashing into danger and, when it is met, dashing out of it with equal eagerness. Even so the Britons are more mettlesome than the Gauls, having been under Roman occupation for a shorter time. Those already conquered are moving toward what the Gauls are now; and those unconquered remain as the Gauls once were.[87]

As ever the weakness was tribalism. Tacitus' comment that 'the ambitions of petty princes divide them',[88] was evidently truer of

Britain than of Gaul. Indeed quisling chieftains, like Cogidubnus of today's West Sussex had proved a valuable tool of conquest, 'using the time-honoured means of Roman diplomacy, by which kings are persuaded to serve as servitude's instruments'.[89] The following sardonic passage on the sedation of the northern peoples – by following a brutal conquest with the introduction of Mediterranean pleasures – is equally a compliment to Rome on her handling of the newly conquered:

> In order that a rude and scattered people might be coaxed toward peaceful paths through comfort, he [Agricola] encouraged the building of temples, markets and houses. The sons of chieftains were educated in the liberal arts; and those who not long before spurned Roman speech began to aspire to rhetoric and adopt the toga. So by slow degrees the Britons were seduced by pleasant pastimes, like strolling through colonnades, relaxing in the baths and attending polished entertainments, till finally the gullible natives came to call their slavery 'culture'![90]

Returning to Scotland, and to geography, Tacitus describes the sudden widening of Britain upon 'crossing' into Caledonia (i.e. after leaving Central Scotland) when it becomes 'a vast and irregular shape'; adding, in a flash of knowledge about the north-west Highlands, 'Nowhere has the sea more mastery, more conflicting motions. Nowhere is land and water more intermingled; the sea among mountains, making them its own.'[91] He also gives a fair summary of Britain's climate:

> The sky is cloaked in cloud, the rain incessant, though the cold not unduly severe. The length of day is difficult for us to grasp. The nights are clear and – in the extremity of Britain – brief, so that a short interval separates dusk and dawn. They even say that if no clouds obscure the sun it shines all night, tracking across the sky without either setting or rising. The soil (save for olives, wine and other warm-climate fruits) permits crops and favours cattle. Seeds sprout quickly in the damp earth but ripen slowly in the damp air.[92]

As described, Agricola spent his first campaigning season, probably that of AD 78, in Wales. In 79 he consolidated Cerialis' conquest of northern England. However, Vespasian's death, in the late June of that year, put a spoke in Agricola's wheel. All campaigning ceased. War was an imperial prerogative and each new emperor must confirm or veto its continuation. Though this meant delays, worse lay ahead. From a Vespasian unable to accept that the British venture should fail, power would pass to a Domitian unable to stomach its success. Nevertheless, Vespasian's policies were for the moment safe in the hands of his elder son; and during the winter of 79–80 one may assume that Titus sent Agricola orders to proceed. The crucial phase of the British plan now began to unfold.

In the spring of 80 Agricola advanced into new territory. His eastern column pioneered the inland route (now the A66), choosing Cheviot rather than coast, since the latter was longer, with forest barring the lower Tweed, while the almost harbourless Northumbrian shore offered little likelihood of naval support. Southern Scotland was 'networked', but compared with Wales resistance proved slight. This remarkable season ended with Agricola's vanguard at the Tay.

A question now arose regarding the Forth-Clyde isthmus. Here Agricola had found the wasp's waist, a defensible line of only thirty-five miles, seven times shorter than the Fosse Way. Doubtless his despatches pointed to the advantages of utilizing this line as a frontier and contrasted it with the severity of the Highland alternative. Titus may have accepted such a view. At any rate the northward advance appears to have ceased and the 81 and 82 seasons were spent consolidating southern Scotland.

Even so, this seems an unduly long pause, best explained by Titus' death on 1 September 81. Again Agricola was obliged to await new orders. His campaign had encountered the double-postponement of two emperors' deaths in two years. All chance of surprising the Caledonians had been lost. To make matters worse, Domitian had decided to lead his own expedition across the Rhine. For this he would require detachments from all four of Agricola's legions. The year 82 was therefore one of dismal delay and manpower reallocation in which, as the army of Britain was pared down, the chances of taking and holding northern Scotland dwindled.

Meanwhile Agricola was pondering the possibility of invading Ireland. We glimpse him standing with his staff at the Rhinns of Galloway and looking across to the last outpost of free 'Celtica', only twenty-five miles distant: 'Often I heard him say how Ireland could be taken and held with only one legion and auxiliaries; and that this would help regarding Britain too, for with Roman arms appearing everywhere, liberty would seem to be nowhere.'[93]

The foremost source of ambiguity remained central Scotland. Should he fortify the isthmus as a frontier or not? Here Tacitus is unusually specific on geography but vague on policy, evidently reflecting the indecision of that year:

> The fourth summer was spent securing what had been so swiftly gained. He could in fact have found a stop-line within Britain itself, had the army been less keen and Roman pride less easily satisfied. For here Clyde and Forth, driven inland by the tides of opposing seas, are sundered only by a neck of land. This was now secured with garrisons and the whole tract taken in hand, the enemy being pushed back into what is in effect another island.[94]

The strategic view from central Scotland was quite different from that further south. In the first place, discovery of the Forth-Clyde isthmus had shown how easy it would be to seal off the Highlands. Secondly, proximity to the Highlands made it clear how difficult their invasion would be. Finally, revelation of the Irish Sea's narrowness made a move in that direction more attractive than before. We may guess that, in view of his loss of manpower to the German expedition, Agricola favoured the last of these choices. Being less mountainous, Ireland would require a smaller force, leaving a reserve to man central Scotland. It is presumably with reference to an Irish invasion that Tacitus tells us he occupied the coast of south-west Scotland 'hopefully rather than defensively'.[95] He had a substantial fleet and was ready to use it. Of the two courses an invasion across *ocean* would have been the more prestigious and in later life he spoke wistfully that it was not chosen. By contrast, the army, always shirking the sea, preferred to march north. '*Penetrandam Caledoniam*',[96] they are heard shouting ('let's get stuck into Caledonia').

The dilemma was resolved by a directive from Rome: Agricola was granted a second term as governor and ordered to proceed with the conquest of all Scotland. This is consistent with Domitian's malice. Agricola was being manoeuvred into the most difficult of the options with a much reduced force. Meanwhile the emperor would lead an army into Germany with more achievable objectives and shorter supply lines.

So, unaware of being on a collision course with the imperial psy-

che, 83 and 84 see Agricola advancing through Strath Allan, Strath-
earn and out into the broad corridor of Strathmore, setting the
pattern for all subsequent invasions by skirting the Highlands in a
right-flanking movement toward Aberdeenshire. The navy's role was
crucial to this east coast strategy. By constant contact with its war-
ships and supply vessels at the Tay, Montrose, Stonehaven and Aberdeen, the army could be fed and supported. Agricola's handling of
combined operations proved to be his strongest card, more successful
in the light of others' failure. Fleet support had been the weak link
in Caesar's British forays.[97] We will recall Germanicus, the drownings
in the Waddensee and shipwrecks on the Frisian Islands. During the
conquest of north-west Spain a comparable strategy seems to have
lapsed owing to fear of the open Atlantic.

> Agricola was the first to use the navy as part of his armoury; and
> it made a stirring sight as it brought up the rear. So the offensive
> was carried by sea and land simultaneously. Many a time the
> infantry, cavalry and sailors would meet over a shared meal, cap-
> ping each others' stories: the one about forest and hilltop, the
> other about wind and wave; conquest of the land on the one hand
> and of the ocean on the other. For their part the British were
> stunned by the fleet's appearance. It was as if their seas and shores
> were being stripped of secrets and their ultimate bolt-holes
> barred.[98]

Attempts have been made to trace the campaign through its marching
camps. Indeed the terrain has yielded little else. This ubiquitous
instrument of Roman mobility is worth describing in broad terms.
Marching camps were usually square or rectangular. Internal layout
reflected the order of march, with the commander at the centre, the
vanguard in the front and the main force behind. Since everyone's
tent and each tent's place were always the same, a standardized
pattern was intended to soothe tired men and speed them to their
rest. All soldiers bore its blueprint in their minds and could recreate
it perhaps in a couple of hours, using the trenching tools which
were standard equipment. An advance party under the *praefectus
castrorum* (camp boss) selected and marked out the site. While the
main body dug the ditches and threw up the spoil into perimeter
mounds, the rearguard unloaded the pack animals and the leather
tents were erected in precise pattern within. Every infantryman

carried a *pila muralia* (wall spear), which was driven into the rampart so that it bristled like a porcupine.

However, camps were not wholly stereotyped. The *praefecti* had their quirks and latitude was allowed in external proportions or the design of gateways, with their various inturned or outturned extensions, intended to impede or deflect attack. For example, one of Agricola's camp bosses favoured a peculiar sickle-and-hammer-shaped opening. In theory such variants allow us to plot a progression of camps, distinguishing them from other campaigns or periods.

Ancient sources tell of camp construction every evening and destruction every morning; the unit refilling the ditches before it marched away. If a camp were left intact the enemy could occupy it, perhaps to lie in wait for a tired Roman force expecting to use it again. But in practice, due to laxity or successive occupancy, demolition was not always carried out. Had it been, Britain would not have inherited so many fine examples. There are also instances of camps superimposed, or of small built into the corners of large.

A camp's size gives an idea of numbers. Since wasted space meant defending a larger perimeter, sprawling layouts would be avoided. Occupation density *sub pellibus*[99] (under canvas) has been calculated as about 300 men per acre.[100] Spacing between camps tends to be about fifteen Roman miles, the standard day's march for fully laden troops. This is a reasonable distance in view of the additional chores of making and striking camp, packing and unpacking, foddering animals, cooking one's own meals and so on.

From the Firth of Forth to the Moray Firth some fourteen marching camps associated with Agricola's campaign curve northwards in a 150-mile arc. Near their beginning is the great base of Ardoch,[101] where six overlapping camps, three clearly visible, show it as the hub of northbound traffic. Of this long line Raedykes, behind Stonehaven, is probably the most rewarding to visit. The furthest known is at Bellie, near the Moray Firth. The furthest visible on the ground is Ythan Wells, Aberdeenshire, whose gorsey dyke signals with yellow flag the empire's northernmost upstanding work: 1,300 miles as the crow flies from Rome, three months' march at standard pace. The Moray Firth may be seen as the limit of a thousand-mile swath, cut by Rome into the Celtic and British worlds.

Here, then, Tacitus' text, the marching camps, and the lie of the land, are the sum of evidence. None is overhelpful. Tacitus is unspecific on geographical detail, though he gives the useful hint that

Agricola 'divided the army into three'.[102] The camps resolve into two main sizes. The larger, around 110 acres, shows the army marching as one. At 300 men to the acre, this is consistent with a total force of 32,000: four understrength legions of about 4,000 each and an equivalent number of auxiliaries. The smaller, around thirty acres, is roughly compatible with division into three. But there are many imponderables. Missing or undiscovered camps, multiple use, varied unit groupings and the likelihood that some camps were built during return journeys, make this a dubious guessing game. It may, however, be pessimistic to say that the story will never be told. Archaeology and aerial survey are a potent partnership; and the camera's eye is sharpened by drought, which increases colour differences in herbage, caused by soil disturbance. Remarkable detail can be wrung from these inscrutable bivouacs, such as the location of rubbish pits, where dateable material might be found. Recent years have been exceptionally dry. Of the ten hottest summers on record, six were in the 1980s. 'Global warming' brings some recompense.

If details of Agricola's march are obscure, his strategy is not. First he must avoid entanglement in guerrilla warfare, which meant avoiding the hills. Second, he must bring the enemy to him, forcing a battle on favourable ground. The accepted way to provoke confrontation was rampage: destroying crops, burning houses, butchering animals and even people. North-eastern Scotland, a tract of lowland in a highland setting, is well suited to such grim tactics. Its rich lands could be devastated while their agonized tenants watched from the hilly grandstand where they had taken refuge. By putting the following sentence into the supposed speech of Calgacus, the British commander, Tacitus allows himself a veiled comment on this sinister aspect of the *pax Romana*: 'What they call "empire" is theft and butchery; and what they call "peace" is the silence of death.'[103] Barbarity was not, it seems, a barbarian monopoly.

Nevertheless, the policy worked: drawing the enemy toward a rendezvous at *Mons Graupius*, somewhere along the line where plain and mountain meet. Where is *Graupius*? Though it has given its name to Britain's biggest massif, the battle site was probably at the foot of a single hill. This must have been big enough to hold a substantial British host, close to a Roman camp, with some flat ground adjacent and rising ground behind. Tacitus describes it briefly: 'The Britons were drawn up in a striking and frightening way: their front rank level with ours while the rest, on rising ground, appeared to tower up behind them; the chariots rushing noisily to and fro across the fields between.'[104] These vague clues could apply to almost any hill near almost any marching camp along a Highland front of nearly 200 miles. Here was a veritable Teutoburg Forest of a puzzle, combining hints from a great historian with clues from a romantic landscape. What could excite scholarly Scotland more? The result was centuries of learned (and sometimes not-so-learned) debate, with everyone adding his piece, including Sir Walter Scott: 'Our Scottish antiquaries have been greatly divided about the local situation of the final conflict between Agricola and the Caledonians. Some contend for Ardoch in Strathallan, some for Innerpeffry, some for Raedykes in the Mearns and some are for carrying the scene of action as far north as Blair in Athole.'[105]

So, between about 1725 and 1975, the sharpest eyes of Romano-British scholarship ranged up and down the line where grass and heather meet, its prestigious pens producing theories neither provable nor disprovable. But at the latter date debate subsided. J. K. St Joseph (1912–94) longtime director of the Cambridge University Committee for Aerial Photography, whose work in Britain (from 1930) had revealed forty-three forts, twenty fortlets, fourteen signal stations and 235 camps, played a strong card.[106] A photographic sortie of 26 July 1975 revealed a new marching camp at Durno, six miles north-west of Inverurie and twenty-three north of Aberdeen. At 144 acres this is the largest known encampment beyond the Forth, big enough to accommodate Agricola's entire force with room for prisoners of war besides. Might this imply that, although forward units had already reached the Moray Firth, all were now recalled and recombined to meet some exceptional event? Above Durno towers the bulk of Bennachie[107] (1,733 feet), a plateau four miles long and two wide, linked by a ridge to the body of the Highlands and commanding views southwards to Stonehaven and eastwards to the North Sea. Pending discovery of weapons, graves, or other finite evidence, this is presently the strongest candidate for the identity of *Mons Graupius*.

Before the battle, Agricola addressed his army, emphasizing the feat of exploration and the pride in trailblazing: 'You have outshone previous armies and I previous governors. Britain's bounds are no longer rumour and guesswork, but as factual as our forts and our strength. We have brought Britain both to light and to heel.'[108] The encounter itself was a tragic preview of Culloden: tribal motley facing trained troops, the unwieldy against the compact, wild passion versus professional calm, 10,000 clansmen slaughtered for the loss of 360 Roman auxiliary soldiers. The legions did not even engage. However, the Britons were so numerous that the majority could not come to grips. Twenty thousand were able to scramble back up the hillside or disappear into nearby forest, where nightfall covered their retreat. With so many left to fight again and the Highlands yet unpenetrated this could hardly be called a decisive victory. At most it was a promising start. Beyond lay an interior made for guerrilla warfare, unsuited to the formal encounter, hopeless for cavalry and demanding a dangerous dispersal of force. Wales, a mere fifty miles wide, had required thirteen offensives. The Highlands are over 120 miles and behind is an even wilder world: a jigsaw of sea and land; as if carved by the hand which had tried to make Greece and tossed it, as a reject, into Europe's opposite corner.

So far, however, the Scottish campaign had gone well; perhaps too well. Before long rumours of glorious *Graupius* would reach a Roman public more interested in the glamour of battles than in their long-term inferences. Agricola now marched on to the Moray Firth and a rendezvous with his fleet. The *Boresti* are thought to have given their name to Forres, near Elgin.

For the victors the night was bright with celebration and looting. For the vanquished the weeping of men and women mingled as they dragged off the wounded and searched for survivors, abandoning their homes and even setting them alight in their rage. The morning revealed the aftermath of victory: everywhere the dismal silence, the hilly solitude, the smoking ruins. Since our scouts met no one it was apparent that the enemy was not regrouping. Accordingly, since the summer was too far advanced for the war to be enlarged, he marched the army down into Borestian territory. There he gave orders to his naval commander to circumnavigate Britain.[109]

These orders doubtless included probing for a Highland back door, which exists in the shape of Loch Linnhe. The army's obvious next step, the Great Glen, would require new thinking and a fresh start. Little could now be done until the April of 85. The battle had been fought at too late an hour on a day too late in the year.

The same spring, which had seen Agricola entering north-eastern Scotland, also saw Domitian's army crossing the Rhine at Mainz.

The emperor led in person. His nominal aim was to chastise the Chattans, a troublesome tribe. Perhaps he also intended to enlarge the Roman hold on Germany's south-west corner. Without venturing deeply into barbarian territory, it was tempting to seek a short cut between the Rhine and Danube frontiers, reducing the long re-entrant via Basle. The improvement would in due course be made and Domitian's campaign was a significant step toward it. This was, however, incidental to the emperor's purpose. Domitian knew that fame would not be won by road improvements but by a victory, like that of his brother at Jerusalem (strikingly shown on the sculptural panels of the Arch of Titus, where they may still be seen). Such *éclat* could now be matched by a rousing success in Germany.

However, the Chattan expedition would merit no arch. The enemy simply retreated into his forest. Ground was gained, but memories of Quintilius Varus forbade a penetration of more than fifty miles beyond the Rhine. So, after two or three seasons of exhausting and frustrating effort, there were no notable battles, no striking successes and few captives or trophies to parade through the Roman streets. Domitian then dashed to the lower Danube, perhaps grateful for a diversion from his German stalemate and a second chance of glory. The ambitious and malicious Decebal, king of Dacia (today's Romania) had used the imperial preoccupation to descend from the Carpathians, cross the river and savage Rome's Balkan provinces; an attack which cost the life of Moesia's governor, Oppius Sabinus. Domitian summoned the Praetorian Guard from its comfortable quarters on the Tiber to meet him on the Danube. An expedition into Dacia was hastily mounted, doubtless backed by inadequate staff work, in which the praetorian prefect, Cornelius Fuscus, was routed and killed, prompting Juvenal's sneer:

> Fuscus, who did his soldiering in banqueting halls,
> Little dreamed himself a banquet for Dacia's crows.[110]

Dio would be scathing about Domitian's role in this campaign:

> He took no part in the fighting, remaining in one of the Moesian cities and living it up, as usual; for he was lazy as well as cowardly; and dissolute toward women and boys besides. So he sent others to fight his battles, claiming any successes for himself and blaming someone else for the reverses. He even celebrated a Triumph, as

if he had won a victory; in which, instead of captured spoils, he paraded 'props' drawn from the government furniture store![111]

A second attempt led to a Roman victory at Tapae, only thirty-five miles short of the Dacian capital. Success at last. But news of a mutiny on the Rhine eclipsed Domitian's moment of glory and sent him scurrying north. This was the rebellion of Antoninus Saturninus, who blackmailed the legionaries of the Mainz garrison into supporting him by sequestering their life savings, deposited in the regimental strongroom. However, the rest of the Rhine army stayed loyal and the rising collapsed. For a second time Domitian marched against the Chattans, who had dared support Saturninus. At this unfavourable juncture the Danube again erupted with the Marcomanns or south Germans, probably prompted by Decebal, attacking from today's Slovakia.

Domitian had now reigned nine years in an accelerating nightmare of reverses, rushing between Rhine and Danube in a manner prophetic of the later empire. Rich in promise, his wars had been poor in results, with no prizes to assuage his insecurity or soothe the envy which corroded his spirit. He had backed the wrong horse. He could, like Claudius, have chosen to visit Britain and reap the triumph of Agricola's 600-mile advance, crowned by victory on the ancient world's northernmost field. Instead the setbacks tipped him into darkness, creating, during his last six years, a time when Rome spoke in whispers, senators chose to potter on their estates and writers pretended their muse had forsaken them.[112] 'He was suspicious of all mankind' (commented Dio, from the safety of a later age).[113] Dio also described[114] how he invited senators and knights to banquets conducted in near-darkness, with the guests' places at table written on imitation gravestones, served by black-painted slaves, with black tableware and the accoutrements of a funeral feast; the host droning on about topics related to death while his guests reclined in shivering silence. Informers were ubiquitous, show-trials frequent, murders and enforced suicides a daily event. Domitian was even said to have executed a man because he had a map of the world painted on his bedroom wall and could be accused of 'dreaming dangerously'![115]

What of Agricola, commander of the only successful front who, in six years, had doubled the area of Britain under Roman control? His successes had coincided with Domitian's early disappointments, fortunately not quite as dangerous a time as these later years. Here was a dutiful but ingenuous soldier, nearing the end of a long and hazardous mission during which every congenial voice had fallen silent and every friendly door had closed.

> These achievements, though played down in Agricola's despatches, were received by Domitian with a mixture of pretended pleasure and disguised disquiet. He knew that his own recent Triumph over the Germans had been a fraud and the subject of ridicule. In place of captives he had purchased slaves who could be kitted out to look like prisoners of war. By contrast here was the genuine article: thousands of casualties inflicted and a decisive victory for all to see. The very thing the emperor most dreaded: that a private citizen's name should outshine his own![116]

It was time for Agricola to return, entering Italy on tiptoe lest his coming should be greeted with a warmth Domitian himself had been unable to inspire. Then, 'so that his entry into the city might not excite attention, he avoided all friends, slipping into Rome by night and by night visiting the palace, as required. There, after a perfunctory peck and not a word spoken he quickly melted into the crowd of creeps round the throne.'[117]

Willy-nilly our general was a national hero. Triumphal ornaments were awarded and the regulation statue put in hand. Spite bided its time. Though only forty-five, Agricola would never work again. Prudently he withdrew to Fréjus and obscurity, dying there at fifty-four (three years before Domitian), probably poisoned by an imperial courier. 'For the remainder of his life Agricola lived not only in disgrace but in actual need, just because the things he had accomplished were too great for a general. That is why Domitian finally had him murdered, despite giving him the triumphal ornaments.'[118]

Tacitus leaves his hero with a phrase famous for its bitterness: *perdomita Britannia et statim omissa*[119] (Britain, no sooner grasped than let slip). His meaning is that *Mons Graupius* clinched the conquest of Britain and the jealousy of Domitian threw it away. But the majority of the enemy had escaped from that battle and unpropitious country lay ahead. History does not judge *Mons Graupius* a Waterloo and questions whether Agricola's depleted force could have won one. On the other hand, there is general truth in Tacitus' judgement, for it had required a painstaking pyramid of effort to put an army into northern Scotland and it would not easily be constructed again. Soon it would begin to topple and the will to total conquest pass, perhaps for ever.

Agricola had made one of Rome's longest advances, extended knowledge, established sixty forts and built some 1,300 miles of road.[120] This may be compared with the 18th-century Highland road-building of Generals Wade and Caulfield: 860 miles in something over a million man/days. Agricola's effort, nearly twice that mileage in a quarter of the time, has been estimated as 900,000 man/days,[121] though allowance must be made for more modest specification.

All would be wasted. Agricola's fate was not to be remembered in a Romanized north Britain, but in the dim earthworks of marching armies and on Tacitus' bright page. At Richborough, Kent, marble splinters and cruciform foundations still recall the tetrapylon, or cross-arch, at Rome's principal port of entry, thought to commemorate Agricola's completion of a conquest begun from that spot by Claudius forty years earlier. But if there *were* a Richborough Monument its salute was unwarranted. Before long the frontier would be back on the Tyne-Solway line where Petilius Cerialis had left it a generation earlier.

The crumbling of Roman Scotland was not, however, instant. Tacitus' adverb *statim* (straight away) is denied by archaeology, which shows Agricola's successor guarding his gains with forts, though none is yet certain north of Stracathro.[122] Agricola was recalled in 84 or 85. In about 87 came the abandonment of Perthshire and a shift in the army's centre of gravity to southern Scotland. Around 100–105, in Trajan's reign, this too would be abandoned. The step-by-step shrinkage of Roman North Britain echoed a larger shift in the continental fulcrum from Rhine to Danube. The fate of what we know as Scotland will be decided in the country now called Romania. Britain was a side-show, opened because Claudius needed a success and reopened because of Vespasian's emotional attachment. Though Tacitus argues, *ad hominem*, of a constructive Agricola and a destructive Domitian, the reduction of the British legions may have been less a matter of Domitianic spite than of Rome's weakness. She had declined from the strike-where-she-liked situation of the late Republic to one of rob-Peter-to-pay-Paul. The army was scattered around the frontiers and the emperors were too fearful of a military conspiracy to risk the establishment of a central pool or strategic reserve. To attack on one front meant borrowing from others. Domitian saw Scotland, as Hitler did North Africa, in terms of priorities.

Indeed resemblances between Agricola and Rommel are too numerous to ignore: the steadfast soldier, the demonic master, the distant war-theatre, the stretched supply lines, the breathtaking advance, the surge of popularity at home, the prize almost within reach; then starvation of resources, frustrations of the start-stop kind; and finally recall, muted praise and death under suspicious circumstances. Both were perhaps happy to leave a darkening stage.[123]

Compared with the inner provinces, Roman Britain has little to show in the way of prestigious buildings, impressive urban sites or engineering marvels. Nevertheless, Agricola's mark on the northern landscape is part of a larger legacy of military remains – especially in relation to active campaigning – of which we should learn to be proud. Most remarkable is the number of temporary camps. Four hundred have so far been identified; three quarters of them from the air since 1950. They vary in size from one to 165 acres and include winter camps, siege camps, construction camps, as well as some fifty 'practice camps', built by soldiers in training. Most, however, were marching camps. Britain is fortunate that warfare and military occupation were largely in remote or upland regions, little disturbed by later ages. This wealth in Wales, England's North and Scotland is in strong contrast to continental Europe, where no more than a handful of upstanding camps survive and relatively few are known, even from the air. The south of England is also poor. In Wessex, where Vespasian is said to have fought his thirty battles, few have been found. Heavy and prolonged ploughing is usually given as the reason, but we may ask why other faint markings, like Iron Age fields, are discernable; and why there is so little imprint on the chalk downs, where ploughing was slight and Vespasian active. We can only assume him to have been lax regarding the drill of nightly camp-making; or unusually thorough in their destruction. More probably he bivouacked within friendly *oppida* and captured forts. Perhaps we should not be asking why lowland camps are few but why upland are many. Here we must not discount the obvious: the mood of moorland Britain, then largely cloaked in forest and even more sombre than now; to say nothing of the truculence of the remoter tribes.

In Rome of the mid 90s the boil of terror ached for the lancet. The empress Domitia, believing her own arrest imminent, finally found courage to do what all Rome had vainly hoped of her father, Domitius Corbulo. He it was who had conquered Armenia, only to die on the whim of Nero. Now his daughter would give tyranny their joint reply. At 5 a.m. on 18 September 96, despite his palace walls being clad in mirrors and the dagger beneath his pillow, Domitian was attacked in his sleep and succumbed to eight stab wounds, inflicted by a slave acting for the empress and her co-conspirators, who included the praetorian prefect. As the news broke that morning senators hurried to the Chamber, jostling to make jeering speeches and to push through a motion *damnatio memoriae*[124] (in condemnation of his memory). This execration carried with it the annulment of the late emperor's laws, suppression of his titles, removal of his portraits or emblems, and erasure of his name from every inscription in the empire. The Younger Pliny described the destruction of his golden statues:

> The pleasure in being present as those proudest of faces bit the dust, of hacking and chopping them with sword and axe, as if each blow were piling on the pain. All got a kick from seeing these likenesses mutilated and dismembered; that hateful, fearful face cast into the furnace and the thought that from this melting down of menace and terror something useful and enjoyable might be made.[125]

Like the 1991 toppling of the statue of Felix Dzerzhinski, founder of the KGB, it was feeble recompense for so much suffered so meekly for so long.

Thus ended Domitian in the sixteenth year of his reign at the age of forty-four, whose father was the genial Vespasian and whose brother had been the darling of the Roman crowd. His memory was treasured solely by the soldiers, demonstrating the army's disinterest in liberty and devotion to dynasties. Of these there had been two since Augustus established the Principate: the Julio-Claudian and the Flavian, the latter ending on Domitian's death without issue.

For a final comment on the loss of Scotland one may perhaps defer to the authority of Edward Gibbon:

> The masters of the fairest and most wealthy climate of the globe turned with contempt from gloomy hills assailed by the winter tempest, from lakes concealed in a blue mist and from cold and lonely heaths, over which the deer of the forest were chased by a troop of naked barbarians.[126]

EPISODE FOUR

The Artist

I**N MATTERS RELATING TO THE** empire's defence, it is misleading
to see Rome solely as a Mediterranean power. Such a view shows
Italy at the centre, double-wrapped by the inner and outer provinces.
Macedon and Carthage have long been eliminated and the nearest
rival, Parthia (Iran) is far away. If, on the other hand, we look more
closely, seeing Rome in a *European* context, her safety seems less
certain and the outside world less distant.

The Celts had been a formidable enemy. Occupation of their lands
brought Rome up against the Germans, resulting in an imperial frontier on the Rhine and upper Danube, only 250 miles from Italy. The
middle Danube was more dangerous still. Its course is a similar
distance from north-eastern Italy, but the Drava and Sava rivers
offered corridors straight toward the empire's centre, while the passes
through the Julian Alps, behind Trieste, are the lowest in the Alpine
arc. Add to this the extent and backwardness of the Eastern European
and Eurasian barbarians, plus their tendency to migrate westwards,
and we see why Rome's critical frontiers were not the remote Euphrates, the Syrian desert or the far Sahara, but the not-so-distant Rhine
and Danube.

Fortunately, grave or multiple dangers had been slow to arise along
this 1,700-mile European boundary. Following Augustus' German
War a long lull settled on the Rhine, allowing Claudius to turn
toward Britain. But before this tiresome entanglement could be
resolved, rumblings across the Danube began to remind the Roman
leadership that there were good reasons to consider the river's middle
and lower reaches as the most endangered sectors of the entire

166

imperial rim. Accordingly Domitian's reign saw a decisive shift in deployment from the German to the Balkan front. It was the terrain beyond its far bank which made the Danube a less favourable defensive line than the Rhine. For substantial stretches Rome's Danubian provinces faced mountain, favouring the attacker and covering his retreat. The late-1st-century disturbances arose from such regions, especially today's Romania, where the southern Carparthians loom darkly beyond the Danubian Plain.

A wider view shows the Carpathians as part of an almost complete mountain circle, two hundred miles across, with peaks over 7,000 feet. Within lies Transylvania, home of the Dacians, a former steppe people of Sarmatian origin, related to Ovid's Getans. Their capital, as well as Dacia's most populous region (today's Hunedoara) lay in Transylvania's south-western corner, dangerously close to Belgrade and the Drava-Sava mouths. Southwards Dacia was less than 250 miles from the Aegean and barely a hundred from the Black Sea. Here was a natural fortress of exceptional strength, looming over the Danubian frontier; as well as a strategic hinge, hurtful to Rome in the wrong hands.

In earlier episodes we have glimpsed the barbarian lands by courtesy of Roman authors. Regrettably their light penetrates the Carpathian ring but faintly. The Dacian Wars are described only by Cassius Dio of Nicaea, the 3rd-century Greek whose account of this period survives in the much truncated form of a *précis* by John Xiphilinus, a Byzantine cleric, made at about the time of the Norman conquest of England. His few pages provide general background but little about Dacia and its people. Lack of information about the frontier lands is, of course, normal. The Roman army was late to arrive on these reaches of the Danube. The river bank and its hinterlands were places of army camps, half-drained bog, part-built roads and barely assimilated natives. We may assume that civilian visitors, especially of the tourist kind, were seldom seen. Beyond lived the wild tribes. Unless strongly escorted on military or diplomatic business, or carrying merchandise destined for barbarian chieftains, crossing the river was an act of last resort. As mentioned in Episode One, an archaic custom had allowed those condemned to death a grace period within which to flee Roman territory; the sanctuary seeming to offer little more than the sentence. This exemplified the *Barbaricum's* reputation; and neither it, nor the frontier in the stricter sense, nor even the outer provinces, were conducive to authors whose tastes, like their readers', tended to flower in more civilized vicinities. Rather than complain at the sparseness of the record, one should perhaps be grateful that Ovid, Dio and Tacitus contributed at all. However, Ovid is long gone and though Tacitus, freed at last from fear, is now writing at full flood, he stands at the stern of his age and his work covers nothing later than Agricola's death in AD 93. From that date, to the commencement of Hadrian's reign in 117, written history runs thin. And yet there is, at the heart of Rome, a major source of quite another kind: a Bayeux Tapestry in marble, dedicated to the emperor Trajan and devoted almost entirely to his adventures across the Danube.

Of Trajan it may briefly be said that he was Rome's first non-Italian emperor. Born in 53 at Italica, near Seville, of good Roman family, his father had commanded the Xth legion when Vespasian's guns were battering the Judaean cities. He served as a tribune in Syria when his father was its governor. Under Domitian he himself governed Spain; and he was probably present at the two Danubian war theatres, Marcomannia (Czechoslovakia) and Dacia.[1] At the time of his adoption by Nerva he was governor of Upper Germany, where he stayed till that emperor's death. Modernity would probably call him a liberal, though in view of his survival in high office under Domitian the cynic might question his sincerity as a champion of freedom. History is not short of soldiers who plead duty in support of tyranny.

Though neither unduly intelligent, subtle nor learned, Trajan was, it seems, one of those rare men able to wear all hats and please all people. As emperor his answers to the twin ills of unemployment and public boredom anticipate the baby-kissing politics of our own day: 'In popularity few have been his equal, for he knew that the Roman people's affections are engaged by two things: the corn dole and the spectacles; and that in successful government jollity looms as large as polity.'[2]

He was serenely self-confident, with the gift of imperturbability and the ability to shrug off criticism. He was a relaxed and affable man, and perhaps also a modest one, though with a weakness for claiming credit for building work.[3] According to one source, 'his name was on so many buildings that they nicknamed him Ivy.'[4] Dio accuses him of being a drinker and a paederast: 'We know of course of his inclinations toward boys and wine. But despite this his reputation remained high, for though he drank hard he stayed sober and his relationships with boys harmed no one.'[5] His popularity with the army was beyond question and this was soon matched by popularity in Rome: with the lower classes for his bread and circuses and with the upper for his decisive rejection of all things Domitianic:

> He envied no one. He killed no one. He favoured all good men and feared none. He ignored slanders. He refrained from anger. He was not tempted by others' money. He had no murders on his conscience. He spent hugely on war and the works of peace. He was approachable and a good mixer. He would share his carriage with others, visit the houses of ordinary citizens and relax there.[6]

The dismantling of terror, begun by the elderly caretaker emperor Nerva (AD 96–8), was accelerated in all spheres of public life. Informers and denouncers were outlawed. Publication of the *Senate Transactions*[7] (the Roman *Hansard*) was resumed. The Younger Pliny speaks of heady ideas such as imperial accountability and equality under law: 'An emperor must deal fairly with his empire, accounting for expenditure and not spending what he might be ashamed to admit . . . There is a notion in the air which I hear and understand for the first time: not that the First Citizen is above the law but that the law is above the First Citizen.'[8] This was the man on whom the Senate would vote the title for which he would be most remembered: *optimus princeps* (best emperor of all): 'As the word "august" reminds us of the one on whom it was first bestowed, so the word "best" will not live in mankind's vocabulary without memory of you.'[9]

Turning to the future emperor Hadrian, twenty-three years Trajan's junior and a distant relative from the same provincial town: the boy's father died when he was ten and Trajan became his guardian. In due course his mother sent him to Rome, where he was laughed at for his provincial accent, lost his head at the sight of so much glamour, overspent his allowance and incurred his guardian's displeasure. But fortune would smile in his direction when Nerva nominated him to carry the news to Mainz of his guardian's adoption. Then, on Nerva's death (after only a sixteen-month reign) he was again despatched to Germany to tell Trajan that the purple toga was his. To bring this, the greatest of all news, was seen as supremely auspicious. In Trajan's eyes, however, he would remain a messenger boy.

Trajan's Column, index of a trans-Danubian epic, stands alone in Trajan's Forum. It is remarkable in all respects but in none more than its preservation: a marble mast, intact amid the forum's ship-wreck. And while St Peter[10] has replaced the emperor at the mast-head, the shaft on which he stands (though chipped by eighteen centuries and gnawed by the petro-chemistry of our own) has eluded major ravage and spoliation. Even its base largely escaped injury by the Vandals and their more recent namesakes.

This last structure, the Column's podium, is a seventeen-foot cube of marble blocks, carved with captured armament and housing the sepulchral chamber for Trajan's ashes and those of his empress Plot-ina. Above the doorway an inscription tells us that the Senate had the Column erected during Trajan's sixth consulate (c. AD 113) 'to show how high a hill required to be excavated to accommodate these great works'. The hill was the Quirinal; the works Trajan's Forum (last and largest of the imperial fora), the vast Basilica Ulpia which lay along its northern side, as well as libraries, markets, shops, colon-nades and other useful or ceremonial features. To accommodate what was by all accounts a breathtaking ensemble of buildings and spaces, it had been necessary to cut away a flank of the hill to a depth of 120 feet. It is clear from the inscription that the original reason for the Column was simply to record this effort, the combined height of podium and shaft being equivalent to the depth of rock removed. In other words, the Column's far more famous function, as a memorial to the Dacian Wars, was an afterthought; and the shaft, originally intended to be plain, was adapted to this new pur-pose by carving on it the frieze, upon which its claim to greatness rests.

The Column consists of seventeen marble drums, each over four feet tall. Slanting across its joins and crossing them with extreme precision, the frieze covers the shaft's entire surface in a spiral of twenty-three bands, approximately three feet wide and 656 long. Its subject is Trajan's conquest of Transylvania, known as the Dacian Wars. It contains more than 2,500 human figures, those in fore-ground averaging twenty to twenty-two inches in height. These are in half relief, with background figures in low relief. Though the frieze is continuous, its action is divided into more than 150 episodes, separated by conventional uprights such as a tree, wall or standing man. The reliefs are thought to have been painted and many of the figures held metal swords and spears. Inside the Column is a spiral stairway, lit from four sides by forty-three window slits, which doubled as lewis holes when the drums were hoisted into place. There are also fourteen larger, round holes, brutally banged into the frieze at irregular intervals; probably for the scaffolding required to rob the marble hands of their weapons. It seems likely that the sculptors worked from a full-scale cartoon, consisting perhaps of a textile band on which the content had been drawn in detail. Opinions differ on whether it was carved drum by drum in the workshop; as one, on site; or in the workshop with a few inches, near each join, left for completion when assembled.

The reliefs are not mentioned by any ancient author. However, Trajanic coins show the Column, with diagonal lines to represent the frieze; their dates of issue suggesting that the final concept was in place at latest within eight years of the end of the Dacian Wars and well inside Trajan's reign. The frieze is remarkable for the number and diversity of its scenes, the quality of its compositions and its narrative skills. Most extraordinary of all is the precision of its detail, though the sculptors were working to only 30 per cent life-size. Equally memorable is the sense of great events, despite the inhibitions of the three-foot band. In terms of technique and artistry it is unsurpassed.

In theory the continuous frieze offered a powerful form of expression. At the symbolic level its upward movement echoes the hard slog, from the Danube up into the Carpathians. At the level of propaganda its continuity allows Trajan's quiet presence (sixty appearances in 165 scenes) to accumulate, with all the insistence of a drumbeat, culminating in the fanfare of his statue at the column's summit. But in other respects this is an inadequate medium. The Column is perplexing to the viewer, its narrative continually disappearing round the corner as well as retreating further and further up the shaft. From any position the story is disjointed, since more than half of each loop is out of sight. To follow it an observer would have to walk twenty-three times round the Column, inviting eye strain and a cricked neck. These irritants were originally mitigated by the Forum's design. Trajan's libraries – one for Greek, the other for Latin books – flanked the Column on two sides. These must have been provided with balconies from which close inspection could be made, at least to about half the Column's height. On the third side towered Trajan's huge temple, the Basilica Ulpia,[11] on which we may suppose there were also viewing provisions, this time to full height.

We must remember, too, that in their original painted form the reliefs would have been bolder and their story clearer.

Owing therefore to the problems of a Column which begins from a base itself three times human height and ends at an altitude which almost defies the unaided vision, attempts to study it *in situ* will almost certainly end in frustration. Fortunately plaster casts are to hand in the Museum of Roman Civilization.[12] These are from matrices made on the initiative of Napoleon III in the 1860s. A second set went to Paris and a third to the Victoria and Albert Museum, London, where the entire frieze is reconstructed in halves, the replicas skilfully mounted round two columnar brick cores. They have stood in the Plaster Casts Hall since 1873 and make a striking sight, but the frieze is scarcely more accessible than the original and the lighting less than perfect. Nevertheless these Napoleonic casts, as well as the photographs of them made in the 1890s by Conrad Cichorius[13] of Leipzig University, are definitive sources for a masterpiece whose sharp and brilliant chisel work has since been dulled by sour air and acid rain.

The Column is plagued by problems of interpretation. Captions, so helpful in the Bayeux Tapestry, are entirely absent. We know that Trajan himself wrote a *Commentary* on the wars, whose original was housed in the adjacent Latin library. It is possible that this lost account and the frieze's narrative were integrated. Modern commentators have produced a confusing range of theories; while counter-arguments have been devised to refute almost all of them, especially in relation to the Column's intentions and meaning. The first and most common-sense supposition was that the frieze tells the story of the Dacian Wars. Though this failed to produce instant clarification it was hoped that, with further study, a cogent narrative would emerge, which would dovetail with field work and archaeology in today's Romania. At the other extreme art historians, following Karl Lehmann-Hartleben,[14] began to interpret the Column in aesthetic terms, seeing it as a work of creative imagination in which neither places nor events played a decisive role. Richmond stood somewhere between. Living and working in Rome on the eve of Mussolini's invasion of Ethiopia, he had a close view of glory-seeking; of propaganda and its place in official art; of the need to rouse the nation, vilify the enemy and extol the armed forces, either as a preliminary to war or as justification in its aftermath. Is the carved shaft of Trajan's Column, therefore, a record of events, a work of art, or an instrument of special pleading? Might it, indeed, be all three?

The Column has been described as a silent movie without captions,[15] a foreign film without subtitles, or a 'talkie' bereft of its sound track. This is not entirely frivolous. Resemblances to cinematic technique are numerous. The transitions from one episode to the next resemble cuts. There are split-screen effects, with two strands of action developed simultaneously. There are tempo changes: gallops or charges alternating with static episodes, reminiscent of the way music and dialogue sequences alternate on the silver screen. There are even abrupt contrasts which the film editor calls shock-cuts. Such devices do not arise from precognition of the cinematic art but through the choice of a continuous band as the means of expression. It presented new opportunities in the sense of flow, timing and accumulative meaning. It is, however, too much to expect that the whole range of conventions resulting from the motion picture's invention, like changes of angle[16] and distance from camera, should be grasped all at once. Though daringly experimental in its progression from scene to scene, the Column clings to a single, visual standpoint: a side-on view, as it were, in medium-shot.

There is also the restraint of band size coupled with viewing distance. On a three-foot strip it is difficult to portray a crowd more than six deep, for beyond this the figures become too small to register. To suggest thousands of men in battle, hundreds of prisoners, scores of casualties; to show us the mountains of Transylvania, with their mighty hillforts; and finally to take us to the walls of the ultimate barbarian stronghold, Royal Sarmizegetusa; the frieze's designer was faced with problems more comparable to those of the stage. In famous lines Shakespeare regrets his theatre's inadequacies and suggests how these might be overcome:

> O pardon! Since a crooked figure may
> Attest in little space a million...[17]

Though the frieze includes many individual portraits in its foreground, in general it tends to work in this way: a clump of trees to represent a forest, a group of soldiers an army, three ships a fleet, a few houses a town, a handful of prisoners a victory. How else could a story involving 750,000 Roman soldiers, as well as the entire Dacian people and their allies, be told with a total of only 2,500 carved figures?

On the whole it is remarkably successful. To convey the impression of a mighty epic with a cast of thousands is in no small measure a vindication of the form chosen, for the continuous spiral gives an effect of totality which triumphal arches, with their separate panels, never achieved. Its designer has no need to apologize for underselling the Dacian, as Shakespeare does for the Hundred Years' War:

> Where – O for pity! – we shall much disgrace
> With four or five most vile and ragged foils
> Right ill-disposed in brawl ridiculous
> The name of Agincourt.[18]

He has, on the contrary, transcended the limitations of an untried and difficult form to produce the greatest of military art works.

In common both with theatre and cinema, the Column must wrestle with the problem of continuity. This may be defined as the guiding hand of consistency, which governs every aspect of action: time, place, direction of movement, costume and background. To reduce misunderstanding all must remain constant unless there is clear reason for change. The Column grasps the principle firmly. Its story is seen from a northfacing viewpoint, with Dacia (Romania) right and Roman territory (Serbia, Bulgaria) left. The Romans attack from left to right while the Dacians counter from right to left. Where parallel action occurs (such as Roman units advancing via two routes) those in foreground are supposedly to the south of those in background. There is also consistency in dress, manner, insignia and grouping, so that individual regiments, or characters like Trajan and Decebal, the Dacian king, are identifiable from scene to scene.

Dio's abridged account of the Dacian Wars, though itself of limited value, corroborates the narrative in useful and interesting ways. There is also assistance from archaeology as well as guidance offered by the topography of Romania. Finally there is the thinking of a century of Column scholars.[19] Nevertheless, despite progress in squeezing information from the frieze's 165 action-packed scenes, there persists a negative tradition, deriving from Theodor Mommsen, the most eminent of 19th-century Romanists, who believed that the plot and therefore the Column's overall meaning were irredeemably obscure. 'We are left', he wrote, 'with the impression of detail half understood and the disturbing sense of a great and moving historical catastrophe, faded for ever and lost even to memory.'[20]

Ian Richmond (1902–65) was in general agreement with this verdict, venturing so far as to conclude that 'there was no intimate connection between the successive scenes'; in other words that their tendency was random and that narrative was not the main purpose.[21] This eagle-eyed observer, born in Rochdale, became director of the British School in Rome at twenty-eight. As a lifetime student of the Roman army he was fascinated by the insight into its duties and methods which the Column offers; for it provides a closely observed record of constructing camps, digging ditches, bridging streams, laying roads and many matters related both to temporary and permanent fortification. It is also a unique source for the appearance of finished works: Roman forts, towers and camps, as well as Dacian citadels. Though the ruins of thousands of Roman and Iron Age military works litter the European landscape, this is our only visual record of how they looked in use. 'The victories', said Richmond, 'are portrayed always in company with the toil which made them possible . . . It tells us something of history, but more of the labour by which history was made.'[22]

In concentrating upon subject-matter of this type Richmond was mining a rich vein, for 20 per cent of the frieze's content deals with the army at work, exceeded only by combat scenes at some 25 per cent. In his eyes, however, the support activities seemed the more important. Indeed, among scholars from the former frontier provinces it has become an accepted view that the Column's purpose was less to portray the Dacian Wars than to exalt the army. Apparently it was normal to emphasize the legions' engineering skills, seeing them as a hallmark of civilization which even Rome's auxiliary soldiers lacked. By contrast, to Italian scholars, close to the forum and far from the frontier, the Column is seen as recording Roman achievement in wider terms than military construction. Such a one is Lino Rossi, a Milanese medical practitioner and amateur Columnist, who took on this subject (including an exhaustive photo coverage, plus investigations in Romania) from his own resources.[23] Though British scholars have damned Dr Rossi with faint praise, his view is not unbalanced by obsession with a thesis and his diagnosis of the frieze's storyline is frequently helpful.

On the other hand, Richmond can never be taken lightly. Especially brilliant are his thoughts on how the Column's information was gathered. Assuming the sculptors to have been professional artists – in fact the best available and probably Greek – it is highly unlikely that they were witnesses to battlefield events. In any case the idea of applying a frieze to the Column was an afterthought. Yet mysteriously, as Richmond observed, it contains 'observation so detailed as to be almost photographic'. As an example of this detail, let us cite a scene in which we look over the rampart of a camp at the tents within. Not only can we see the leather panels with which the tents are made but also the knots with which the panels are tied and even the configuration of each knot. Did the sculptors have advice on such matters? This is belied by elementary mistakes. On more than one occasion legionaries are shown building turf ramparts. But instead of laying the turves flat they are being erected on edge, as if they were rigid blocks. This and similar errors would not have been made had the sculptors been working to military guidance. To what then *were* they working?

Richmond had no doubt that the Column drew on eyewitness evidence of a different sort:

> The scenes must be the result of working up the contents of an artist's wartime sketch-book ... Each is based clearly upon a careful sketch, which must have been made in the war area from factual details on the spot, because nowhere else can such things have been seen or imagined in accurate combination.[24]

It is an attractive suggestion that Trajan had a war artist on his staff: the anonymous genius to whom this Episode is dedicated. It is, of course, impossible to prove his presence; or indeed that there was not a *team* of artists (though the existence of a fully developed Roman press corps may strain credulity). Assuming Richmond's guess to be correct, he must have had exceptional gifts of reportage and the ability to commit what he saw to paper with the utmost speed. It is a talent comparable to that of the 19th-century draftsman-journalists, who were able to produce hand-drawn records of events like state occasions for their magazines in a remarkably short time; scenes sometimes involving hundreds of people, with scores of foreground faces rendered as recognizable portraits. Though we have no direct evidence for such experts in antiquity, the skills needed to supply the Column with its wealth of observation could not have been born, fully fledged, in this solitary instance. We may therefore suppose a tradition of graphic reporting whose fruits have not survived elsewhere.

That a civilian hand was at work is suggested not only by standards of draftsmanship far beyond anything elsewhere known of the soldier; but also, as we have said, by misinterpretations, particularly regarding constructional activities. Another example is a scene in which sawn lengths of bough or tree trunk, intended to be laid crosswise on a rampart top to make a walkway, become functionless circles; that is to say the rows of round timbers, seen end on, are depicted as a decorative pelmet along the rampart's parapet. Such misunderstandings almost certainly arose from the original artist, though it is sometimes possible that they occurred in the translation to marble. In any case, these are exceptions. The majority of events are seen with an eye both sharp and true and appear to have passed from sketcher to sculptor, from paper[25] to permanence, with uncanny veracity.

Nevertheless, despite Richmond's faith in the Column's exactitude, there remain scenes at which the war artist could not have been present, or which could not have happened as he shows them. One is a Dacian surprise attack on a diversionary front; another the army crossing the Danube on two pontoon bridges laid side by side. These bridging points were almost certainly at separate locations. In any case even the ablest of war correspondents cannot witness everything. We must therefore accept a degree of manipulation, albeit by someone close to actual operations; and indeed the experienced Column critic comes to sense it.

Be these matters as they may, it is feasible that the sketches were assembled into a picture book (perhaps supplementing Trajan's own, written account) and that this would be in the normal form of a continuous scroll, wound from one rolling pin onto another. It is also feasible that such a scroll contained the Second Dacian War on one side, with the First on the reverse, to be read on the wind-back. Such a book may have inspired the frieze, for the latter resembles nothing so much as a scroll wrapped round a shaft. On the Column the narrative of the First War ends exactly half way up, with the Second War occupying the top half: possibly reflecting a division in a book.

Turning to the story told on the Column we will recall, in Episode Three, ominous clashes between Domitian and Decebal during the period AD 85–92. Following Trajan's succession (in AD 98 and already in his early forties), 'he could', as Dio comments, 'see how Dacian power and pride were continuing to grow'.[26] Ambitious as ever, Decebal remained a menace to Roman security in the entire Balkan area. Unfortunately for the king, his was a bid for power which would meet, in the new emperor, a matching quest for glory. Trajan mustered his strength for a pre-emptive attack on the Transylvanian stronghold, launching it in the spring of 101. The narrative depicted on Trajan's Column now begins. But before joining Trajan's army on the Danube bank, it is timely to consider the character of the Dacians and their Transylvanian homeland.

In about 500 BC a Sarmatian splinter-group, thwarted perhaps by Thracian cousins already occupying the south-eastern Balkans, branched northwards from the Black Sea and penetrated the Carpathian passes. That they included or were closely related to the Getans is suggested by the name of their future capital, Sarmizegetusa, which may have meant 'Sarmatian-Getan place'. Whatever their composition they had found paradise: a green bowl with the Carpathians its rim; watered, sheltered, fertile, and rich both in useful and precious metals. Here was a land offering all the steppe lacked; and the new arrivals responded by settling down to farm it, mine it and work its metals.

Some two centuries later Celts began to cross the Carpathians from the opposite or Balkan direction. Luckily for the Dacians, Celtic numbers were small enough to be absorbed yet large enough to make a contribution; leading to significant improvements in ironcraft, husbandry and defensive architecture, with new plough types, the potter's wheel and techniques of large-scale fortification. It was the beginning of a cultural miracle, continued and augmented by Greek and Roman influences; for Transylvania's bounty was matched by her position, close to the outposts of the classical world yet protected by a fearsome mountain circuit from their predation.

In about 80 BC a unified kingdom began to emerge under Burabista; and from then until the Roman invasion a distinctively Dacian culture flourished. The soil, the iron deposits, the gold and silver mines, were amply and creatively exploited. Writing was adopted, using Greek and Roman characters. Quality pottery was produced, with painted, geometric designs. Medicinal botany exceeded the average standards of the day. There was a calendar, based on Dacian astronomical measurements. Coinage had been issued for 150 years, though by the 1st century BC extensive trade with the empire led to the adoption of Roman currency. Borrowing from outside practice, the Dacians now excelled in citadel construction, typically of hillfort character, with ditch-fronted walls: some of squared blocks with towers, modelled on the Pontic cities; others of irregular masonry, immensely thick and internally cross-tied with wooden beams in the Celtic manner. The capital was ringed by major fortresses, some enclosing impressive religious sanctuaries. Religion was polytheistic: not far removed from Mediterranean paganism, though resembling the northern religions in the practice of human sacrifice. Ptolemy tells us they boasted forty cities. Sarmizegetusa (Gradishtea) had piped water and was defended by mighty walls of Celtic type, both turreted and galleried. With the accession of Decebal in AD 87, Dacia could be called the most developed nation-state in Europe outside the Mediterranean, perhaps the only one.

Around the beginning of Domitian's reign Decebal was already drilling a national army of paid professionals modelled on that of Rome. As we have seen, he would not hesitate to use it. It may be overstretching parallels to call this king a 1st-century Saddam Hussein; yet both were cool gamblers who defied the superpower of their day. The stakes were high: for Saddam a fifth of world oil; for Decebal a chance to slip his mountain leash and take control of the lower Danube, the Black Sea ports and even the Aegean. Both believed bluff and distance would protect them. Both placed trust in secret weapons: in Decebal's case abundant gold with which to attract the foreign specialists needed to match Rome's war machine. Trajan too was a gambler. To muster an overwhelming force he would be obliged to draw down his other frontier garrisons to danger level. The cost, as it transpired, would be loss of Scotland; the prize, Dacia's mines, last great booty within Rome's reach.

Let us return to the heroic helix, and particularly its content. Because the sculpted band slants upwards from a horizontal base, it must taper in, requiring half a turn to reach full width and curiously resembling the 'fade-in' at the beginning of a motion picture. Its opening scene offers the only known portrait of a Roman frontier: the Danube bank, with its watchtowers and guards, seen from the river, as it may have appeared from the barbarian side. There are stone watchtowers, surrounded by circular palisades of pointed stakes, with wooden balconies. From each balcony door a long firebrand slants skywards. All are alight, suggesting the hours of darkness: probably just before dawn on a morning in April, 101.

Still on the first spiral, we see a Roman fortress. From its front gate, in one of the most striking images in military art, stream legion-

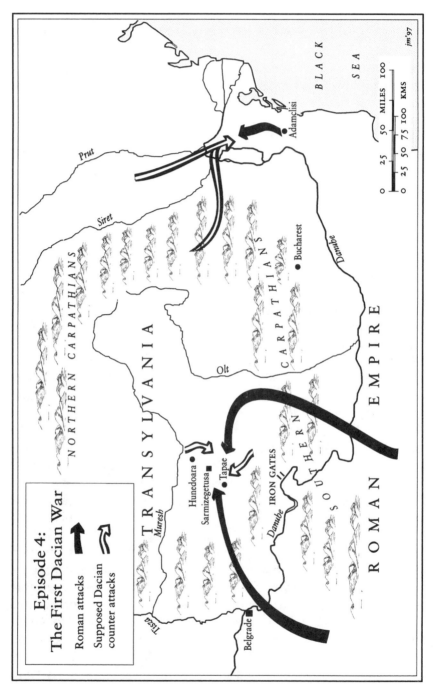

Episode 4:
The First Dacian War

Roman attacks

Supposed Dacian
counter attacks

aries and guardsmen, marching across the Danube on two boat-bridges, side by side. Why *two* bridges? Why double a laborious piece of engineering for a few hours gained in crossing time? And why is Trajan leading the further task force and relegated to the background? The reason is surely that this is a convention for simul-taneous invasion on two fronts, with Trajan in charge of the upstream crossing. In fact we are fairly sure his departure point was Viminiacum (below Belgrade). The other army, under Lucius Quietus, crossed 125 miles downstream, at Drobetae (Turnu Severin) in today's Romania. The two locations are separated by the Iron Gates gorges and the mountains through which the Danube has cut its dramatic path. The strategy is clearly a pincer movement against the Dacian capital, Royal Sarmizegetusa, situated some seventeen miles south-east of present-day Hunedoara. Trajan's group, from the west, faced the easier mountain crossing but the tougher fighting; the second group, from the south, the stiffer climb through the Tran-sylvanian Alps, but a back-door approach to the capital.

In spiral two, on Dacian soil, Trajan holds a war council, followed by a religious service. A barbarian emissary arrives on a mule and a circular object hanging from his saddle is thought to be the large mushroom upon which, according to Dio,[27] was written a message from the Dacian king telling Trajan to turn back. In a moment of humour (rarest of commodities in monumental art) the courier slips while dismounting and is shown, in slapstick manner, sprawling on the ground. This is the first of several small concurrences between Dio and the Column, suggesting a common source, probably Trajan's lost *Commentary*. The emperor now addresses the army. Scenes of camp-building and other construction work follow.

Spiral three shows Trajan advancing through foothills. Torrents are bridged and soldiers, cutting avenues through dark thicket, remind us of the later name 'Transylvania' (land beyond the forest). The enemy retreats and Trajan diverts to inspect an abandoned hillfort, small but with ominously impressive walls and arched gate-ways. Captured by the vanguard and held by the hair, the first pris-oner of war is thrust into the emperor's presence. A deserted city, believed to be Tibiscum (Caransebesh) now comes into view. Roof-tops peep over the tall, silent, multi-angular ramparts. Swirling round them from two directions the Roman armies, which have advanced by different routes, now recombine. Their meeting tells us the moun-tains have been crossed.

In the Bistra Valley (spiral four) the Dacians turn and give battle at Tapae. They fight desperately: tousled, bearded warriors in flapping cloaks and baggy breeches, with round shields and, probably, wielding sickles (later prized from their marble grip by metal robbers). Rome prevails and the way to the capital seems open.

Nevertheless Sarmizegetusa is ringed by powerful citadels and, in spiral five, further advance is barred by one of them. Trajan, accompanied by a staff officer, views it from across the valley. The intervening ground is sewn with mantraps. On the battlements are displayed a captured standard and a row of Roman heads. Within is a large larder, on stilts, and a huge, wooden watertank: signifying the siege-resistant properties of these strongholds. Above all flutters the sinuous dragon flag of Dacia. The Romans do not attack, but burn the surrounding villages. By a stroke of luck the king's sister falls into Roman hands.[28] Trajan ushers her aboard a boat whose bow points westwards. On this note the story of the first campaigning season ends; and in the absence of an obvious victory we assume its objectives were not achieved. Having failed to break the defensive ring Trajan dares not wait for winter to close the passes behind him and makes a timely retirement to the Danube. Wintering beyond the Carpathians, with Dacian strength still intact (an outcome toward which Decebal was obviously working) would have meant almost certain Roman destruction.

Spiral five opens with cinematic suddenness. Dacian warriors, their mounts and a wagon are floundering in the freezing Danube. Some drown, but many survive to attack a Roman fort whose defenders fight desperately from the walls. The wily Decebal has launched a winter counter-offensive. But where? At such a juncture the lack of captions is especially irksome. However, had this been a silent movie, it is likely that a card would now read: 'Winter, further down the Danube.' For evidence of this we have Adamclisi to thank.

Hard by the Romanian village of Adamclisi, forty miles inland from Ovid's Tomis, is the most important group of ancient remains in the lower Danube region. Here is the so-called Altar: a war memorial, attributed to Domitian, where it is supposed that the emperor was mauled by this same Dacian king in one of his earlier breakouts from the mountain ring. Now, more than a decade later, is it possible that Decebal was drawn back to the scene of his early success, like Hitler to the Ardennes, striking southwards toward the lightly defended Black Sea ports? For the Altar is not the only monument in this curious corner of the Pontic steppe. There is a second, known as the Mausoleum, attributed to Trajan: a mound which, when dug,[29] revealed a circular structure whose design resembles Roman tombs of the 1st century. Inside were found only ox bones, suggesting a ceremonial purpose; and there was also the base of a stone upright, indicating that this too was some kind of cenotaph. There is, however, more. Two hundred yards away, on this same, windy hill, stands a third ruin, far more famous: the *Tropaeum Traiani* (Trajan's Trophy). This is a victory monument, whose purpose appears to have been to commemorate the diversionary campaign of the winter of 101–2, depicted on spirals six and seven of the Column.

The *Tropaeum* took the form of a circular drum, stone-faced on a concrete core 100 feet in diameter and 130 high. At its summit was a hexagonal shaft which carried the trophy: a Dacian captive at the feet of a faceless, three times life-size Roman warrior, clutching an ensemble of captured weapons. The dedication, dated AD 108, is to Mars the Avenger, indicating that Trajan's victory was seen as a retrieval of Domitian's defeat of a generation earlier. Possibly the Mausoleum had been provisional, the more ambitious *Tropaeum* replacing it after the war's end. Richest by far of its gifts are two rows of sculpted stone panels, recovered from rubble around the base. Out of an original fifty-four tablets in the lower row, forty-eight have survived, of which only four are badly damaged. These were hung round the drum's middle and consist of war scenes. The upper row had a further twenty-six tablets, thought to have stood around its parapet like crenellations, each containing a full-figure portrait of a prisoner of war. There were, in addition, two decorative bands: one with foliage and wolves' heads, the other with interlaced palmettes.[30] The entire monument is now to be seen in the form of a lavish, full-scale *in situ* reconstruction, completed in 1977; encasing the much eroded core. For a modest tip, the custodian may be persuaded to open a door in the modern shell, revealing something of the original masonry within. Carvings and decorative stonework are displayed in a specially designed museum.

The connection between these tableaux and the Column was first recognized by E. Petersen in 1905.[31] Prior to this, spirals six and seven were perhaps the most mystifying, for all they tell us is that Trajan embarked somewhere, disembarked somewhere else, defeated persons unknown and re-embarked. The clue is wagons, common to both versions. Their presence (and, on the Adamclisi portrayal, that of women and children) implies that this was a migratory movement; an invasion of Roman territory induced by the promise of land. In addition the panels reveal the invaders as a mixture of peoples: Dacians, Sarmatians of other tribes, and Germans. The only place where these coincided was Bessarabia (Moldova), since the Basternians, a totally isolated German tribe, had somehow found their way into that region.[32]

Decebal then, in his hour of peril, had succeeded in rallying his allies and persuading them to support him in opening a second front in the form of Danube crossings, perhaps just above the delta. We need not suppose a battle at Adamclisi itself. This was merely a symbolic location, hallowed by earlier events. Many of the panels show trees: to be exact, an unlikely selection of palms and oaks, suggesting pursuits as varied and far afield as the delta and the Carpathian foothills. Recalling Ovid's 'bare and leafless landscape without tree',[33] it is unlikely that the main fighting was in steppe surroundings.

Comparison between Trajan's Column and the Adamclisi panels is of great interest: seemingly two versions of the same story, seen through different eyes and chiseled by different hands; one by master craftsmen, the other in all probability by common soldiers, perhaps military masons, who combined active service with the function of regimental tombstone carvers. As one might expect, the difference in execution is as striking as that between world-class orchestra and bar-room piano. Crudely carved in pocked and pitted limestone with lumpy, Frankenstein-like figures in stiff poses, the *Tropaeum*'s panels verge on the grotesque. Surprisingly the ornamental bands above and below the tablets are of accomplished workmanship, perhaps by Greek sculptors from nearby Histria. The panels themselves were seemingly entrusted to someone whose technical ineptitude was compensated by battlefield experience; and this naïve authenticity enhances their value as evidence.

The Adamclisi artist sees things closely. His characters, usually full-figure and numbering from one to three persons per panel, are about 80 per cent life size. They are therefore two-and-a-half times bigger than on the Column (though the Column's finer chisel work often allows more detail). He was incapable of elementary perspective and more than rudimentary composition. Crowd scenes or complex movements were out of the question. His technique allowed no departure from a rigid viewpoint or a single plane of action. Costumes suggest winter, but, apart from solitary trees,[34] there is no sense of surroundings. This is in marked contrast with the Column, which shows or implies forests, streams, mountains, wild animals, villages, towns, time of day and weather with amazing skill and care. On the other hand, the Adamclisi scrutiny, though confined to simple events, is realistic and uncompromising. It sees no glamour in war. Its scenes of hand-to-hand fighting are brutal. The Column is by artists for the Roman public; the *Tropaeum* by soldiers for soldiers.

Such differences tell us much of both: for example, about intention and propaganda role. In this sense the *Tropaeum*'s sentiments are the more trustworthy, inasmuch as they were farther removed from sponsorship and censorship. What differences did this produce? The emphasis of Adamclisi is on combat and ceremonial. Its panels feature Trajan; but there is only one address, no religious services and no camp-building or other constructional activity. We therefore conclude that the Column's preoccupation with pious observance and engineering achievement reflects a government view of what ought to be seen; while the *Tropaeum*'s interest in battlefield prowess and victory parades reflects what the soldiers wanted to see.

Since the tablets were retrieved piecemeal, with some carted off to Bucharest, their order round the drum is uncertain. Nevertheless, the intention was clearly sequential. The panels fall readily into groups and it is not hard to guess their drift. The army advances toward the scene of disturbance. Trajan meets the migrating barbarians, who beg for land. He rejects their appeal. A battle follows, among wagons. Then pursuit, slaughter and shepherdless flocks. Finally a parade with captives, followed by celebratory scenes, with trumpeters and standard bearers.

It is revealing to compare the two sources in their portrayal of the barbarians. The Column is remarkable for its perception of the background, yet Dacians themselves are depicted conventionally. Though seen as more powerful and capable than most enemies, this is an off-the-peg portrait, with the barbarian looking much as in other examples of official art. He is tousled, bearded, heavy featured, with a short hooked nose, high cheekbones, beetle-browed and always scowling and sombre. There are cap wearers – who, according to Dio, were the aristocracy – and the bareheaded commonality. (The Dacian cap, conical and floppy with its point drooping forwards, was not unlike that of Snow White's seven dwarfs.) But despite differences of rank and age there is little facial variety. It is as if the artist found them – as newly arrived Westerners did the Japanese – seemingly identical. Doubtless, being derived from a small genetic pool, they did to some extent look alike.

The Adamclisi artist was more familiar with and fascinated by the enemy. Relatively speaking, greater space is devoted to his portrayal. Not only do we see more weaponry, costume and other features but, as has been said, people of three racial origins are depicted. The *Tropaeum* may therefore be considered the richer and more accurate ethnological source. The Dacians and their Sarmatian cousins, some stripped to the waist, wield the double-handed battle scythe[35] like some fearsome hockey stick (whereas the Column favours the sickle, preferred by the Transylvanian Dacians and more suited to close combat in wooded terrain). Their breeches are heavy and plaited vertically. They wear boots and tight-fitting leather helmets with neck flap, rather like a dustman's cap, though with a chinstrap. Some have long, belted tunics, apron-cut and split high up the sides. The Sarmatians wear shin-length riding coats, probably of sheepskin with the fleece turned inwards, split to the navel. Some Dacians have pudding-basin haircuts, as shown also on the Column. Others have wild hair and all wear long beards. The Germans are bearded, too, though neatly trimmed, their hair swept into the distinctive Suebic or south-German knot, on the right-hand side. They are tall and trousered, with a double rope-belt and a v-shaped cape of poncho type covering chest and stomach. The tidy appearance of these Basternian Germans denies Tacitus' verdict: *sordes omnium* (they are all filthy).[36]

Returning to the Column: it is unlikely that the supposed war artist was present at this diversionary campaign. Accordingly its presentation is subtly different, with greater than normal drama and compression. Mistakenly the Pontic Dacians and their allies are dressed exactly like the Transylvanian Dacians. By contrast, on the Roman side, there are precise and seemingly accurate data: a first aid post; a cart-mounted *ballista* on the move; a prison pen, filled with captives. In short it seems likely that this entire parenthesis had been synthesized from the accounts of others and beefed up with incidents transposed from the main theatre. The campaign ends with Trajan granting citizenship to a group of joyful auxiliary soldiers.

The Column's designer had now to break the thread and start afresh: to end the winter campaign on the lower Danube, get Trajan back upriver and commence the spring assault on Transylvania. In order to signal this decisive switch he uses a 'shock-cut', from the joyful auxiliaries to Roman prisoners being tortured: naked men, bound, face upwards, with hot irons applied to the flesh. The tormentors appear to be high-class Dacian women, perhaps priest-esses, with hair in buns, richly dressed in ankle-length costume similar to that worn by the king's sister. The setting is mountainous, perhaps the capital itself. Finally the action returns to the lower Danube, where the emperor embarks on a warship whose prow points upstream.

Back on the middle Danube (spiral seven) Trajan again leads the army across a bridge of boats. The campaigning season of 102 has begun and a second invasion of Transylvania is underway. So the frieze returns to the main story, re-establishing it with a scene which cleverly echoes the start of the first season. This time, however, the troops, streaming off the pontoon bridge, separate into what appears to be three columns of march, with Trajan in the nearest. For this the Vulcan, Tergova and Turnu Rossu passes all have their advocates; but the presence of supply carts with the upriver group suggests a less mountainous route for the left flank. This could only be the front-door approach via Tapae, the way taken by Trajan in the previous spring. Heavy *matériel* implies that this column's role will be siege or blockade, while the less encumbered armies, including Trajan's, will swing in from the rear.

In spirals eight and nine Trajan's force crosses the Carpathians by an arduous, flanking route, aiming to approach the almost impreg-nable environs of the Dacian capital from the less heavily fortified, eastern side. Again the Dacian army retreats, leaving local dignitaries to sue for peace. Trajan's force breaks into groups, in single file, with roughened marble signifying the uneven ground of mountain passes. Spiral ten sees the army across the divide at last. Another of the central citadels is encountered. A fort is built and gun-pits dug. An infantry attack is accompanied by an artillery duel, in which Dacians man a captured or copied *ballista*.

In spiral eleven a final assault on the hilltop redoubt begins. Ger-man irregulars, half naked and armed with clubs, lead for Rome, backed by oriental or African archers and slingers. While the Dacians are lured out to fight before their palisades a legion attacks from the rear, storming a gateway under locked shields: the celebrated *testudo* (tortoise) formation. The Romans appear to have won a decisive victory and taken key strongholds commanding the approach to Sarmizegetusa.

Realizing that the game is up and wishing to preserve his capital and some vestiges of influence, the king pleads for an armistice. In spiral twelve, under the part-glimpsed walls of Sarmizegetusa, the Dacians kneel in mass surrender: rank on rank, with arms imploringly outstretched. Behind them on a rock stands Decebal, his palms raised skywards. So ends the First Dacian War.

A penultimate scene shows families being brought down from the hillforts. Resettlement in valleys was a standard first step in the Roman pacification of mountain country. Meanwhile other Dacians are dismantling walls in obedience to the peace terms. But some remain in hiding on the hill and their whispering implies an intention to subvert the treaty. Dio describes the surrender:

> Trajan took some hillforts, where he found the weapons, engines and standards captured from Fuscus.[37] Because of these reverses and the fact that his own sister had fallen into Maximus' hands,[38] Decebal now accepted all the Roman conditions, though only as a ruse to buy time. So he consented to the surrender of armaments, engines and engineers, the extradition of deserters, the demolition of forts and the evacuation of captured land. Hencefoward he would align himself with Roman foreign policy, cease to harbour deserters and desist from employing fugitives from within the empire; for the biggest and best part of his army had been made up of those enticed from Roman territory. All this followed from his meeting with Trajan, to whom he prostrated himself, swore submission and surrendered his sword. After concluding this peace the emperor left the camp at Sarmizegetusa. Having placed garrisons throughout the conquered territory he returned to Italy where he celebrated a Triumph and received the title *Dacicus*.[39]

So Dacia was reduced to protectorate status. Though there appears no intention to depose Decebal and annex his kingdom, precedent suggests this would follow, either when the Roman grip had tightened or upon his death. Dio reveals a factor which an official source like the Column would never admit: the embarrassingly large scale of Roman desertion to the Dacian side. Soldiers, veterans and engineers had long been improving Decebal's defences, equipping him with artillery, drilling his men and even fighting alongside them. This appears to belie all we have said about fear of the lands beyond the frontier. Dacia was, however, an exception. Where the less advanced regions of the European *Barbaricum* offered Roman runaways the likelihood of slavery or death, Decebal promised gold, plus a respected role in a stable state. The deserters' motive was no doubt gainful employment rather than opposition to Rome. Since the ancient world had not invented political viewpoints in the modern sense, there was little ideological basis for treason. By the same token there was little ideological or moral basis for loyalty, especially among provincials of non-Roman origin. The empire's subjects were, after all, a miscellany of conquered or overawed races, largely cemented by Roman success.

The final scene, a victory salute, is followed by an angel-like figure of *Victory*, flanked by trophies. This ensemble, half way up the Column, separates the First and Second Dacian Wars and is equivalent, in terms of modern theatre, to the interval. Some two-and-a-half years now pass unrecorded. Dio takes up the story; and we note that defection works both ways:

Because Decebal was reported to be breaking the treaty in all its clauses the Senate once more declared him an enemy. Rather than delegate the war to others Trajan again took personal command. But this time many Dacians began to desert to the Romans and Decebal soon seemed ready to throw in the sponge. And yet the stumbling block was that he would neither give up his arms nor accept personal captivity. As a result he continued to muster men and call on the adjacent peoples to join his cause.

Though losing in the field, Decebal attempted to hit back by means of terrorism, slipping deserters into Moesia[40] with orders to assassinate Trajan. The emperor was an easy target due to his accessibility and his wartime habit of holding open situation-conferences. But the plan miscarried thanks to the arrest on suspicion of one, who revealed the others under torture.[41]

The Column's narrative recommences with Trajan's embarkation by night from an Italian Adriatic port. It is the spring of AD 105. Two spirals are now devoted to the emperor's journey back to the war theatre. His itinerary may have been via Greece, to the head of the Aegean, then overland. These spirals can be closely inspected at the Victoria and Albert Museum, where the replica is divided into two and the beginning of its second half is at floor level. Unfortunately, from the standpoint of historical events, this is the least important part of the frieze and was probably included as makeweight. Because the first war was eventful and hazardous, while the second was relatively quick and easy, their stories are of unequal length. The designer was thus obliged to pad the second half of the narrative with these two bands at the beginning and two more, devoted to mopping-up operations, at the end.

With spiral fifteen the scene switches to Dacia, where hostilities have already begun. Roman forts are under fierce attack. The enemy's intention is to cut the new Danube bridge. This project, pushed forward during the 'phoney peace' of 103–4, is the first known work of the Syrian-Greek engineer and architect, Apollodorus of Damascus. The bridging point was Drobetae (Turnu Severin) between today's Serbian and Romanian banks and just below the Iron Gates gorges, where routes branched out toward the key passes into Transylvania. At almost a kilometre (1,087 yards, including approaches) it would be the longest permanent bridge in antiquity.

A second project, no less remarkable, was the widening of the cliff road through the Iron Gates of Orsova. This deep, limestone gorge, eighty miles long, formed by the Danube cutting through the southern Carpathians, separates the middle Danube of Hungary and Serbia from the lower of Romania and Bulgaria. Today its whirling waters are stilled and their level raised by the dam of the Djerdap power station. During the Roman period the Iron Gates had frustrated efforts to build a continuous frontier road. Tiberius, Claudius and Domitian all attempted to cut a path into the vertical face on today's Serbian side; finally creating a throughway only three feet wide, increased to six by planking, supported on timber brackets keyed into the cliff from joist holes below. Presumably this had been stripped away by spring floods and the crashing ice for which the gorge is infamous. It was a link Trajan must mend, for his entry points to Dacia were at either end of it. Accordingly, over a distance of twelve miles in the canyon's sheerest stretch, the ledge was widened to six feet, producing a permanent rock road, dependent on wooden cantilevering for its safety-rail only. The ledge and beam holes were well preserved before the reservoir engulfed all trace; excepting a commemorative inscription, which was raised above the new high-water mark and may still be read.

Trajan's projects made unwelcome reading in Sarmizegetusa;

especially the bridge, whose destruction was considered a matter of urgency. The Column shows the Romans stubbornly holding the bridgehead fort of Pontes. Behind is the bridge itself, its stone piers and timber spans depicted in meticulous detail, their number scaled down from twenty to five. Even carpenters still working on the super-structure are thrown into the line and fight with their axes. At this desperate moment, in finest Hollywood style, Trajan and his escort gallop to the rescue along the Iron Gates road. As they thunder by, two masons, seemingly unconcerned, are still smoothing the cliff, while a third is cutting the lettering of the inscription.

In spiral fifteen, then, the bridgehead is under attack, Trajan arrives in the nick of time and the day is saved. After dedicating the bridge the emperor gives audience to ambassadors from friendly or fright-ened tribes. These are of both German and Sarmato-Dacian racial groups, distinguishable by dress and hairstyles. The setting, in the bridge's shadow, is at once a propaganda exercise and a threat, for not only was the bridge an accomplishment beyond barbarian capability, but also a warning that technology gave Rome the keys to all lands east of the Danube and Rhine. Students of the Column have proposed that Apollodorus appears in this scene, standing behind Trajan (viewer's right). If true it is his only known portrait.

In spiral sixteen the army spills across the Danube for a third time, now by the bridge. On the Dacian bank the units divide into two strands, separated by the rusticated marble which represents moun-tain. Once again Trajan leads the further or left arm of a pincer which will meet near the enemy capital. The crossing was in the spring of 106; and in spiral seventeen, after scenes of footslogging on upward paths, a transition to high summer is implied by legion-aries with sickles, reaping the alien corn (another cinematic trick, in which tedious time is overstepped and its passage implied by a seasonal symbol). Crossing the mountains and fighting his way toward Sarmizegetusa has cost Trajan three months. But now a change is seen in the enemy's attitude. On the walls of a stronghold close to the capital the defenders are shouting at one another, with vigorous gestures, arguing whether to resist or surrender.

Sarmizegetusa comes into sight, its awesome ramparts stretching much of the length of spiral eighteen, perhaps four times longer than those of lesser citadels. The Romans fell trees and construct siege towers. The two army groups reunite before the walls. These appear to be of polygonal blocks, some variant of the *murus gallicus*. In the foreground a heap of rough stones, probably core filling, implies last-minute efforts to strengthen the defences. Upon this are strewn three sets of bizarre equipment, whose function surely mystified the artist who recorded them and has puzzled commentators since. They consist of poles, with discs at each end. The poles are nailed together to form triangles. Across the centre of each lies what seems to be a trident. Other poles are supposedly attached to objects resembling casks or small barrels!

Here the artist may have linked separate items, thrown together on a heap, into one fanciful structure; the 'poles with barrels' being large mallets or tamping instruments; the 'tridents' being rakes or forks and the 'poles with discs' being the bracing members by which the inner and outer wall-faces were tied together.[42] Again we see an uncannily photographic eye without the specialized knowledge to support it.

The walls are stormed and breached; and spiral nineteen shows disheartened Dacians already setting fire to their own defences. Further along the rampart distraught defenders raise their hands to heaven. Others are grouped round a pot, ladling out the contents, presumably poison. In spiral twenty the Romans occupy and loot the city. Trajan receives another salutation.

Spirals twenty-one to twenty-three are largely devoted to pursuit of the Dacian remnant through forest and mountain, beyond the river Muresh and into north-western Transylvania. Hard fighting still lies ahead; and the drama is heightened by the presence of the king, who has escaped the *débâcle* and leads his hard-core loyalists in a desperate rearguard action. During twenty-one, however, there is a flashback to a very different scene, also described by Dio:

Decebal's treasure was found buried beneath the River Sargetia, which runs past his palace. Prisoners of war had been used to divert the river. A pit was then dug in the bottom to take gold and silver in great quantities, plus other valuables impervious to water. The river bed was reinstated and the stream returned to its course. The royal robes and other perishables were hidden in caves and the same prisoners – used for this work also – were then butchered to ensure secrecy. But when Bicilis, a courtier who knew what had happened, was captured, he gave away the secret.[43]

Dacia was rich in precious metals. The *massif* north of the royal capital is to this day called the Muntsii Metalici (Metal-Bearing

Mountains). The Column shows goblets, plate and other valuables being loaded onto mules. This was estimated as more than half-a-million pounds of gold plus a million of silver; in cash terms 700 million *denarii*:[44] Rome's last great loot from a foreign war. Meanwhile, in a mountain retreat, Decebal addresses his followers for the last time. Some kill each other in suicide pacts. Spiral twenty-two sees the king and his bodyguard cornered in a wood by Roman cavalry. Under a tree, bareheaded and on one knee, Decebal cuts his own throat with a diagonal sweep of the sword. A Roman officer, arm outstretched, leans from his galloping horse in an attempt to take him alive. He is a second too late. Decebal's head is displayed on a tray in the Roman camp. It would later be sent to Rome, there to be rolled down the Gemonian Steps, a fate usually reserved for the bodies of executed criminals. The Dacian Wars are over.

In 1965 the tombstone of this same cavalry officer, one T. Claudius Maximus, was discovered in northern Greece.[45] It describes the incident and carved upon it is almost the same scene as on the Column: a small but important confirmation of the latter's historicity.

The last turn of the topmost spiral, twenty-three, shows Roman army veterans, marching into Dacia. Before them a Dacian family is fleeing the country. The men carry large bundles. One drags a reluctant child by the wrist. A man and woman look longingly backwards. Men and boys drive cattle and sheep before them. As the spiral tapers toward 'final fade-out', the leading animal wanders from the Dacian homeland, perhaps through one of the north Carpathian passes into the Ukrainian plain and exile. On this poignant note the frieze of Trajan's Column ends.

Comparing the Column's first and last scenes we are reminded of the frontier Rome had given up and that which she would now take on. The new boundary would be a huge bulge protruding into Sarmatian territory. Three hundred inbending river miles had been bartered for five hundred outbending mountain miles. The northern Carpathians, which touch 7,000 feet, are not a single ridge but a tangle of peaks up to fifty miles deep. The army had no experience of defending Alpine crests, extremely difficult to supply and almost untenable in winter. Trajan's answer was to keep his forts within the Transylvanian basin and guard its mountain approaches through watchtower networks. The plan seems to have worked, for the Dacian province would last 165 years, as long as Rome had strength to hold it. Trajan's victory was followed by sixty years of almost unbroken peace on the Lower Danube.

The other military imperative was to prevent Dacia becoming a vacuum. Hence the implanting of veterans. In fact these were only the van of a migration without precedent in the conquered territories: poor Italians to plough the new province and Dalmatian miners to win its metals. Those Dacians who remained became an underclass, their identity diluted or lost. So pronounced an ethnic and cultural displacement provides antiquity's closest approximation to the land-runs and gold-rushes of the 19th-century New World; though government control of mineral exploitation and the huge army presence made it less of a free-for-all.

Our evidence is less archaeological than philological: disappearance of the Dacian tongue and the persistence of Romanian, a wholly Romance language, closely resembling Italian in sound and substance. Situated in the Greek-speaking half of the empire, Dacia would stay culturally Western. Some 3,000 Latin inscriptions have been found, compared with only thirty-five Greek. Though later surrounded by Slav, Magyar and Turk, part Orthodox and part Moslem, Romania has survived as an island of Latinity in speech and sentiment, as well as in her very name. Even her Black Sea province of Dobruja, Greek from the Bronze Age, today speaks Romanian; and it is one of history's small ironies that Ovid's verses may be better understood in modern Constantsa than in the Tomis of his own day. The survival of Romanian is especially remarkable in view of the eventual loss of Latin from all other Roman frontier provinces.

Romanian does not resemble Italian in all respects. It seems normal to look inwards to the Romance languages, toward an Italy or a France at the heart of the West; drawing on them for the vocabularies of sophistication. With Romanian one looks outwards, beyond the Balkans; and one will not be surprised to find a simpler tongue, as if Italian had survived only in the Apennines or Alps. Trajan's name is enshrined in the language. The word *Trajan* signifies anything Roman and by extension almost anything old: a defensive work, an ancient road, a *tumulus* or barrow; even a snowdrift, in the sense that this may resemble a barrow. Hence the verb *introeni* = to be snowed under (literally, to be *entrajanned*!).[46]

The spring of 107 saw Trajan back in Dacia, organizing the new territory. The Roman capital would be Sarmizegetusa, some twenty-five miles from the mountain stronghold of Royal Sarmizegetusa, now razed and desolate. Three legions remained in the province; and though two would be withdrawn within a decade, an unusually large complement of auxiliaries meant that her garrison would be similar to Britain's: 30–40,000, or one tenth of the Roman Army. Nearly 100 fort sites are known in Romania, compared with Britain's exceptional total of 250. Roman Britain was, of course, twice as big and held twice as long.

Visitors to Romania may wish to see Sarmizegetusa Regia, capital of the indomitable Decebal. It lies in the Orashtie Mountains at 4,000 feet; on a steep, high hill, densely clad in majestic beech: centrepiece of a clutch of Dacian citadels, cunningly concealed within the inner Carpathian foothills. They are approached from the north via the town of Orashtie (Hunedoara Province). From there a secondary road runs south to the village of Costeshti. Alas, Sarmizegetusa is some sixteen miles deeper into this upland tangle, via an unsurfaced forestry track of dwindling merit whose second half is negotiable by off-road type vehicle only. Even the nearer citadels, like Blidaru, involve a 2,000-foot climb. The remains are greatly reduced by Roman demolition. This, plus the absence of signposting and the low quality of local advice, makes the casual visit a questionable proposition. Sarmizegetusa, though a milestone in the story of Roman expansion, is still among antiquity's least accessible and most undeveloped major sites.

The Roman capital, *Ulpia Traiana Sarmizegetusa*, is on Route 68 to Caransebesh, some twenty-eight miles south of Hunedoara. A well-preserved amphitheatre, the Forum of Trajan and a palace of the Augustales (priestly college) are on view. Ten miles west, on this same road, is the *Poarta de Fier a Transilvaniei* (another Iron Gates), the pass commanding the western approach to the royal strongholds, where the battle of Tapae was fought. On the Danube, at Turnu Severin, are the remains of the Drobeta fortress and the surviving abutment of Apollodorus' bridge. In the Dobruja there is of course Adamclisi, famous for its three monuments. The carved panels, formerly scattered, are now assembled in the village museum. Nearby stand the ruins of a municipality founded by Trajan and called Tropaeum Traiani after his monument of the same name. The ruined circuit of its 4th-century walls, with some two dozen towers, survives. On the coast are the remains of the Pontic cities of Callatis (Mangalia) and Histria (Istria), the latter twenty-five miles north of Constantsa on the coast road. At Constantsa (Tomis) itself are the Archaeological Museum of the Dobruja, a stretch of Trajanic city wall and some fine 4th-century floor mosaics. At Hirshova are the remains of the lower Danubian fort of Carsium and south of it, between the villages of Topalu and Dunarea, those of Capidava.

It is time to resume centre stage and, in returning to the Eternal City, to ask who was the author of Trajan's Column. Surely so copious a masterpiece must have been the work of many: whoever brought back the visual material from Transcarpathia, whoever edited it and whoever fixed it in stone. Possibly the sculptors were summoned from a studio in Asia Minor, where centres like Aphrodisias[47] supplied statuary to the Roman world. There must also have been a co-ordinator to select the scenes, set the style and supervise the work; and who more suitable than Apollodorus, architect to the imperial court and author of Trajan's Forum? There is, however, a clue to the contrary. The Column's depiction of his Danube bridge is flawed. Crucial struts, intended to counter the downthrust of the arches, are shown as if positioned the wrong way round. If this typifies our artist's blindness to technicalities, it also makes a fool of the bridge's designer and few would believe that had Apollodorus been in charge of the sculptural project he would have let the error pass. Doubtless his hands were full elsewhere in Trajan's Forum: a commission so abundant that even the Column was a minor addition. Failing Apollodorus, commentators have invented a master-sculptor, even calling him 'the *maestro*': perhaps the specialist charged with the Forum's decoration, while Apollodorus looked after its buildings. Some have gone further and argued that the supposed *maestro* must have been answerable to a 'column committee', appointed by the Senate; for the dedicatory inscription tells us that the Column was sponsored by that body. The existence of a committee, with conflicts between itself and the *maestro*, could explain the Column's contradictions: great artistry negated by excessive content and incomparable execution wasted through prohibitive viewing problems. Surely so brilliant a professional would have chosen a more accessible medium (such as a continuous, horizontal frieze, housed in an arcade) or at least a wider band and a simplified narrative. But we know that the senators had already commissioned a column for another reason (to mark the depth of rock excavated) and doubtless clung to their original choice. It is also conceivable that a senate committee, fawning on the emperor, would insist that no detail of his war be omitted: an approach regretted by art critics but applauded by historians and students of warfare.

Hadrian had followed Trajan perhaps three times across the Danube and over the Carpathians. Even then his standing seems not to have been high, for a suitable bearded officer in his late twenties has not been identified among the Column's scenes. Doubtless this helped heap coals of fire on Hadrian's head. Later events make clear the growing hatred of ward for guardian; the secret envy of his easy popularity, the concealed contempt for his facile intellect and showy adventurism. Now, at the war's end, with crowning irony, we find Hadrian assigned the task of glorifying a campaign which he detested; having been elected *praetor*, with special responsibility for the victory festivities. These included Triumphs, games and other events lasting more than a year, four triumphal arches and seven commemorative coin issues!

Trajan, Apollodorus and Hadrian: the victorious commander-in-chief and 'best emperor of all'; the busy architect at the zenith of his brilliant career; and the jealous, touchy, under-recognized young Spaniard, treated by Trajan as an errand boy. Dio offers a tantalizing vignette of the three together. He describes Trajan deep in conversation with Apollodorus; poring no doubt over some architectural drawing. Hadrian, the country cousin, chanced upon them and offered a suggestion. This irritated Apollodorus, who sent him off with a flea in his ear. It was a trivial matter, but it would one day cost Apollodorus his bridge, his career and his life; for we subsequently learn that:

Hadrian banished and later put to death Apollodorus, the architect who had masterminded Trajan's projects in Rome. It was given out that he had done some wrong; but the truth is that once, when Trajan and Apollodorus were in deep discussion about some architectural point, Hadrian had chipped in with a comment which caused Apollodorus to snap, 'You know nothing about these matters. Away and draw your gourds!' When Hadrian became emperor he remembered this taunt.[48]

'Your gourds' referred to one of Hadrian's youthful attempts at architectural drawing. He had apparently been fascinated by a feature known as the pumpkin dome, examples of which would later be included among the outworks of his famous Villa, near Tivoli, where they may still be seen.

The Dacian Wars were followed by a seven-year peace. Accepting Dio's view that Trajan was motivated by glory, this would be a time of anti-climax and chafing ambition, sufficient to tempt him toward the ultimate challenge to Roman arms: conquest of Parthia. This campaign was launched in 113, initially with dazzling results: four new provinces, carved out of Armenia and what is now Iraq; confining the enemy to what is now Iran and bringing the Roman army to the Persian Gulf. Needless to say it opened a long and mountainous left flank, east of the Tigris, which extended as the Romans advanced; and from it the Parthians continued so effectively to promote resistance that, as Trajan reached objectives in the south, his northern gains began to crumble behind him. The setback was a signal for Jewish revolts in the Roman east, threatening even Syria, a province crucial to Trajan's rear. He hurried back, reaching Antioch in the winter of 117. There he suffered a severe stroke. It was decided to repatriate him by sea, but not far along the coast of Asia Minor he died. His ashes were taken on to Rome and deposited in the podium of his Column.

Though Trajan had neglected to nominate a successor, Hadrian held the high cards. He was presently governor of Syria, which not only meant he was close to events but also that he inherited command of the large army assembled for the Parthian conflict. His progress to the purple was unopposed.

Hadrian's reign brought changes in foreign policy which would astonish all Romans and dismay those who held her martial traditions dear. It had been a century since the Varian Disaster shattered the assumption of endless empire. During that period, emperors had shifted uncertainly between consolidation and acquisition, with acquisitors motived by popularity at least as much as by territory. Now here was a highly unorthodox emperor, willing to risk unpopularity by forgoing glory and putting Rome on a pacifist path: renouncing offensive war, rescinding Trajan's eastern conquests and seeking prosperity behind firm frontiers.

An alternative way of seeing Hadrian's policies is as reactions to his predecessor's. Indeed Hadrian's measures were sometimes so emotional that one can seldom be sure whether he believed in the rightness of a course, or whether it attracted him because it was contrary to Trajan's. Besides playing down all aspects of his guardian's achievement and repudiating his foreign policy, Hadrian phased out his festivals and games, closed his theatre, dismissed his officials and executed his more prominent generals. Perhaps they had voiced opposition to appeasement and expressed outrage at the return of territories won with their soldiers' blood. Even Dacia, packed though it was with Roman immigrants, was now in question; and it was with difficulty that Hadrian's advisers dissuaded him from its abandonment.

Apollodorus was doubly doomed. The new emperor believed himself a creative genius and glowered at all who excelled in the artistic or intellectual fields. According to Dio, he even 'abolished' Homer![49] Malevolence focused first upon the Danube bridge, which Hadrian ordered to be dismantled lest the barbarians use it against Rome; though all other crossings of the Danube and Rhine were left intact. Accordingly its timber arches were removed, leaving only the stone piers: so soundly placed, despite the strong current, that parts remained visible until the 19th century and one of the abutments still stands. Its designer was murdered or forced into suicide by imperial agents. While Hadrian's reign cannot be compared in terms of terror to those of Nero or Domitian, he would not lag far behind them in pettiness and spite.

On the other hand, there was nothing trivial about taking the Roman empire onto the defensive. Augustus had shied from so controversial a course, preferring to hand on the task to Tiberius in the form of posthumous advice. Even now, twelve reigns later, it required courage to translate the first emperor's last wish into practice. This was only made possible by the recent failure in Parthia and the ignominy it brought to the war party. A counter-current, favourable to change, had been created. But how long would it flow and how soon would Rome's fighting spirit reassert itself?

Hadrian's armistice succeeded; for the reign of his successor, Antoninus, marks the apogee of the empire's prosperity. It should also have begun a new era of *détente* with the outside peoples. 'Good fences make good neighbours', as the saying goes; and Hadrian's efforts to strengthen the frontiers did not preclude improved relations, doubtless cemented by economic aid which was intended to reduce dangerous differences and promote the adoption of Roman ways. Alas, progress in these directions was impeded by ingrained attitudes on both sides. The thawing of the immense *Barbaricum*, most of which was far beyond Rome's reach, would prove to be a process requiring more centuries than the empire had left to live.

Dacia had been the most capable and promising of Rome's European neighbours. With earlier goodwill or gentler handling the natural stronghold might have been converted to a friendly bulwark against yet more dangerous enemies beyond. By contrast, Trajan's way resembled that of Cortez and Pizarro, of whom it is said that they beheaded civilizations as casually as a walker lops a wildflower with a swing of his stick. The scent of gold had reached the Roman conquistador also.

Trajan's Forum, on which the wealth of Dacia was squandered, is today a sad space at the heart of Rome, haunt of flickering lizards and stray cats fed by elderly ladies. Of Apollodorus' architectural masterpiece only the market with its semicircle of shops remains remotely intact; and only the Column, splendid in isolation, profits from the ruin of its surroundings. Resisting 1,900 winters, it has fared less well in the hydrocarbon haze and corrosive rain of the last three dozen, especially where its topmost spiral takes the drip from the capital above. Since 1987 the entire shaft has been surrounded by scaffolding and encased in plastic sheeting. Surely a prudent and enlightened course would be protection within a cylindrical building, incorporating a rising walkway for continuous viewing, with suitable lighting and multilingual commentary.

Such is the inspired if oversupplied spiral, with its brede of marble men overwrought, sepulchre for an emperor, cenotaph for a king and simultaneous memorial to a victorious army, a forgotten nation, a team of anonymous sculptors, a confused committee, a perplexed designer and an unknown master of reportage; as well as being a monument of world stature and our richest record of events beyond the Roman rim.

Barbarians and Romans

IT WAS 800 YEARS SINCE Romulus had given his name to the Eternal City; and she was tiring. Trajan's wars had been especially strenuous. Despite Hadrian's tours of inspection, his pep-talks, his efforts to keep the soldiers on their toes with drills, manoeuvres and the building of defensive works, the army began to relax. The 2nd century would be among military history's most complacent; almost without improvements in defensive works, weaponry or tactics. Though still largely dormant, the *Barbaricum*'s size and the profusion of its people meant that any policy which did not guarantee military superiority must eventually lead to ruin.

Central to this self-deception was the imperial frontier, with its supposition that the army's proximity would suffice to make the outside world behave. It had taken strength and watchfulness to make and maintain clear borders, without grey areas or debatable lands; to create a world which was either Roman or not Roman, a division so distinct and so zealously guarded that it would be as safe to plough the first field behind the front line as any in Latium. None the less, for all its majesty and authority, the peace imposed by Rome will not long outlive the 2nd century. Time reveals it as an extended truce, a respite from the gruesome norms of human conduct. Though two predominantly peaceful centuries were a formidable achievement, the effect would be to pond up external pressures which must one day overflow. In any case it had been optimistic to believe that Mediterranean standards of stability could indefinitely be imposed north of the Alps and in – or beyond – the Balkans. Iron Age man had little taste for order. Indeed it remains questionable whether even his post-atomic counterpart has the skill or the will to do better.

Human nature is slow to change; as may be seen in our language. A glance at that indispensable work of reference, Roget's *Thesaurus of English Words and Phrases*, shows how unequal are the vocabularies of peace and war; from which we may deduce which of those pursuits has most exercised minds and bodies. The vocabulary of peace occupies five lines of synonyms on the printed page, that of war twenty-eight. Searching further: under 'harmony', 'concord', 'mediation', 'passivity' and related meanings there are forty-five lines; while 'discord', 'disunity', 'combat', 'armament', 'retaliation' and so on, yield no less than 287! So, in one major language at least, there are five-to-six times more words available to hawks than doves; a telling comment on our dedication to violent solutions during the millennia in which English and its parent tongues evolved, not to mention the ample additions from the warlike, cold-warlike and terrorist jargons of recent years. Returning from words to facts: though Rome's emperors tried their best to do so, no age or country can insulate itself from eternal verities. It is one of the strangest developments in military history that a state, summoned from mid-Italian obscurity by the trumpet of Mars, should have ended by devising a strategy dedicated to passivity and a tactic based on sitting and waiting; though the techniques of war wait for no one.

In short a single defensive line, without secondary or in-depth support, would prove progressively vulnerable as the empire weakened. Subdividing the army and posting it in penny packets along a 4,000-mile perimeter not only promoted the habit of dispersal but also blinded the high command to the importance of centrally held reserves. Rome had spun a web round western Europe, the Near East and Mediterranean Africa, yet neglected to put a spider in the middle. The empire's geography, the moral importance of Italy at its heart, the middle Danube and upper Rhine as the likeliest and deadliest points of entry: all indicated a need for counterstrike provisions based on northern Italy. There the Alps would perhaps have dictated a twofold grouping, with a powerful army at each end: one in north-western Italy or at Basle and another in north-eastern Italy or at Ljubljana. However, the implementation of anything resembling a centralized strategy would be postponed until the western empire's dotage, when it was too late to be decisive. The truth is that large clusters of legions were unwelcome to a regime founded in suspicion and obsessed with fear of usurpation and conspiracy. The caesars slept more soundly in the knowledge that their regiments were scattered.

It will not be till the 3rd or 4th centuries that meaningful improvement occurs; albeit erratically, with each autocrat imposing an often contradictory view. Positive developments will include enlargement of the imperial bodyguard into a rapid-response force and conversion to heavy cavalry, with mounted regiments deployed behind each major front. Rome will cease to be the empire's military headquarters and subsequent capitals will be more realistically positioned in relation to external dangers. Finally there will be division of command within a partitioned empire: first, experimentally, into four; then, more permanently, into two. But despite modernization and increased flexibility, Rome will never assemble a united force. More typically, she will continue to improvise and compromise, mustering armies in reaction to news of attack and punching with fingers rather than fist.

However, till the late 2nd century, perimetric defence continued to seem valid simply because no crisis arose to prove it otherwise. Unlike the Maginot Line, which was tested within a decade, the imperial frontier was not placed in serious question for a century-and-a-half. Prior to the Marcomannic War of AD 167–75, the absence of deep fortification or strategic reserves was disguised and seemingly made unnecessary by developmental factors: Rome's forwardness and unity contrasted with barbarian backwardness and bickering. As Tacitus had put it:

> Nor have we weapon stronger against the strong than this: that they share no common purpose.[1] Long may it last this – if not love for us – at least detestation of each other. Fortune grants us nothing greater than our enemies' disunity.[2]

Rome's strength lay in diplomacy, breadth of experience and staying power; barbarian weakness in divisiveness, myopia and transience, as well as ignorance of organization, logistics and siege techniques. Yet all was changing and the long span of peace, supposedly braced by the girders of Roman vigilance and readiness, would sag surprisingly soon.

First, however, with the resplendent reign of Hadrian's successor, Antoninus Pius (139–61) the empire reached the watershed of its well-being and stability. The Augustan dream of a benign balance between emperor, senate and army; the Hadrianic hope of a creative correspondence between provinces and centre, city and country, Roman and barbarian, seemed at last to be working. Economic penetration of the outside world and the outward spread of Romanization were proceeding. Three questions nevertheless persisted. Had the Romans matured sufficiently to value peaceful objectives? Could the office of emperor, so subject to the quirks and swings of each incumbent, provide continuity for the achievement of such goals? And would the European *Barbaricum*, with its dark currents of disturbance, allow time for the improved relationships to root? The answer to all three questions will be in the negative and would soon be given. Under Antoninus' successor, Marcus Aurelius (161–80), the European theatre erupted. The Marcomannic War had its epicentre in today's Czech and Slovak lands, anciently part of Germany, postulated by archaeology as the least hostile of all frontier stretches. Here was a region rich in cross-frontier activity; a sector most penetrated by mercantile and diplomatic effort; with nearly forty known Roman or part-Roman sites reaching up to a hundred miles beyond the Danube.[3] They are thought to have included commercial depots and military or diplomatic missions, whose mixture of south Germanic and Roman-style buildings points strongly to coexistence. These findings confirm what Tacitus had written (in the context of Marcomannia) of 'divers Roman businessmen, coaxed abroad by the hope of some franchise; seduced into staying first by the money to be made and finally by oblivion of their own homeland'.[4] In short, here were the beginnings of a Romano-Germanic co-operation which might in time have reduced economic and cultural differences to the point of peaceful merger.

This possibility was exploded for ever by the Marcomannic conflict. Not only was north-eastern Italy invaded but, more ominously, the attacks spread along the entire front between Black Sea and North Sea. Though Marcus eventually won the war, it revealed two unfavourable developments. First, the tribes had learned to sense Roman adversity and act together. Curiously, the disturbances were in some cases discontinuous, with one warlike tribe apparently responding to another across gaps of several hundred miles.

The second fact was that the frontier failed: its thin membrane punctured in a dozen places, wherever strong force had been applied. Events revealed it as overstretched and undermanned. Its forts were outdated; with *castella* in no way matching what the Middle Ages would call castles. The entire system had been evolved against weak, divided and demoralized enemies during the 1st century and never upgraded during the 2nd.

Neither defensive works nor strategic thinking would find remedy in Marcus' son and heir, the idle and dissolute Commodus (180–92) of whose accession Cassius Dio lamented: 'My history now descends from realms of gold to those of iron and rust, as did Rome's fortunes on that day.'[5] Henceforward, despite noble exceptions and striking recoveries, the state will begin to stumble in the face of its own weaknesses: the absence of a reliable rule of succession, excessive power in unworthy hands and inability to control the army. The milestones on this descending path would include assassination, *coup* and counter-*coup*, civil war, appeasement of the barbarians with gold and employment of barbarians to fight barbarians, culminating in the eventual loss of Roman control.

Returning, however, to the War: its abiding question is why Marcomannia (Czechoslovakia), so propitious for cross-border friendship, should have detonated with such abruptness and violence. Did it signify a backfiring of the slave trade and a breakdown of the three-tier model of Roman control through 'prestige goods dependency'? An explanation better matched to outcomes is perturbation, caused by disturbances in the Eurasian living space, outside the Roman view. The deep *Barbaricum* of Eastern Europe and beyond, was a seismic zone of unpredictable tendency. Age-old impulses to flee from hunger or danger by migrating, usually in a westward or southward direction, had been long frustrated by the Roman empire's presence.

More specifically, responsibility for transforming the middle Danubian tribes from friends to foes may lie with the Goths. This Germanic confederacy originated in southern Sweden, where names like Gothenburg and Gotland survive. They crossed the Baltic, and Claudius Ptolemy, writing around AD 150, locates them on the lower Vistula. A hundred years after the events of Marcus' reign they would arrive on the north Pontic coast; and though their route between is guesswork, it probably lay through today's southern Poland, passing close outside the Sudeten Mountains, adjacent to today's Czech and Slovak Republics. It is therefore probable that the transit of this powerful nation displaced east-German groups like the Vandals and Langobards, who in turn drove the Marcomans and neighbouring Quadans hard against the Danube; overwhelming Rome's intelli-

gence network, brushing aside her diplomatic screen, forcing the
river and putting her extended army to the test of all-out conflict.
Without reserve regiments, reinforcement of the middle Danube
could only be made by transfers from other frontier sectors, weakening them and inciting yet more tribes to attack. If there is substance
in these surmises, the Marcomannic War was a remarkable preview
of 4th and 5th-century calamities.

Before moving on to the late period we must attempt to answer
a crucial and difficult question: how did the transformation from
Roman to barbarian dominance come about? From the Augustan to
the Antonine Age we have seen a majestic Rome facing divided,
bewildered and largely passive tribes. The Celts were still reeling
from Caesar, the Germans dazed by Drusus and Germanicus. On
the rare and probably minor occasions when Roman territory was
infringed, it was on a raid-and-return basis, like boys daring an
orchard wall; though from Marcus onwards, the view is of growing
menace and ever more damaging raids. In the 4th century, however,
the character of incursion changes from raids to migrations, and the
barbarian goal from loot to land: a wish to be part of the empire
and partake of its wealth and security.

In fact the emergence of barbarian power has never been satisfac-
torily explained; and the absence of a clear answer has clouded the
long-standing conundrum of why the western empire succumbed.
Our two impressions – of the earlier and later barbarian – are bewil-
deringly disconnected, for we have little knowledge of the outside
peoples during the period of change which might explain their dramatic gain in strength. Indeed we are seldom sure of the extent to
which we are witnessing gains in barbarian or losses in Roman
strength. One of the blackouts in the written sources most crippling
to ancient history occurs during the 3rd century. It is especially
irksome for the fifty years from 235 to 285, though never so total
that the gravity of events cannot be guessed. Indeed, these were
sufficiently serious to merit history's description: the 'Third Century
Crisis'. Its characteristics were a seething army, provinces defecting
and emperors or pretenders averaging one a year. Though these
weaknesses – and the raids upon imperial territory which they invited
– shocked the Roman command into improvement and drew a heroic
response from soldier-emperors like Claudius II, Aurelian and Pro-
bus, more meaningful in the long run was the readiness to buy off
the barbarian so that Roman could be left in peace to fight Roman.

This folly would not end with the 3rd century; for in Kiplings words, 'once you have paid him the Danegeld, you never get rid of the Dane.' On the other hand, the drain on hard currency was less decremental than might appear. Owing to his taste for Roman trade goods, the barbarian and his money were easily parted; and what governments gave, businessmen could sometimes win back. Be this as it may, an even more dangerous change in barbarian military capability was now afoot.

In the 3rd century unfamiliar names begin to appear opposite much of the European frontier: seemingly new tribes, but in fact new names for combinations of the old. They are exemplified by the Alamans of south-western Germany, meaning 'all men' and signifying a fusion of the Suebian tribes into a coalition, so long and vividly remembered that *allemand* will enter the future French language, meaning 'German'. At a time of internal weakness it is improbable that the Roman army was sufficiently aggressive to provoke such alliances. It seems more feasible that interruptions to cross-border trading, caused by the commotions within the empire, upset the tribal equilibrium, promoting unstable conditions in which the formation of one coalition would almost certainly be followed by others. In this event we have the irony that commercial relationships, created to ensure the loyalty of puppet chiefs, should recoil on Rome as soon as her merchants and officials failed to keep their part of the bargain.

More widely, it is arguable that whenever Rome sneezed the *Barbaricum* caught a cold; for stoppages in commercial traffic between large partners and small (as between the empire and individual tribes; or between Rome and China, in which barbarians were middlemen[6]) were so destructive to the smaller economies that trouble was virtually guaranteed. M. G. Raschke[7] has proposed that bolts of Chinese silk became, as it were, the cash of the Asian steppe, on whose existence basic transactions came to depend; and it is likely that interruption to the silk traffic aggravated all problems in the vast space between China's western and Rome's eastern approaches. Similarly a faltering in Roman bribery payments, or hitches in the wine and slave trades, would not only create headaches for Quisling chieftains but also filter-down effects of grave consequence for the tribes as a whole. The seriousness of mercantile matters is born out by the little we know of cross-frontier treaties, in which the granting or withholding of access to markets was evidently a prime diplomatic lever, as in the peace terms of AD 175:

The Quadans were refused the right to attend markets for fear other tribes might mingle with them and spy out the Roman disposition[8] [and] Marcus restored to the *Marcomanni* half the neutral zone along their frontier, allowing them to settle up to five miles from the Danube. He established places and days for markets and exchanged hostages . . .[9]

In view of barbarian commercial addiction we may imagine the empire's neighbours under acute stress, with Rome comparable to a drug dealer who becomes so involved in gang feuds that he forgets to supply his customers. The Third Century Crisis must therefore have been critical for the barbarians too: a time of trouble in the empire, but of even more fateful upheaval outside it. These commercial upsets, the scenting of Roman weakness, the impulse toward coalition and finally migration, would be the ingredients of the western empire's destruction. Overextended, with declining wealth and her technical lead over the outside peoples eroding away; an ageing state, whose civilian majority had forgotten how to fight, now faced an unhinged barbarian world in which all had learned to be warriors from childhood.

However, the migratory fluxes, which signalled the destabilization of central and eastern Europe required an outside push to give them irreversible motion. We have already noted their origins, on the extreme wings of the empire's European horizon: in the Scandinavian and Black Sea regions. Jordanes, chronicler of the Gothic nation, would refer (in the late 6th century) to Scandinavia as 'the Scandza Peninsula: a man-manufactory, a womb of nations'.[10] The Goths would be neither the first nor last to emerge from this hungry corner. It is possible that they were responding to even larger folk movements, comparable to those impelling the steppe peoples, a thousand miles to their south-east. The relationship (in the Ural-Altaic language group) between Finnish, Hungarian and Turkish – and all of them with Mongol – demonstrates that there was more than one route for wanderers from Asia. It is therefore possible that the northernmost Germans were already being squeezed by arriving Finns; though a more common explanation is that crop failure promoted the Scandinavian exodus. Migrating south-eastwards and encountering Ukrainian winters even colder than those of their homeland, the Goths pushed on, reaching the Black Sea by the 4th century. There, in the last and greatest misadventure of European prehistory, they would collide with the next arrivals on the inexorable conveyor belt of the Eurasian steppe.

The Huns entered Europe's south-eastern approaches in the 370s. Their arrival was disastrous for the Goths who, disastrously for the Romans, were driven into the Balkans. A catastrophic Roman defeat at Hadrianople (Edirne, western Turkey) in 378, led to a Gothic takeover of the Danubian provinces and attempts on Italy via the eastern Alpine passes. Meanwhile the Huns, who had based themselves in Hungary, conquered northwards into eastern Germany and today's Poland. This displaced further people, notably of the Vandalic coalition, who fled westwards, appearing on the Rhine in 405. Theirs was another portentous name: from the German *wandeln*, to wander. A sweeping left hook, through Gaul, Spain, across the Straits of Gibraltar and along the northern coast of Africa to Carthage (in due course followed by the seaborne invasion of Rome) put the Vandals among military history's immortals and presaged the end for Italy. By the mid 5th century, Ravenna, the western empire's last capital, had become so flooded with barbarian officers, bodyguards, opportunists and refugees that Romanity was quietly drowning in Germanity; to the extent that Goths were able, almost absent-mindedly, to take charge of the governmental machine. Throughout the West, Roman provinces were dissolving into Germanic kingdoms and the hazy outlines of medieval Europe beginning to emerge. The Romans and the outside peoples, who had clashed and mingled during the empire's creation, did so again during its disintegration, producing new aptitudes, releasing new energies and reaping an immediate peace dividend. With the end of the centuries-old Roman-barbarian conflict, the tax burden ceased and a defensive commitment, whose crushing cost was all but destroying town and country, was lifted at last. Land-sharing and other accommodations between Frank and Gaul, Visigoth and Spaniard, Ostrogoth and Italian, appear to have been accomplished amicably. The Church was at once a salve, a cement and an agency for continuity. In any case, because the barbarian brought few institutions or ideas, he would need to draw deeply on those of conquered Rome. Because his confederations embodied mixtures of dialects and customs, they would make no unified impact on classical culture; demonstrated by the survival of Romance language throughout western Europe. Only in Noricum (Austria) is there evidence for an evacuation of the Roman population in the face of Alamanic attack, resulting in a German language gain. Only in post-Roman Britain was there a fight to the death between native and invader, leading to an eradication of Romanity from the entire east and centre of the island; though roads and other infrastructure remained.

It is revealing to think back upon the bad press given to the outside tribes by Roman authors. Naturally this had worsened with the military situation. Barbarians were seen to be gripped by *Schadenfreude* and intent on destruction; as repeatedly stated or implied by Ammian (*c.* 325–95), greatest of late Roman historians:

> It is as if bugles were blowing all round the Roman world [. . .] the cruellest tribes awoke and burst the nearest frontiers [. . .] the barriers were down and savagery pouring like lava-streams from Etna [. . .] the caged beasts had broken their bars and were rampaging over Thrace [. . .] numberless peoples, long assembling to put a torch to the Roman world and encompass its destruction [. . .] this ravening age, as if the Furies had incited the world and madness was spreading into every corner.[11]

Similarly St Jerome (*c.* 340–420), from a different standpoint:

> How many mothers, Christian virgins and gentlewomen have become the sport of these wild beasts? Bishops held to ransom, clerics murdered, churches sacked, horses stabled at the altar, holy relics scattered?[12]

This was perhaps true of earlier attacks. The Huns were especially to be feared; and the fourteen-day sack of Rome by the Vandals, which gave birth to the term 'vandalism', darkened the image further. By contrast, the evacuation of Noricum and the trek of its citizens across the eastern Alps shows a kinder barbarian face. The Italy to which they were retreating was already an Ostrogothic kingdom. With the exception of Britain, as successive parts of the empire fell into barbarian hands, the hands became gentler. It was not the conquerors' intention to destroy their new home. By the 5th century the invaders had adopted a 'promised land' view of Rome, more comparable with a Mexican view of America today.

Most early 20th-century historical work on the so-called migrations period was French or German, giving us the equivalent but different expressions, *invasions barbares* and *Völkerwanderung-*

zeit, each reflecting its own national experience. The French emphasizes the onslaught and horror; the German implies readjustment, as Europe sought to resume the natural patterns of flow and resettlement which the imperial frontier had so long obstructed. With the passing years our century has presented us with a far wider choice of interpretations than was offered by these early labels. After all, we are still not far removed from the migrational storm which followed the New World discoveries; and well placed to understand that our own restless age is largely a product of its disturbances. The making of countries like the United States reminds us how stimulating demographic upheaval can be.

A further, almost comparable human commotion followed the Second World War, prompted by the collapse of colonialism, the fall and rise of ideologies and the burgeoning of aspirations; with the spread of communications tempting aspirants to move and of cheap transportation, bringing temptation within reach. Countries not affected by these 20th-century migrations are rare. To a degree they are fortunate. On the other hand, there are economic miracles related to movement into places like California, West Germany, Hong Kong and Taiwan which confirm yet again that migrations need not be destructive, for it is usually true that incomers work harder than incumbents.

With this complex human tide, released since 1945, has come a new vocabulary of flux: refugees, job-seekers, guest workers, foreign advisers, brain-drainers, expatriates, displaced persons, illegal aliens, unlawful immigrants, gate-crashers, tax exiles, Zionists, pursuers of the American dream and so on. In some cases there is no parallel with late antiquity, in others the resemblance is marginal. However, two of our late 20th-century categories of vagrancy do seem to fit 5th-century circumstances, namely 'economic opportunists' and 'asylum seekers': those seeking a better life and those fearing for life itself. Both imply civilian rather than military impulses and neither suggests destructive intent. A place to settle, land to till, safety from the great churning of tribes which attended the close of the Iron Age: we may guess that food and fear were uppermost in barbarian minds, as they are for the needy and desperate of our own day.

Was this the reality of the barbarian invasions? Is it closer to the truth than the essentially martial 19th-century image of sword-waving hordes, hurling themselves against the empire's defences? Were the Angles and Saxons, with a drowning coast in front and frightened tribes behind, a military conspiracy against Britain; or were they a sort of 'boat people'? Did the Vandals plan their sensational march from the Rhine to Carthage; or were they refugees, set into motion by terror and hunger, who merely stumbled against doors which chanced to be unlocked? Of course, while today's migrants tend to respect the strength of their host countries, the barbarians came armed and ready to fight for their promised lands. And yet our own century is not without its homeland seekers (like the creators of the Boer Republics, Pakistan and Israel), prepared if necessary to go to war. One way and another, we are well placed to understand the migrations period.

Perhaps not surprisingly the view of Rome as a noble flame, quenched by barbarism, is no longer in fashion. The 'Dark Ages' have been replaced by a creative merger in which Roman and barbarian combine with unexpected ease and (except for Britain) proceed with relative calm into the 'post-Roman' or 'sub-Roman' era. On the contrary, we now accept that the 5th century's most destructive event was the Byzantine reconquest of Ostrogothic Italy. Today, more aware of other cultures, accustomed to exotic faces and foreign languages on the street and at school, striving for solutions of togetherness, we are readier to allow the outside nations a hearing. So we should be; for the Romano-barbarian mergers of the 5th century made Europe; Europe made the New World; and all Western peoples are their children.

List of Abbreviations

Agr.	Tacitus, *Agricola*
Amm	Ammianus Marcellinus
An.	Tacitus, *Annales*
ANRW	*Aufstieg und Niedergang der Römischen Welt*
Arch.	Vitruvius, *de Architectura*
BAR	British Archaeological Reports
dBG	Caesar, *de Bello Gallico*
Ex Ponto	Ovid, *Epistulae ex Ponto*
Ger.	Tacitus, *Germania*
Hist.	Tacitus, *The Histories*
JW	Josephus, *The Jewish War*
JRS	*Journal of Roman Studies*
NH	Pliny, *Natural History*
Res Gestae	*Res Gestae Divi Augusti*
RFS	Congress of Roman Frontier Studies
RFS, 1	1st Congress of Roman Frontier Studies (Univ. of Durham, 1949)
RFS, 6	*Studien zu den Militärgrenzen Roms I* (Bonn 1964)
RFS, 9	*Actes de ixme Congrès International d'Etudes sur les Frontières Romaines* (Mamaia, 1972)
RFS, 13	*Studien zu den Militärgrenzen Roms III. Internationaler Limeskongress* (Aalen, 1983)
Strat.	Frontinus, *Strategematon*
Suet.	Suetonius, *The Twelve Caesars*
Tac.	Tacitus
Velleius	C. Velleius Paterculus, *Roman History*

Notes and References

PROLOGUE: Romans and Barbarians

1. 56.32.2.
2. Excepting – if science be broadly defined – Lucretius (99–55 BC) author of *de Rerum Natura*; Pliny the Elder (AD 23–79), antiquity's foremost recorder of nature and knowledge; and Ptolemy (Claudius Ptolemaeus of Alexandria), 2nd-century geographer and astronomer.
3. L. Musset, *The Germanic Invasions* (London, 1975) 203.
4. *Arch.*, 10.1.1.
5. In the light of present knowledge it may be assumed that the *amphorae* found in the Bay of Jars, Brazil, are from a random ship, blown off an African coastwise course (as was Cabral, Brazil's discoverer, in 1500).
6. *Hist.*, 16.
7. *Immensa Romanae pacis maiestate*, *NH*, 27.1.3.
8. Tac., *Hist.*, 4.64–5.
9. Tac., *An.*, 4.5.
10. Cicero, *pro Marco Fronteio*.
11. 5.26.3.
12. *dBG*, 6.13.
13. *Pharsalia*, 3.339–423.
14. Probably 2,100 miles, from Germany to the Ukraine.
15. 75.1.3–5.
16. Strabo, *Geog.*, 3.4.16: 'concerned not with rationality but with animal needs and instincts'.

17. Pliny the Younger to Lucius Verus, 7: 'I class them rather as thieves than enemies.'
18. Strabo, 3.3.8: 'the journey to their lands is long [. . .] and they have lost all instinct for sociability.'
19. *Idem*, 4.4.2: 'as always those who live toward the north are more aggressive.'
20. *Philippic*, 1.14.
21. *NH*, 3.5.39.
22. Velleius, 2.117.3.
23. *JW*, 2.363.
24. *Agr.*, 30.4–5.
25. Dio, 61.33.3.
26. id., 62.5.5.

EPISODE 1: The Poet

1. Usually pronounced with short o as in Thomas.
2. *Durus cautibus, horrens Caucasus, Aeneid*, 4, 366–7.
3. Pliny, *NH*, 5.31.18.
4. *Geography*, 11.5.6.
5. *NH*, 6.14.5.
6. id. 6.5.15.
7. *Geography*, 11.2.33.
8. *Artimisia absinthium*; German, *wermut*: both names with alcoholic connections. In Ukrainian, wormwood is *chernobyl*. The 1987 nuclear incident caused headshaking in the Soviet Union, owing to the prophecy in *Revelation*, 7.10–11.
9. Originating as a literary movement in the early 3rd century BC: Theocritus *Idylls*, 1–11.
10. Especially *John*, 10.11.
11. *Judges*, 6.3–5.
12. *History*, 4.71–72 (text reduced and paraphrased).
13. So Amm., 31.2.13: *in immensum extentas Scythiae solitudines* (in the measureless wastes of Scythia); and c.f. Gibbon, *Decline and Fall*, Vol.2, Ch.12, 358.
14. 3.351–383.
15. G. D. Williams, *Banished Voices* (Cambridge, 1994) 19.
16. He did, however, manage a monograph on the local fish and animals, *Halieuticon*, of which a 136-line fragment survives.
17. A hereditary knight, not unlike a British baronet.

18. *Tristia*, 4.10.26.
19. id., 4.10.21.
20. e.g. *Don Juan*, 5.5.7–8: 'There's not a sea the passenger e'er pukes in / Turns up more dangerous breakers than the Euxine.'
21. Moore, *Life of Byron*, 1.347.
22. *Tristia*, 4.10.57.
23. 56.4.
24. *I, Claudius*, (London, 1934).
25. *An.*, 10.1.
26. *Tristia*, 4.18.68.
27. id., 3.2.6.
28. Aurelius Victor, *de Caesaribus*, (4th century) 39.44: *pestilens frumentariorum gens* (the pestilential race of 'corn merchants'). The existence of such a service is rarely attested and was never officially acknowledged.
29. *Tristia*, 2.207–10.
30. id., 2.103–4.
31. id., 3.5.49–50.
32. id., 1.2.97–8.
33. id., 4.1.64.
34. id., 4.1.69–70.
35. Oscar Wilde, *The Ballad of Reading Gaol* and *De Profundis*.
36. *Tristia*, 5.7.9–21.
37. *The World of the Scythians* (Oxford, 1991) 65.
38. *Ex Ponto*, 4.9.84.
39. *Hist.*, 4.64–5.
40. id., 4.70.
41. id., 4.75.
42. id., 4.67.
43. Strabo, *Geog.*, 17.1.43.
44. Amm., 32.1.1.
45. Herodotus, 4.69.
46. Equivalent to Diana, Roman goddess of hunting and of chastity.
47. How steppe cavalry found its way west during the migrations period and how the sword symbol may have ended up as King Arthur's *Excalibur*, see B. S. Bachrach, *A History of the Alans in the West* (Minneapolis, 1973), 111.
48. Amm., 31.2.23.
49. id., 22.8.4.
50. id., 31.12.18.

51. *Iliad*, 13. Homer's phrase, 'the proud mare-milkers', almost certainly refers to the Scyths.
52. Strabo, *Geog.*, 7.4.6.
53. id., 'it yields thirtyfold, however crudely ploughed.'
54. id., 7.3.7.
55. *Hist.*, 4.28. Sindica, today's Krasnodar.
56. *Panegyricus*, 12.3–4.
57. Amm., 16.10.20.
58. id., 17.12.1.
59. *Hist.*, 1.79.
60. id.
61. Amm., 17.12.13.
62. *Hist.*, 4.46.
63. The Dobruja's annual rainfall is sixteen inches (400 mm).
64. Quoted by A. Alfoldi. *The Moral Barrier on Rhine and Danube*, RFS-1, 13.
65. *Tristia*, 3.10. 7–12.
66. A style now associated with China and Japan.
67. This tactic, said to have won the Battle of Hastings, probably also had steppe ancestry: Bachrach, *op.cit.*, 92.
68. *Tristia*, 3.10.51–70.
69. id., 3.10. 19–34.
70. id., 4.4. 55–60.
71. i.e. falsely named 'hospitable'.
72. *Tristia*, 5.10. 14–22.
73. Dryden, *Love Triumphant*, 138.
74. *Tristia*, 4.1. 71–84.
75. *Ex Ponto*, 1.2. 17–22.
76. *Tristia.*, 5.10. 23–38.
77. id., 5.7. 47–8.
78. id., 5.10. 43–4.
79. id., 4.1. 66–70.
80. id., 4.10. 111–114.
81. id., 1.1. 39–44.
82. id., 5.7. 47–64.
83. *Ex Ponto*, 4.8. 18–22.
84. *Tristia*, 4.1.94.
85. id., 5.2.65–72 and 77–8.
86. *Ex Ponto*, 1.2. 57–8.
87. *Tristia*, 3.12. 25–34.

88. id., 3.10. 75–6.
89. Ex Ponto, 3.8.15.
90. id., 3.1.23–6.
91. Suetonius, *The Twelve Caesars, Augustus*, 63.
92. Ex Ponto, 1.2. 81–7.
93. The *ara pacis Augustae*, a sculptural masterpiece, recovered in the 16th century.
94. *Res Gestae*, 2.13.
95. Velleius, *Hist.*, 2.126.3.
96. Ex Ponto, 2.5. 17–18.
97. e.g. *Aeneid*, 1.278 and 6.851.
98. *Fasti*, 2.683–4.
99. *Tristia*, 2. 197–200.
100. Ex Ponto, 1.8.10. *In propinctu* could also mean 'in readiness for battle'.
101. Unlike *Tristia*, the *Pontic Letters* were addressed to individuals.
102. Ex Ponto, 4.7. 7–12.
103. id., 4.9.75.
104. id., 4.9. 80–85.
105. id., 4.13. 18–28.
106. Mother of Apollo.
107. Ex Ponto, 4.14. 57–62.
108. id., 4.14. 23–4.
109. *House of Fame*, 3.1.97.
110. Frances Meres, *Palladis Tamia*, (London, 1598), 282.
111. *The Fall of Icarus*.
112. *Pygmalion* (1912).
113. Leonard Digges (1588–1635).
114. Wm. Cody (1846–1917), who boasted killing 4,280 buffalo in eighteen months.
115. Dio, 55. 4–21.
116. *An.*, 1.6.
117. Suet., *Aug.* 19.65.
118. *Tristia*, 1.3.85.

EPISODE 2: The Lawyer

1. Usually pron. Tyoot in English, Toyt in German.
2. There is at least one bust of Ovid extant (Uffizi Gallery, Florence).

3. First proposed by Philipp Cluverius, *Germaniae Antiquae* (1631).
4. The Hünnering.
5. Staatliche Museen, Berlin; with copies in the Kulturgeschichtliches Museum Osnabrück, which also houses objects from the Varus battlefield.
6. Particularly to his *Oath of the Horatii*, painted Rome 1785 (Louvre, Paris).
7. By the Fr. Sculptor F. A. Bartholdi (1884).
8. Like Czar and Shah, a word derived from Caesar.
9. *Ger.*, 46.
10. id.
11. id., 1.1.
12. *dBG*, 4.17–19.
13. id., 4.19.
14. Some ten miles downstream from Coblenz.
15. He crossed again in 53 BC.
16. *Geog.*, 7.1.2.
17. Wear, Wye, Vézère, Isère, Isar, Yare, Oise, Ouse, Isonzo, etc.
18. Strabo, *Geog.*, 7.2.1.
19. *Pourrir* = to rot.
20. e.g. 'the inscrutible oriental'.
21. An expression having its origin in Dryden, *Conquest of Granada*, 1.1: 'Ere the base laws of servitude began / When wild in woods the noble savage ran.'
22. In Gk. *elektron* (associated with words for 'sun'), origin of our term electricity, due to its generating a charge when rubbed. Latin *sucinum*, related to *sucinus* = sappy, seems closest to amber's true origin.
23. Compare glass; Ger. *glantz* = lustre; Fr. *glace* = ice.
24. *Ger.*, 45; following Pliny, *NH*, 37.11.42.
25. *An.*, 3.53.
26. *NH*, 37.45.
27. *An.*, 2.62.
28. Notably the Pyhrn Pass (nr. Windischgarsten) due south of Linz.
29. J. Wielowiejski, *Der römisch-pannonisch Limes und die Bernsteinstrasse*, RFS, 13 (1983) 799.
30. *Ger.*, 5.
31. id.

32. Evidently replicas, all bearing the same date and still being minted, reputedly in Italy, by some astute entrepreneur.
33. *Ger.*, 5 and 42.
34. id., 23.
35. id., 72.
36. *Decline and Fall*, 9.358 and 359.
37. *dBG*, 4. 1–2.
38. German *kochen* (to cook) = Latin *coquere*.
39. *Ger.*, 16.
40. Long bridges.
41. *dBG*, 1.48.
42. From clinch or clench, secured by pinning sideways. Planks were overlapped rather than edge-joined.
43. Danish Nat. Mus., Copenhagen.
44. *Ger.*, 19.
45. id., 20.
46. id., 37.
47. Boswell, *Life of Dr Johnson*, (for the year 1778).
48. *Ger.*, 13 and 14.
49. Of Franconia-Thuringia.
50. Sp., *tudesco*.
51. Amm., 27.2.2. avers it was dyed.
52. *Ger.*, 13.
53. *Jewish War*, 7.78.
54. *Ger.*, 13.
55. Amm., 27.10.5.
56. *dBG*, 6.23.
57. Ger., 15.
58. *Geog.*, 7.2.3.
59. *Life of Caius Marius*, 17.1.
60. *Ger.*, 9.
61. Jove's Day, seen more clearly in It. *Jiovedi*.
62. M. Todd, *The Northern Barbarians* (Oxford, 1975) 19.
63. P. Salway, *Roman Britain*, (Oxford, 1984), 544–5.
64. *dBG*, 4.1. The largest German group; opp. the middle Rhine.
65. *Ger.*, 5.
66. e.g. Pliny *NH* 5.10.3., 6.15.40; Tac. *Ger.*, 1.6–8; Strabo, *Geog.*, 2.5.12.
67. Surveyor = *agrimensor* (lit. 'field measurer').

68. *NH*, 6.38.210.
69. id., 3.5.39.
70. *Arch.*, 6.1.12.
71. *Ger.*, 33.1.
72. *Aeneid*, 1.278–9.
73. id., 6.851.
74. *Aug.*, 18. Dio (51.16.5) tells us that part of Alexander's nose fell off during the ceremony.
75. id., 31.
76. *Life of Caesar*, 58.
77. *Ger.*, 46.
78. 20.30.26.
79. *An.*, 2.6.
80. Then called Lake Flevo.
81. i.e. the 'Wading Sea'.
82. Tac. *Ger.*, 17.
83. Iceland?
84. Reported by the Greek explorer of the North Sea and beyond, Phytheas of Marseilles, *c.* 300 BC.
85. As perhaps befell Caligula (Dio, 59.21.3).
86. Dio, 55.1.33.
87. The 'supreme souvenir': when a commander, in hand-to-hand combat with the enemy commander, seized his armour or similar spoils.
88. Velleius, 2.105.
89. J. von Elbe, *Die Römer in Deutschland* (Berlin, 1977), 107.
90. The author's assumption. There is no direct evidence that Varus was charged with this function.
91. *Tristia*, 4.2. 1–2 and 16–17.
92. 2.117–18.
93. The rebellion of Tacfarinas, AD 14–24.
94. Nearer the truth would have been 'deciding where cities might be founded'. There is no record of a Roman town in trans-Rhenine north Germany during the Augustan or any other period; nor of wintering beyond the Lippe.
95. 56. 18–19.
96. 2.118.
97. id.
98. 56.19.
99. Dio, 56. 20–22.

100. Suggested by W. John, *Die Örtlichkeit der Varusschlacht bei Tacitus*, (Göttingen, 1950).
101. A tactic of desperate defence, by which the enemy is made to pay twice; eg. Rorke's Drift, Natal, 1879.
102. 56.22.
103. A lineage of battlefield suicide: his father, S. Quintilius Varus, after fighting on the losing side at Philippi; his grandfather's fate unknown.
104. 2.119
105. Either today's Haltern or Hamm.
106. Frontinus, *Strat.*, 2.9.4.
107. Velleius, 2.111.
108. By Dio's time the western Rhine bank was called Upper and Lower Germany.
109. Dio, 56.23.
110. To reduce unsettling changeovers.
111. *Aug.*, 23.
112. Known as the *Res Gestae*, inscribed in his temples and best preserved at Ankara.
113. *Hist.*, 1.89.
114. At the time of writing, a century later.
115. *An.*, 2.88.
116. Correctly, Boudicca.
117. Meaning his ancestry included the opposing leaders at the time of Actium; *An.*, 2.53.
118. *An.*, 1.13.
119. Pron. 'vike' by English tongues; 'fake' by Dutch.
120. In military areas also the name given to civilian settlements near forts.
121. The next tribe westward from the Cheruscans.
122. *An.*, 1.60–61.
123. *Henry V*, prologue to act IV.
124. Quotations on Caecina battle from Tac., *An.*, 1.63–8.
125. id., 1.70.
126. id., 2.23–4.
127. In Tac., *An.*, 2.10 and Strabo, *Geog.*, 7.14.
128. *An.*, 1.11.
129. 56.33.5.
130. *An.*, 2.26.
131. Suet., *Tiberius*, 43 (*caper* = billy goat).

132. *An.*, 2.26.
133. J. F. C. Fuller, *The Decisive Battles of the Western World* (London, 1954), 181. Also E. S. Creasy, *The Fifteen Decisive Battles of the World* (London, 1931), 19.
134. *Die Örtlichkeit der Varusschlacht* (Berlin, 1885).
135. W. Schlüter, *Römer in Osnabrücker Land* (Osnabrück, 1991).
136. *An.*, 1.60. See also Livy, 1.165–70 and 1.184–5, on Trasimene (217 BC), when a Roman army was caught on constricted ground (*saltus*) between lake and hills.
137. J. A. S. Clunn, forthcoming: *Auf der Suche nach den verlorenen Legionen*, epilogue. His account proposes that Varus committed suicide in a temporary camp at Felsenfeld, a few miles east, on the previous day.
138. *Hist*, 28.5.8.
139. Amm., 21.11.12.

EPISODE 3: The Soldiers

1. The tour of Greece is described in Dio, Bk. 52.
2. Museo Nazionale.
3. Dio, 59.12.3.
4. *Vespasian*, 5.
5. It was usual for a commander to march in the middle.
6. The job of the second in command. Vespasian was perhaps a busybody.
7. Tac., *Hist.*, 25.
8. Today's Sousse, Tunisia.
9. Suet., id., 4.
10. *JW*, 6.331.
11. Strabo, *Geog.*, 2.5.8.
12. Suet., *Nero*, 18.
13. *dBG*, 4.22.
14. Leaving place-names from Brentwood to Borehamwood via Theydon Bois, Northwood, Cheshunt and so on.
15. The divisions we call England, Wales and Scotland did not exist. Their names are used here for convenience only.
16. Twenty centuries have not invalidated this view.
17. *dBG*, 5.12.
18. *Caligula*, 46.

19. Gk. *thanatos* = death. Related in garbled form by Procopius, *de Bello Gothico*, 1.4.20.
20. Dio, 60.19.
21. *Claudius*, 17.
22. Dio, 60.19.1.
23. 55.19.4.
24. *Claudius*, 17.
25. 153 BC.
26. 19.2.3. At the siege of Amida, on the Tigris, AD 359.
27. As artillery would launch another future emperor: Napoleon and the siege of Toulon.
28. *Vespasian*, 4.
29. A post-Roman term. Approximately Hampshire, Wiltshire and Dorset.
30. Older readers may recall the difficulties with gut-stringed tennis rackets.
31. Amm., 23.4.5.
32. Josephus, *JW*, 5.63.
33. The anonymous *de Rebus Bellicis*, 18.5.
34. 23.4.14.
35. For a recent exposition, S. James and V. Rigby, *Britain and the Celtic Iron Age* (London, 1997) which, despite new insights into British separateness, fails to face serious problems posed by language and place-names.
36. Fr. = Wales.
37. *Et gallos quidem, qui Celtae sunt* (as for the Gauls, who are the Celts); Amm., 15.11.12.
38. The Galatians of St Paul's *Epistle*.
39. S. Piggot, *Ancient Europe*, (Edinburgh, 1965), 16.
40. The *Conn Cétchathach* cycle, 8th century AD.
41. Livy, 1.36.1 and 1.44.3.
42. *Eclogues*, 66.
43. Nr. Christchurch, Hants.
44. Most notably the gold *stater* of Cynobellinus, minted about 25 AD.
45. *Geog.*, 4.1.2.
46. As proven at the Iron Age Experimental Farm, Butser, Hants.
47. A name deriving from the eponymous Greek colony of Emporion.
48. *dBG*, 7.23.

49. By comparison, Britain's largest medieval castles (Dover, Windsor and Caerphilly) are in the thirty-acre class.
50. *Geog.*, 4.4.3.
51. Chainmail seems to have been a Celtic invention.
52. *dBG*, 5.21.
53. Pliny, *NH*, 4.14. 102.
54. Mature Celtic style, 500 BC to the Roman conquest. Continental and centred to the north of the Alps.
55. *dBG*, 4.5.
56. *Ger.*, 28.
57. 62.9.2.
58. *Agr.*, 12.
59. *Hist.*, (intro) 5.
60. 72.14.
61. Welsh *Derwydd* = druid and *derwen* = oak.
62. *Amm.*, 15.9.8 and Strabo, 4.4.4–5.
63. *dBG*, 4.33.
64. *Geog.*, 4.5.2.
65. S. C. Standford, *Native and Roman in the Central Welsh Borderland*, RFS, 8 (1989) 52.
66. *Vespasian*, 4.
67. Today's Jodefat, ten miles north of Nazareth.
68. *JW*, 3.166–7.
69. id., 243–9.
70. Suet., *Nero*, 40. also C. Cavafy's poem on these same events: *Poems* (Athens, 1948) and various anthologies.
71. 3.118.
72. Father of one of our sources, the historian G. Suetonius Tranquillus.
73. Dio, 61.33.3.
74. Tac., *An.*, 14.29–30.
75. 62.2.
76. 62.5.
77. Compare Tac. *Hist.*, 4.17: 'Slavery might serve for Syrians and the East, but many in Gaul had been born before there was such a thing as Roman taxes.'
78. 62.6.
79. Tac., *An.*, 14.33.
80. *Hist.*, 4.74.
81. No longer believed to have been at Stanwick, where a 1980s

dig uncovered enough Roman material to suggest that this Brigantian stronghold remained pro-Roman.

82. *Agr.*, 20. For the same method applied in North Africa, see *An.*, 3.74.
83. id., 9.
84. id., 3.
85. Though the generally more important *Histories* and *Annals* are partially missing.
86. *Agr.*, 11.
87. id.
88. id., 12.
89. id., 14.
90. id., 21.
91. id., 10.
92. id., 12.
93. id., 24.
94. id., 23.
95. id., 27.
96. id., 24.
97. Due to storms, *dBG*, 4.29, 5.11, 5.23.
98. *Agr.*, 25.
99. Lit. 'under skins'.
100. Though there are different schools of thought.
101. Near Braco, Perthshire, some six miles west of Gleneagles.
102. *Agr.*, 25.
103. id., 30.
104. id., 35.
105. *The Antiquary*, Ch. 4.
106. *The Camp at Durno, Aberdeenshire and the Site of Mons Graupius, Britannia*, 9 (1978), 271–87.
107. Pron. 'ben-a-kee'. Stress on final syllable and the ch guttural.
108. *Agr.*, 33.
109. id., 38.
110. *Satires*, 4.111.
111. Dio, 67.6.
112. id., 67.4.
113. id., 67.6.
114. id., 67.9.
115. id., 67.12.
116. *Agr.*, 39. 1–2.

117. id., 40.
118. Dio, 60.20.3.
119. *Hist.*, 1.2.
120. Estimated by S. S. Frere, *Britannia* (London, 1967) 135.
121. G. S. Maxwell, *Sidelight on the Roman Military Campaigns in North Britain*, RFS, 13 (1983), 62.
122. Near Edzell (ten miles north-west of Montrose), the empire's most northerly fort. Invisible on the ground.
123. *Tu vero felix Agricola, opportunitate mortis* (happy in the timeliness of your death). *Agr.*, 45.3.
124. Earlier passed on Caligula, later on Commodus.
125. *Panegyricus*, 52.4–5.
126. *Decline and Fall*, Ch. 1, 7–8.

EPISODE 4: The Artist

1. T. Nagy, *Traian und Pannonien, ein Beitrag zur Geschichte Pannoniens*, RFS, 13 (1983) 377.
2. Fronto, to Lucius Verus, 17.
3. The Column's emphasis on construction may thus be in part a personal quirk.
4. *Epitome de Caesaribus*, 41.13.
5. Dio, 68. 7.6.
6. id., 68.6 and 7.
7. The *Acta Diurna*, begun by Julius Caesar. No trace remains of this priceless source.
8. *Panegyricus*, 20 and 65.
9. id., 88.
10. Sculptor Torrigiano, erected by Sixtus V in 1587.
11. From Ulpius, Trajan's family name.
12. *Museo della Civiltà Romana*, Piazza G. Angeli, EUR, Rome.
13. *Die Reliefs der Traianssäule* (Berlin, 1896–1900).
14. *Die Traianssäule: ein römisches Kunstwerk zu Beginn der Spätantike* (Berlin-Leipzig, 1926).
15. A. Malissard, *La comparison avec le cinéma: permet-elle de mieux comprendre la frise continue de la Colonne Trajane? Mitteilungen des deutchen Archaeologischen Instituts*; 83 (1976).
16. There are, however, changes of elevation, for example to allow the viewer to see inside encampments.

17. Hy. V: 1, Prologue, 16 etc.
18. id., IV, Prologue, 53.
19. Cichorius, 1896; Petersen, 1899; Stuart-Jones, 1910; Davies, 1920; Lehman-Hartleben, 1926; Richmond, 1935; Patsch, 1937; Rossi, 1971; Syme, 1971; Gauer, 1977; Lepper and Frere, 1988; Settis *et al.*, 1988; to mention but a quarter of contributors.
20. *Römische Geschichte*, Bk. 5, Ch. 6, 205 (1919 edn, Berlin).
21. *Trajan's Army on Trajan's Column* (London, 1935), 3.
22. id.
23. *Trajan's Column and the Dacian Wars* (London, 1971).
24. op. cit., 3 and 4.
25. i.e. papyrus or other temporary medium.
26. 68.6.1.
27. 68.8.1–2.
28. Mentioned by Dio, 68.9.4.
29. By G. Tocilescu in 1900.
30. A common classical motif and origin of the English word pelmet.
31. *Nuovi Risultati Storici della interpretazione della Colonna Traiana, Roma*, 2.3.
32. Tac, *Ger.*, 46.
33. *Tristia*, 3.10.75.
34. Here we have a contradiction in that the oaks are shown in leaf.
35. Eng. scythe, from *Scythia*.
36. *Ger.*, 46.
37. Domitian's Praetorian Prefect, killed in the earlier fighting.
38. Laberius Maximus, one of Trajan's commanders.
39. 68.9.3.–10.2.
40. The adjacent Roman province.
41. 68.10.3.–11.3.
42. As, today, outward-tending walls are sometimes held by cramping irons, with discs showing at each end.
43. 68.14.4–5.
44. The *denarius* is believed to have been the biblical 'silver penny', specified in *Matthew* 20.2. as a worker's daily pay.
45. M. Speidal, *The Captor of Decebalus: a new inscription from Philippi*, J R S, 60 (1970) 142–53.
46. R. Vulpe, *Les Valla de la Valachie, de la Basse Moldavie et du Boudjak*, RFS, 9 (1972), 267.

47. K. T. Erim, *The School of Aphrodisias, Archaeology*, 20 (1967) 18–27.
48. 69.4.
49. 69.3.3.

EPILOGUE: Barbarians and Romans

1. *Agr.*, 12.
2. *Ger.*, 33.
3. F. Križek, *Die Römischen Stationen in Vorland des Norisch-Pannonischen Limes bis zu den Marcomannkrieg*, RFS, 6 (1967), 131–7.
4. *An.*, 2.62.
5. 72.36.4.
6. Amm. 23.6.68. This curious passage describes the Chinese donating silk to the barbarians, presumably as payment to maintain peace on their frontiers.
7. *Roman Commerce with the East, ANRW* (Berlin, 1987).
8. Dio, 72.11.3.
9. id., 72.15.1.
10. *Getica*, 4.25.
11. 20.4.6., 31.4.9., 31.8.9., 31.10.1.
12. *Letters*, 20.

Index

Ancient versions of place names are given in italics, modern versions in upright letters. While lesser Roman characters are usually given under *cognomen* (surname) celebrities are indexed under the name by which they are best known.